Patterns in Interior Environments

Patterns in Interior Environments

Perception, Psychology, and Practice

Patricia Rodemann

JOHN WILEY & SONS, INC.

New York • Chichester • Weinheim • Brisbane • Singapore • Toronto

Library of Congress Cataloging-in-Publication Data:

Rodemann, Patricia.
     Patterns in interior environments : perception,
psychology, and practice / Patricia Rodemann.
        p. cm.
     Includes bibliographical references and index.
     ISBN 0-471-24162-8 (hardcover : alk. paper)
      1. Interior decoration—Psychological aspects.
     2. Pattern perception. I. Title.
ML2113.R64 1999
747'.01—dc21   98-33560

*This book is dedicated to my late father,
Dr. H. William Rodemann, whose eternal childlike curiousity
and interest in many topics, peoples, places, and times was a
blessing to thousands. He was a humble, kind man who valued
education and educating — a gift that keeps on giving.*

In Appreciation

*A special thanks to previous employers, clients, colleagues,
friends, and associates for their much-appreciated support.*

Contents

Foreword

The 1960s saw the start of a revolution in design thinking. This did not simply represent another in a long line of changes in design style. Rather it represented a change in fundamental thinking about the way one approaches design. Instead of relying on designer intuition and hunches, this approach called for the creation of a scientific knowledge base to guide design. In the Environmental Design Research Association, social scientists, designers, and others came together to initiate this new scientifically based approach to design.

A number of critically praised designs proved to be dismal failures for the users, indicating the flaws in the intuitive approach to design. Just as other disciplines, such as medicine, replaced mystical approaches with science, so these pioneers saw that design could benefit from the development of a scientific knowledge base.

Science is not the only way of "knowing," but it is the only approach that builds a knowledge base to guide future actions. It builds and tests theory to help us understand, predict, and act on things. For design, the scientific approach entails at least two directions: First, and most directly, one can raise and test specific hypotheses of interest; second, one can take a broader scientific approach to the full design enterprise. This involves a cyclical process in which one develops design goals clearly in a brief or program, creates a design that fits the program, and then systematically tests the design in a postoccupancy evaluation (POE). The POE provides information for improving future programs and designs.

Though design research has produced valuable information and designs that work better for the consumers, one area of research has created some controversy: that which has directly attacked what designers claim as their stronghold—visual quality and appearance. Designers may well have special training and expertise in "aesthetics," or creating design as an art object. However, if one broadens the definition of aesthetics to consider the meaning of things to people, one finds a way to study visual quality scientifically. One can define and measure the independent variables, the visual features of an object; one can define and measure the dependent variables, the human emotional responses to the object; and one can then systematically examine the relationship between visual features and human response.

In this book, Patricia Rodemann has taken such an approach to pattern design. She has accumulated vast amounts of data on human responses to different kinds of pattern and product designs, and she presents information on various subgroup responses.

Some readers may question the consumer-based approach to design, thinking that designers shape and create public taste. Though this avant-garde theory of art continues to hold sway, research shows that it is flawed. Studies that I and others have done indicate that expert designer judgments do not always stand the test of time. In cases where consumer research and the designer view clashed, subsequent research showed that the findings for the public held over time (cf. Nasar, 1997, 1998). In sum, the guidelines in this book offer solid directions for the selection, design, and understanding the impact of pattern design for various populations.

Jack L. Nasar
City & Regional Planning, Ohio State University
July 10, 1998

Preface

This book wrote itself out of years of experience and the promptings of people in the audiences at several speaking engagements who said: "You ought to write a book!" or "Do you have a book?" or "Isn't there a video I can take back to the team at my office?" The final impetus came from my mother, who said, "Well you should write something like that! I've never seen anything with pattern psychology. Get with the program!" And two weeks later, "Is it written yet? Well, how are you doing!?"

There have been many times over the years when walking onto the set of a merchandising photo shoot that the color of those little design boards and pattern swatches came to life. Yet it was so different from the design boards and renderings themselves. The sheer impact of pattern on walls, textiles, and furniture, coupled with color and context, transformed the whole into an entirely different animal, as they say. In one example, a gorgeous hued design, an exciting floor plan, and a splendid rendering turned into a barely salvageable project with significant constraints. Why? As design coordinator, photographer, and I turned the corner and glimpsed the room, we all experienced a severe case of "pattern shock." Because of the sheer scale of the design, colors that seemed subtle on an 8" × 10" sample were suddenly overwhelming. The overpowering effect of "something happening" to the walls and draperies made the coordinator exclaim, "My, *my* — I think we need a *very* big armoire." The photographer mentioned something about diffused lighting and a soft focus, and I became very interested in large-scale props.

I mention this incident because it was that the time, in the '80s, as a designer responsible for thousands of interior design settings representing the companies' products, that I realized something much bigger was going on. Who was buying these designs? Where did they live?

What did they look like? How was their home designed? I would never see these anonymous people. This curiosity led to graduate school in design research. Surely there had to be *some* study on the subject. It would be simple: satisfy my curiosity and be done with it.

But there was not. Beyond perception psychology, neurological and psychological studies, the only other discipline engaging in a study of the built environment was environmental psychology—with landmark studies by Clare Cooper, Weisner and Weibel, and plenty of excellent articles and books by Sommer and Sommer, Kaplan and Kaplan, and others. Many of the studies leaned toward the heartily academic, architectural, or experimental. The application got lost on a broader scale. And I realized, we needn't be afraid of pattern; something innate to us as humans craves design. Chapter 1 of this book addresses the earliest considerations of pattern research and descriptive language, and presents some of my initial findings.

Discussions with many design professionals proved fruitful. They all had stories to tell. Even the company controller had stories, and I was able to gather a host of anecdotal examples. It became a bit of an obsession. A visit to the Environmental Design Research Association (EDRA) conference was interesting but intimidating. Here were all these famous authors and researchers. A subsequent public-relations event and student competition through my employer introduced me to many of the leading architects, judges, panelists, and visionaries with their own formidable reputations. How did this all jell with the consumer? It seemed there were two worlds—the world of mass-produced products, homes, and commercial strips, and the world of the caring experts.

Surely, there were marketing studies that pulled it all together? Beyond *The Clustering of America*'s demographic links to consumable products and sociological implications, there didn't seem to be many design-behavior links. We know certain zip codes are more apt to consume cigars, wrestling magazines, and dog food and drive hunky vehicles with big tires, but what does their living room look like? What colors are in the patterns in their kitchen? Which pattern types do they prefer versus the urban sophisticate on the West Coast with a postgraduate degree and a higher consumption of wine, smoked salmon, and high-brow design magazines? Chapter 2 looks to demographic considerations—some very generalized findings from specific national research studies; the differences in preference by region, income, age, gender, and so forth. It is a little taste of the type of thing I began to uncover.

At the time of my initial thesis studies, the National Symposium for Healthcare Design was just getting under way, under the tireless shepherding of Wayne Ruga—oriented toward the impact of the environment on healing and the need to link the designed environment with promoting well-being. Studies under Ohio State University's (OSU) Joe Koncelik, now director of the Georgia Rehabilitation Institute, reiterated the powerful impact of research on product design. Studies with The Ohio State University's Jack Nasar pushed the impact into both the cognitive and broader social realms of environmental design, city and regional planning.

Seminars through the American Society of Interior Designers (ASID) and the then Institute of Business Design (IBD) by Sivon Reznikoff on fire-safe design, by Cynthia Leibrock and Jain Malkin on medical/dental/health-care design, by Lorraine Hiatt on design for the elderly and Bettyann Raschko on barrier-free access, the late Carleton Wagner on psychology/psychophysics of color, Sim Van Der Ryn on sustainable communities, William McDonough and others on environmentally conscious design and biodiversity, and Tony Torrice on day-care/children's design were eye-opening. This was not just the "looking-good image business"; it was a deeply serious and life-affecting one, with impacts felt as a result of our decisions for potentially hundreds of years to come. In the course of my research, as I reviewed thousands of designs daily, I came to wonder whether humans might have a natural response mechanisms that transcended taste, trends, and the whims of the fashion industry marketers. In Chapter 3, I am most concerned with the inital responses to specific pattern types, from florals to historic designs, and all the contextual "baggage" that goes with our perceptions of specific categories of design.

I recalled the consciousness-raising influences of Richard Neutra, Victor Papanek, Bernard Rudofsy, Paolo Soleri, and others from the 1960s and '70s and how they might view a link between interior and behavior—beyond consciousness raising—to the beginnings of activism and the tangible. A retail-design seminar on the go-go '80s focused on design as a *cause* of behavior. By using "all the design tricks in the book," we could enhance retail sales significantly; by tapping into cultural cues, we could increase restaurant sales. I recalled a professor's story from an undergrad design-school class that by sawing off the front legs of the chairs ½" to tilt patrons forward, a noted designer increased "turn time," so that patrons would not linger long. Though potentially sinister, there also were positive implications and outcomes that might emerge.

By this time, my interest was more than piqued, and things were beginning to come together. What about the average people that members of the local ASID chapter do not work with? Could there be more serious impacts in the home? What about those grim parts of the world largely defined in shades of gray and so financially strapped that clean running water is a scarce luxury, where orphanages look worse than our prisons? How was the environment impacting the minds and lives of those children, when we in the developed one-third of the world already knew that rich stimuli, coupled with love and touch, grow brains and shape lives? Closer to home, what about reemerging, redefined role of the corporate design team—how did those impacts play out? What was being specified, and were there studies to measure the results? What happened to products ripped out and discarded; how could we make better, more enduring selections? Attending seminars on design for hospitals, hotels, offices, Alzheimer's patients, and hospice environments followed. During my own short stay in a hospital, I shuffled around the place and wheeled the IV bottle with one hand and a notepad in the other. The areas that had just been redone were calming, casually traditional, inviting. The pattern impact was gentle and interesting; the color palette, softly pleasant.

Full-scale on-site pattern installation for the research studies proved to be no easy undertaking. A discussion with a design had been anything but affirming. He argued that 'impactful patterns' were jazzy and wonderful in the right context, and sniffed as he exclaimed that *all designers knew this basic stuff*. Except that we were not only talking about design professionals. Factory women sewing striped shirt patterns were feeling sick. What about all the consumers in the focus groups I held in community centers, and the countless interviews conducted during lunches and after hours? At the very least, it would offer some tangible information toward the thesis now evolving into multiple research projects—regardless of how the hypotheses worked out.

The weekend I installed one of the reactive patterns, crews were testing the ear-splitting audible fire-alarm system in an adjacent factory. Between the completely random and unanticipated noise, the visual impact of working inches from the design, and the fumes from the adhesive, there *were* effects! Two days later, I was schlepping camera equipment to sites to visually record behavior.

Later, as I stepped back from study three, and reviewed hours and hours of video tape, it also became clear that people who do not know they are being taped do strange and amusing things. This gave a rich behavioral database that made all those books on environmental research methodology come to life. I'll leave this up to the reader's imagination!

An interview with George Paulson of the Ohio State University Neurology Department confirmed some of the medical results, and the linkage between the brain and design. Chapter 4 is more theoretical and scientific, and addresses how the eyes/brain process visual pattern stimuli. This train of thought continues with psychological and cultural influences on perception, plus lifestyle data and perceptions of both pattern suitability for the home and commercial environments in Chapter 5.

I began my foray into the archives of neurology and experimental psychology, perception psychology, and many academic directions, discovering the infitesimal opportunity to specialize—and enjoying life as a bee—hitting all the potentially related disciplines in search for deeper understanding. The post-occupancy studies were eye-opening, but suddenly all spaces had become a post-occupancy study, and all design production at work much more than trends, deadlines, markets, and sales revenue. This was an exciting time, and it opened the door to so many possibilities in research, design, environment and psychology that I hope will take root in the lives and hearts of others. Chapter 6 is designed as an overview of the cultural, historic, and environmental influences of design and the link between the era of the home, exterior, and interior styles and the evolution of design. In chapter 7, we discuss common pattern rules, principles, and techniques inherent in pattern design along with things like shape, scale, sequence, and observations on particular design renditions. For some, these chapters will seem basic, but there are specific new and original research links that help us to see pattern differently. Chapter 8 explores color combinations used in specific patterns styles/types and from distinct historic eras. It is an interesting overview of demographics, styles, and combinations of colors, but is not intended to be the definitive story on color psychology. Chapter 9 explores the patterns associated with specific styles and style language, and is supported by solid demographic research. In Chapter 10, I address specific traits and effects that are important in environmental design—issues of control, self-expression, and some personality-type associations—as a hint at other projects and possibilities. Mostly, it's fun.

Today, following a Memorial Day weekend poring through 635 pages of research data on yet another national study covering textiles, furniture, flooring, color, pattern, style, and shopping behavior, I recall the same weekend a few short years ago, when I was struggling to complete all these scale models and thinking that there had to be an ultimate benefit for someone else in it. *It is time we view the built environment as a highly influential habitat in shaping human behavior, development, and well-being. Pattern is an integral element, coextensive with color, light, and cognitive processing. Human have evolved with a built-in response mechanism, which we are only now beginning to understand more fully and to appreciate. If this inspires you to look at your environment differently, approach other environments differently, and impact other lives—developing minds, healing spirits, enhancing creativity and productivity—this book will have served its purpose.*

Introduction: Pattern. More Than Meets the Eye.

Take a look around you. Right now, at the space you're in: What patterns, textures, color combinations define that space? What material is on the floor, the walls, the ceiling, the windows, the furniture—both in finishes and upholstery? How would you describe it? Is it pleasing? What is the personality of the space?

Now, close your eyes and think back to a childhood place. Maybe it was your room, a parent or grandparent's home, or a place you visited. Which pattern designs do you remember? One woman remembers large antique cabbage roses at her grandmother's place. A corporate executive remembers his childhood bedspread with cowboys—a room with a Wild West theme. I remember a green toile—what a story that scene told. And why, oh why, did the French men wear wigs, ribbons, and velvet knickers in the 1700s? How did *that* make it to the walls of an Atlanta bungalow in the 1950s?

MEMORY LANE

Antique Roses

Cowboys

French toile

Can you think of times, places, the people connected with a look, or examples where a pattern design stood out or was otherwise memorable—good or bad? We all recall examples of oversized 1960s-style bright flowers—still in good condition on a wet-look vinyl wall-covering of an office building restroom in dire need of renovation. What does each pattern say about the occupants of a space? And what is the longevity of the design? *Can we use pattern and be timeless? Which patterns are we more likely to view as "background," "complement," or "statement?" Can pattern design affect behavior?*

Where do you live now, and how have you used pattern? Where do you work, and how does the pattern-design use vary? If you are a design professional, think about the recommendations or selections you have made for clients. Research on the use, the effects, the perceptions of pattern design is relatively new. This is a fascinating journey. I promise you will not view pattern the same way again.

Our man-made interior environment is product intensive. Modern manufacturing techniques have contributed to the widespread availability of an almost overwhelming library for product selection. Manufacturers spend extraordinary amounts of time and money developing designs meant to excite the consumer and result in a sale. More than 100,000 wall-covering choices are available to the consumer. Textile consumers face an equally daunting selection, from tablewear to draperies, upholstery to bedding. The selections in floor-covering are equally abundant.

The lifespan of these design creations is longer than many in the industry would like: six to thirteen years, according to current research; and sometimes up to twenty years or longer in the case of a piece of furniture. The designs of our interior environments have implications reaching far beyond the longevity of the product and the usage of the space.

Pattern design is used for more than the enhancement of residential, institutional, and commercial interiors. A significant part of the "interior package," pattern design contributes to creating environments for selling, learning, healing, relaxing, spending, eating, negotiating, playing, performing complex tasks and many more specific behaviors. In this sense, pattern design becomes as functional as it is decorative—as important in marketing a space as residing and performing within it. Thus, exposure to the psychological effects of the built interior environment is also potentially significant, especially if that space is a task-sensitive working environment in which a ten-year daily exposure could total 20,800 hours based on a 40-hour work week.

It is estimated that Americans spend 95% or more of their time indoors. When they are not in the workplace, they are in other commercial settings or in the home. The individual is potentially exposed to

443,840 hours of pattern and color during the course of an 80-year lifespan, assuming 16 waking hours and 95% of the time indoors. Very little research has been done on the actual effect of pattern design on behavior.

Environmental psychologists suggest that our interaction with architecture and interior environment and the resulting behavior works in the following way: 1) We are receptors of perceptual stimuli; 2) the natural environment is mediated through the built environment; 3) the built environment enhances or discourages interactions between individuals and influences individual behaviors. Many corporate facility managers will attest to the financial importance of increasing worker productivity while reducing corporate square footage and overhead costs. Internal space utilization efficiency and "high-yield space" have become hallmarks of effective interior space design. There are unwritten rules for pattern design in the corporate interior.

In the health-care setting, decisions on the "right color palette" and the "right patterns" are often made to initiate specific psycho-physical responses associated with a calming effect: the lowering of blood pressure and heart rate, the reduction of eye fatigue, and the promotion of healing.

Research documentation and substantiation for these selections appears to be minimal and often anecdotal. As is true in the hospitality industry, a conscious attempt is made to market to and attract specific clientele based on the "cultural symbols" or icons associated with a particular type of environment.

In spite of the plethora of pattern design selections for residential use, little or no research had been done with consumers. Interior selections for the home are often made from a study of shelter magazines and consultation with a retailer who is more interested in what customers buy than other factors. Other choices are made based on cost, impulse, or subjective factors. According to recent estimates, fewer than 6 percent of Americans use the services of a professional designer. The design professional may come from a variety of disciplines, often with several conflicting agendas — budget, aesthetics, time constraints, availability of product, installation concerns, and subjective input. Pattern design is a vital part of the materials-selection phase of the project.

In my research, I have come across some dramatic examples of the effects of pattern design on people. In commercial settings, the results can be profound. The vice president of operations for a children's hospital tells of a "cute" flooring pattern selection installed in the 1970s with documented ill effects on the balance and movement perception of seriously ill patients. Small sick children sitting in the play room or crawling across the floor vomited. The pattern was an optical geometric ladybug motif. When the faulty pattern selection was replaced, the incidence of nausea, dizziness, and the need for staff assistance declined.

The chief of interior design for a veterans' hospital relates how recovering Vietnam War veterans became distraught and the incidence of postwar stress syndrome increased when patients viewed a leafy-pattern wall-covering. The design triggered unpleasant memories of combat in the jungles of Southeast Asia.

A CPA experienced a sense of agitation and mild claustrophobia in his office in a large accounting firm. He relates this feeling to an especially bold geometric wall-covering in contrasting shades of purples, and reports a feeling of fatigue after spending just three to four hours in the space. Undoubtedly, hue is also a factor, which we will address.

A public-relations executive spent a high dollar amount on her kitchen–dining room renovation project and was persuaded by the designer to use a bold overall paisley design. She later admitted to hating the design because the pattern appeared to crawl—from the moment she saw it through the window from outside of the house. The woman ate in her family room for two years because budget and pride did not allow for an immediate change.

A young mother decorated her son's room with a plaid wall-covering design on the wall behind the head of his bed. She admits to not looking at the wall during installation because it gave her migraines. A photo had sold her on the design, and the colors were right.

I began my foray into pattern research after visiting a performing arts center where the entire floor appeared to be undulating in rolling waves—a purely perceptual-optical effect triggered by the small geometric pattern. My colleague described a similar effect in a "tilting" restaurant where the wall-covering and flooring designs created an uncomfortable illusion. After many patron comments and a drop in sales, the product had to be removed. There was a lawsuit. Examples such as these abound. Whereas the interior environment is decorated out of an apparent need for self-expression and a visually rich environment, contemporary society has evolved its own set of "rules" and assumptions regarding pattern application. In the chapters that follow, we will address these rules, assumptions, cultural considerations, and consumer behaviors. It is also important to understand the economic impact in addition to the behavioral impact. *Design drives the marketplace and the marketplace drives design.*

To illustrate the impact of market size and sales volume on pattern design, let's examine some industry statistics for wall-coverings, textiles, and floor-covering alone: The U.S. value of shipments for all textile mill products had a value of $79,742,000,000 in 1995, according to the U.S. Bureau of the Census. Carpets and rugs had an industry value of

$10,732,000,000 in 1995; and upholstered furniture for the home had a value of $24,613,000,000. Upholstered furniture for the office added $8,943,000,000 to the tally. This did not include partitions and related office furnishings and fixtures.[1]

The focus of this book is to take a new look at pattern from design to demographics, psychology, perception, neurology, and physiology; to look at consumer choices and motives, cultural and historic developments in the use of pattern design. Patterns surround us; they are *everywhere*.

References

1. U.S. Bureau of the Census. 1997. "1992 census of manufactures and annual survey of manufactures manufactures summary, by industry: 1992 and 1995," in *Statistical abstract of the United States,* 117th ed., no. 1219, prepared by the Economics and Statistics Administration of the Bureau of the Census. Washington, D.C., 739–40.

CHAPTER 1

The Patterns We Select. The Patterns That Surround Us.

Why do we select the patterns we do? In the course of fourteen years of research on patterns, it has become apparent that pattern design is an expression and extension of ourselves. Choice of pattern is personal. Patterns are symbolic and are imbued with cultural meanings. They are inextricably linked with style and color, with texture and memory. Pattern memory is a cognitive hierarchy of meanings, settings, times, and details. Like a jigsaw puzzle of the interior, pattern must fit into its place within a greater schematic. We shop with preselection criteria in mind—a mental shopping list. Many times a consumer will say, "I'll know it when I see it," to a frustrated store clerk. One wall-covering industry veteran has attempted to facilitate the search process by publishing a subject-selection index for dealers: *The Wallpaper Pattern Guide and Source Directory*.[1] This reference is organized by key words, from *abstract* all the way to *zodiac*. Computer CDs and in-store kiosks also help to facilitate a search by design topic. For purposes of my thesis research, I initially simplified a massive pattern sort of thousands of samples into six two-dimensional pattern-design categories. This system was later expanded and subsequently revised through several thesis research projects to arrive at the current pattern-design groupings with subcategories. Subcategories may be ranked and grouped in hierarchies by their simplicity/complexity, order/abstraction, and other design criteria. There are many systems for categorizing across many industries, for several purposes. My general system follows:

Pattern-design categories

A. Florals

1. Random overall smaller florals and floral trails
2. Large traditional florals
3. Contemporary free-form abstract florals
4. Stylized florals
5. Bouquets and nosegays

B. Botanical and Natural

1. Leaves, weeds, ferns and vines, pinecones
2. Fruit and berries, cherries
3. Bees, beetles, insects, and birds
4. Trees, shrubs, bamboo
5. Still lifes

C. Geometric

1. Gingham
2. Plaid, tartans
3. Checks: open, buffalo check, checkerboard
4. Diamond
5. Diagonal
6. Houndstooth
7. Tile motifs

D. Stripes

1. Ticking stripes
2. Broad stripes
3. Narrow stripes
4. Free-form abstract
5. Variegated, alternating

E. Graphic miniprint and small designs (<½")

1. Chevron
2. Flame
3. Dot, circle, miniprint, swiss dot, calico

4. Tiny bud or nosegay

5. Snowflake

F. Symbols and medallions (> ½")

1. Shields, crests, coat of arms

2. Bows

3. Garlands, wreaths

4. Nautical, flags

5. Stylized single-leaf motif

6. Fleur de lis, trefoil, quatrefoil, cinquefoil

G. Stylized overall continuous designs

1. Overall/calico print

2. Paisley, foulard

3. Fretwork, Celtic motifs

4. Filigree, Moorish motifs

5. Arabesques

6. Sunrise, scallops

H. Abstract/contemporary

1. Abstract overall watercolor

2. Brushwork, scribble, crayon

3. Painted effects, cloud design

4. Swooshes, splashes, swirls, splatters, and modern motifs

5. Blends and mixes in abstract rendition

I. Natural texture/faux effects

1. Stucco, plaster

2. Marble, granite, stone effects

3. Wood or wood looks

4. Suede or leather looks

5. Skins, alligator, reptilian

J. Material/textile effects

1. Woven, Haitian cotton, burlap

2. String, *strie*

3. Silk, satin

4. Satin moiré, damask

5. Casement, loomed, jacquard

6. Tapestry

7. Basket weave, cane

K. Pictorial, novelty, and scenic

1. Art murals, landscapes
2. Natural scenes: bird, animal, seashells
3. Novelty pictorial: houses, pots and pans, ships, maps, balloons, angels, trains
4. Sports: golf, football, baseball, hockey, tennis, basketball, soccer
5. Children's themes: teddy bears
6. Licensed designs and characters

L. Documentary/historic/architectural/cultural

1. Colonial, Federal, Adam: egg and dart, acanthus leaf
2. Chinoiserie, Oriental, Asian
3. French and English: toile, Wedgewood, Staffordshire
4. Victorian: swag and garland, rosettes, draping, tassels
5. Classical: Greek fretwork, Greco-Roman
6. Mission, Arts and Crafts
7. Art Deco, Art Nouveau
8. African, Moroccan, batik
9. Folk art: primitives
10. Other ethnic, cultural, historic

M. Combination design category

1. Floral stripe
2. Paisley stripe
3. Botanic stripe
4. Stylized and floral
5. Abstract and historic
6. Other (carpets and upholstery)

N. Borders

I have tried to be inclusive without being redundant or causing future classification problems. Each study presented same and different pattern renditions, though major category headings remained fairly consistent. There appears to be a *cyclical correlation with pattern popularity,* in that there seem to be different types of designs in peak production and sale during certain historical-cultural time periods (i.e., the 1960s featured oversize florals; 1970s, geometrics).

There *are* differences in the pattern types, repeat, scale, and matches used in upholstery, flooring, bedding and curtain fabrics, tablewear, and wall-covering. There *are* differences in print techniques, weaves, finishes, and textures. I researched *all* applications. The initial focus began with the largest surface areas—walls and floors—and moved on to include countertops, cabinetry (wood finishes), and both printed and woven textiles. It also bears mentioning that *the size of a space and the length of time one is exposed to a given design impacts one's response to it.* In a "speed space," such as a public bathroom or a fast-food restaurant, an otherwise distracting pattern design may serve a valuable *purpose*: to keep 'em moving! In a fast-food setting this facilitates getting customers' attention, and getting them through the line, to the cash register, to the table, and out the door.

$$Sales = Turns^{margin} = Profit$$

I have used a variety of research techniques: semantic differential, adjective checklists, bipolar adjective pairs, rating scales, scale models, slides, design boards in focus-group settings, postoccupancy evaluations, interviews, longitudinal studies with hidden video camera, behavior mapping, and mail surveys with color photos. Many early projects began with small groups at a modest cost. I used representative swatches to scale and full-size repeats on design boards, wherever possible. The installations were commercial spaces. Full-color mail surveys were sent to thousands of consumer households that represented projectable demographics. I have reviewed thousands of designs, in both same- and multiple-color palettes for printed textiles, wall-covering, upholstery, and floor-covering.

I have examined responses to pattern by region, market size, gender, household income, ethnic background, occupation, age, educational level, personality type, life stage, and lifestyle. The first study reviewed the *different responses to pattern based on age,* and found that age does have an influence on response to pattern stimuli. I found a fairly significant *difference in response based on health/vision factors and prior experience.* The methodology involved focus groups of about nine people rating full-scale neutral-hued designs using bipolar adjective pairs and a three-point rating scale as an initial phase of a thesis study.

Semantic differential was also used. The mean age range of the first research group was 27–31; the second group was 76–80, and the third group was 38–42. These groups viewed pairs of patterns. Below are some of the adjectives we arrived at initially, based on review of Kasmar's adjective checklist.[2] Typically, one "measures" value (degree), activity, and strength (positive/negative direction) semantically. Though these were, in a sense, preference studies, other implications emerged.

Bipolar Adjective Pairs Opposites		Selected Adjective Pairs Opposites	
orderly	chaotic	appealing	unappealing
appealing	unappealing	busy	calm
advancing	receding	comfortable	uncomfortable
hospitable	inhospitable	restful	disturbing
flashy	subdued	positive	negative
harmonious	discordant	familiar	unfamiliar
relaxed	tense	pleasing	annoying
healthy	unhealthy	soothing	distracting
serene	disturbed	refreshing	wearying
comfortable	uncomfortable	nice	awful
dynamic	static	livable	unlivable
exciting	unexciting		
directed	undirected		
complex	simple		
changeable	unchangeable		
restful	disturbing		
rhythmic	arrhythmic		
quiet	noisy		
positive	negative		
familiar	unfamiliar		
depressing	exhilarating		
inviting	repelling		
busy	calm		
inspiring	discouraging		
pleasing	annoying		
soothing	distracting		
calming	upsetting		
refreshing	wearying		
sedate	flamboyant		
fatiguing	invigorating		
livable	unlivable		
nice	awful		

In study one, subjects checked the appropriate blank; in study two they highlighted the most appropriate adjectives for each pattern type.

Study One: Combined Group Responses to Selected Designs

Pattern Type	Unappealing	Neutral	Appealing
Contemporary floral	33%	24%	33%
Gingham geometric	43%	19%	4%
Diamond miniprint	0%	17%	83%
Marble print texture	25%	25%	50%
Casement weave fabric	8%	8%	83%
Pictorial newsprint	66%	16%	16%

	Busy	Neutral	Calm
Contemporary floral	33%	24%	33%
Gingham geometric	4%	19%	43%
Diamond miniprint	83%	17%	0%
Marble print texture	25%	25%	50%
Casement weave fabric	8%	8%	83%
Pictorial newsprint	66%	16%	16%

	Unfamiliar	Neutral	Familiar
Contemporary floral	33%	24%	33%
Gingham geometric	43%	19%	4%
Diamond miniprint	0%	17%	83%
Marble print texture	50%	25%	25%
Casement weave fabric	83%	8%	8%
Pictorial newsprint	16%	16%	66%

	Annoying	Neutral	Pleasing
Contemporary floral	33%	24%	33%
Gingham geometric	43%	19%	4%
Diamond miniprint	0%	17%	83%
Marble print texture	25%	25%	50%
Casement weave fabric	8%	8%	83%
Pictorial newsprint	66%	16%	16%

	Distracting	Neutral	Soothing
Contemporary floral	33%	24%	33%
Gingham geometric	43%	19%	4%
Diamond miniprint	0%	17%	83%
Marble print texture	25%	25%	50%
Casement weave fabric	8%	8%	83%
Pictorial newsprint	66%	16%	16%

	Wearying	Neutral	Refreshing
Contemporary floral	33%	24%	33%
Gingham geometric	43%	19%	4%
Diamond miniprint	0%	17%	83%
Marble print texture	25%	25%	50%
Casement weave fabric	8%	8%	83%
Pictorial newsprint	66%	16%	16%

	Awful	Neutral	Nice
Contemporary floral	33%	24%	33%
Gingham geometric	43%	19%	4%
Diamond miniprint	0%	17%	83%
Marble print texture	25%	25%	50%
Casement weave fabric	8%	8%	83%
Pictorial newsprint	66%	16%	16%

	Unlivable	Neutral	Livable
Contemporary floral	33%	24%	33%
Gingham geometric	43%	19%	4%
Diamond miniprint	0%	17%	83%
Marble print texture	25%	25%	50%
Casement weave fabric	8%	8%	83%
Pictorial newsprint	66%	16%	16%

N=21; three age groups. Rodemann, Patricia. © 1991. Master's Thesis, The Ohio State University, Columbus, Ohio. Studies One through Five.

Study One: An Example of Response by Age Group

	Floral	Geometric
Group I Median age: 27	50% livable 16% dislike 16% "awful" 66% pleasing	33% livable 50% dislike 50% "awful" 0% pleasing
Group II Median Age: 40	33% livable 16% dislike 50% "awful" 16% pleasing	16% livable 50% dislike 66% "awful" 0% pleasing
Group III Median Age: 77	11% livable 33% dislike 33% "awful" 11% pleasing	0% livable 77% dislike 88% "awful" 0% pleasing

Rodemann, Patricia. © 1991. Master's Thesis, The Ohio State University, Columbus, Ohio. Studies One through Five.

This was a small initial study, and only two pattern types per category were reviewed with the selected adjectives. Research subjects discussed at length during the focus group what they found appealing or not appealing in each of the designs. But this preliminary study began to suggest some interesting commonalities and disparities across all age groups. When all the pattern designs within the above categories were tested with a second control group of patterns, 66 percent of all groups strongly agreed the geometric design—in this case a ticking stripe—showed a perception of movement, compared with 8 percent for the graphic design and 8 percent for the pictorial. Furthermore, 50 percent of all groups strongly agreed that after viewing the geometric they perceived afterimages, compared with 16 percent for the graphic design. None of the other pattern types caused a similar response. This is addressed further in chapters 3 and 4 on the psychophysical response to pattern design.

The second thesis research study[3] sought to refine, broaden, and retest the initial findings in the first one, but using other slightly different methodologies. Study two used interview technique with an interviewer-administered questionnaire with an adjective check list, more patterns per category, and a scale model. The subjects' ages ranged from 25 to 75 years. There were four patterns in each design category. Patterns were tested in a slide format for a larger life-size approximation; but again real product mounted on 20" x 30" boards proved far superior.

The second study also found that *age has an influence on response to pattern stimuli*. Above the median age of 47, context, conditioning, and familiarity appear to play a larger role in selection than in the under-47 age group. Familiarity, typicality, context, and symbolism play an important role in pattern "meaning" and also design ratings. Two important measures emerged as a gauge of tolerance to a given pattern design: busy or "busyness," and distracting or "distraction." In all age groups, patterns perceived as busy and distracting led more frequently to optical annoyance, weariness, and fatigue. The findings substantiated the trait of certain patterns to initiate common negative responses that transcended preference considerations. This was, again, a psychophysical response, and an unanticipated finding.

Other findings emerged from the interviews. *The importance of "timeliness" and a dislike for dated looks, dislike of "artificiality," and an express distaste for high contrast or unrelieved dense, dark surfaces emerged as new considerations regardless of the type of setting*. But people will tolerate patterns they do not particularly like if they are appropriate to a given setting: retail, restaurant, theme setting, or short-time exposure areas like restrooms. Context and time exposure to a design are extremely important.

$$\text{pattern design} + \text{color} \times \text{length of time exposure}^{\text{context}} =$$
$$\text{physical} + \text{psychological effect} \rightarrow \text{behavior}$$

The third thesis study[4] sought to determine what would happen when the two most "reactive" patterns were installed in similar office spaces. The research methodology included behavior mapping and filming by hidden camera. These patterns are called "acuity" designs and are used in neurological research to determine damage to the optic nerve/visual brain center from trauma, stroke, or disease. The "acuity patterns" are widely available—in popular use—across many product categories and are easily recognizable. Surprised?

Because these were graphics offices, graphics patterns were not uncharacteristic and introduced some artistic whimsy. A few employees were aware of the general auspices of the study; customers were not.

The third study sought to determine how significant behavior and response would be full scale in real-life settings. The behaviors measured included: a) nonverbal (body language), b) social/behavioral interaction, c) attention/arousal, d) task behaviors, e) group/personality orientation, and f) time spent in each setting. We recorded before, during, and after the test condition. After the study was complete, staff and customers were surveyed by questionnaire.

Graphics Research Site A (ticking stripe) provoked unanticipated reactions by staff and research subjects. Though staff members provided full support of the experiment, and expressed mild curiosity and pleasant demeanor, things changed when the researcher left with the hidden camera still running. There were glances of displeasure, avoidance behaviors, expressions of anxiety, and negative comments.

Graphics Research Site B (checkerboard) staffers found the pattern design to be distracting, busy, exhibit movement, and appear to vibrate. The design became overbearing, wearying, and disruptive, and no one felt they would be comfortable with the pattern on all four walls. (Study three is examined further in chapter 4.) The "perceptions" consumers reported moved from semantic ratings into observed behavior.

The third study found correlations between

$$pattern^{x,y} \rightarrow behavior^z$$

through the following measures: a) time tolerance, b) interaction between people, c) task behaviors, d) intended versus actual purpose, e) context, f) familiarity, g) semantics, h) health factors—especially visual, and i) perception/comfort levels.

More important, the pattern designs may have affected business negatively during their installation. This was noted in comparing numbers of visits and dollar sales.

The fourth thesis study[5] sought to undertake a real postoccupancy evaluation in a nonstaged, professionally designed space. This space was a music-rehearsal area at a performing arts center with an acoustic dot pattern wall surface. The survey used an administered questionnaire technique similar to a mall intercept. Performers described the wall surface as wearying and disruptive. Painting the surface to lessen the visual contrast would probably have lessened any reported effects. Subjects felt not only that the design appeared to move (86%) but that the walls had a "swimming effect," which led to feelings of fatigue and annoyance.

It was significant that so many subjects responded in the same fashion to the same type of surface. It was also a point of interest that none were aware of the overall auspices of the research project or intent and there were no changes to the space.

The fifth thesis study[6] led to a professional-practice mail survey. More than 1,000 surveys were sent to specifiers in health care, hospitality, architectural, and corporate and interior design firms. Key-word analysis revealed that most professionals believe the surfaces of a space: are an integral component; create the atmosphere; are the material that's most visible and subject to heavy wear and tear; are important in creating a mood regardless of the space; affect selection of all the other materials, and wrap it together. It appears there are *strong opinions on suitability of certain pattern types for specific spaces.* Pattern usage is heavily context- and location-dependent, and usage varies by project type. Ninety-three percent of professionals surveyed felt that surface design has the ability to affect occupant behavior significantly and that it is a conscious part of their design specification. However, few consumers use the services of design professionals.

Because commercial pattern design specifications are heavily context dependent, it is assumed that what is specified for a casino is not specified in a senior center and what is specified for a south Florida hotel is not specified for a Northeastern hospital specializing in childhood diseases. This professional-practice study shows which pattern categories are specified most. How do the wrong designs get specified and installed by professionals? What other things do we need to know about design/behavior for commercial and residential spaces?

Seventy-five percent of the design professionals say pattern-design selection is more than a casual decision on their part. Are there consumer expectations about specific pattern types for commercial spaces? I also began to wonder which patterns consumers were installing in their own homes and what they were planning to change, if pattern design is such a contextual decision.

This led to large-scale consumer studies covering a variety of design-selection and usage considerations in a broader context. What is happening in the larger market? Which patterns are being selected in the 1990s, and how do they differ from a few years ago? What is happening with overall style? What are the demographic correlations? Is there a way to measure pattern "personality"?

Study Five: Professional Design Specifications of Pattern Types

Pattern Category	Never	Seldom	Sometimes	Specify Often
Floral	23%	34%	27%	16%
Stripe	1%	20%	52%	21%
Plaid/check	24%	40%	30%	6%
Graphic	4%	17%	48%	30%
Printed textures	4%	11%	41%	45%
Solid color textures	6%	8%	33%	51%
Historic/cultural	32%	39%	21%	8%
Novelty	40%	40%	18%	2%
Borders	15%	19%	35%	30%

N=278. Rodemann, Patricia. © 1991. Master's Thesis, The Ohio State University, Columbus, Ohio. Studies One through Five.

Pattern Types Most Represented in the Home Today in Rank Order
1. Medium-Large Scale Floral
2. Geometric Designs (Plaids)
3. Mini-prints
4. Abstract/Watercolor
5. Botanical
6. Stripes
7. Fabric/Textile Effects (Damask)
8. Stone/Marble/Faux
9. Natural Textures
10. Novelty/Graphic
11. Sports/Kids/Characters
12. Historic/Architectural
13. Ethnic/Cultural

N=3,500. Rodemann, Patricia. © 1996. Study Six.

Several new national design research projects were developed, both for clients and independently. My findings are basd on some 4,500 pages of statistical data and fourteen years' experience. For study six,[7] full-color mail surveys were sent to more than 5,500 consumers via a nationally representative demographic database drawn from more than 500,000 households. Photographic representations of patterns, styles, and color reproduction supplemented the rich database for extensive evaluation. Finally, in late 1998, I fielded a survey (study ten)[8] to 500 new movers as a follow-up to the thesis survey to capture another more specific snapshot in time.

This is just the beginning. Which patterns are consumers planning to change/add next? In which styles? Colors? In flooring, wall-covering or textiles? Where do they shop? And who are they? Because my research is multifaceted and ongoing, this book represents the proverbial tip of the iceberg, with an ever-changing and fascinating statistical tale behind these findings.

References

1. *The Wallpaper Pattern Guide and Source Directory*, P.O. Box 5107, Clearwater, Fla. 33756.

2. Kasmar, Joyce. 1988. The development of a usable lexicon of environmental description. In *Environmental aesthetics: theory, research, and applications,* edited by Jack Nasar. New York: Cambridge University Press, 144–55.

3. Rodemann, Patricia. © 1991. Master's Thesis, The Ohio State University, Columbus, Ohio. Studies One through Five.

4. ibid.

5. ibid.

6. ibid.

7. Rodemann, Patricia. © 1996. Study Six.

8. Rodemann, Patricia. © 1998. Study Ten. Thesis follow-up research project.

CHAPTER 2

Who Selects Which Type of Pattern?

As depicted in Grant Woods's painting *American Gothic,* we understand intuitively that some people are born and raised with a more austere outlook on design than others. Culturally, there is plenty of input from our earliest childhood perceptions. We are bombarded with stimuli from both within the home and the media. Even sitcoms are carefully designed to portray a specific look and define a specific character or role through pattern designs and color combinations.

We wink knowingly when faced with the interior that looks like the set of *Married with Children* or the client who is too close to Al Bundy in terms of product selections. There are distinct differences in consumers' overall design selections, with a predisposition based not only on occupation but also region, age, income, educational level, gender, and ethnic background.

Personality, temperament, cultural exposure, and our individual characteristics combine to then determine our specific selections. We all know the vibrant personality type that also embraces color, pattern, and a diversity of styles without fear. This type is leading-edge, and will wear jewelry, hat, and vest along with blouse, scarf, suit, textured hose, and matching shoes. This person's home reflects a similarly adventurous attitude, featuring patterned furniture, wall-covering and borders, Oriental carpets, and a fascinating blend of art and accessories.

Conversely, a more casual consumer type may be more comfortable in jeans and a chamois shirt. His or her home reflects the same style ethic in a mix of textures, neutrals, and natural materials.

As we examine individual pattern selections, we see specific demographic profiles begin to emerge for each category and type. It is quite apparent that there is a different "pattern personality" and demographic makeup between the woman in her 20s and the man in his 70s.

However, both may be planning changes in their home decor within the next year or two: bedding, area rugs, a sofa or slipcovers for the chairs, borders in a bathroom, wallpaper in the kitchen, draperies for the dining room, place mats for the kitchen table, accent pillows in the family room, laminate kitchen countertops, a desk with a specific wood finish for the home office. All involve color, pattern, or finish selections. Consumers carry a mental shopping list with them. My research has shown that they will look at magazines, direct mail flyers, window displays, and vignettes in the store well before they actually make a purchase. Only about 10 percent buy home furnishings and home decor on impulse.

Chapter 1 examined the mix and predominance of pattern types in the consumer's home today. Consumers were not planning to buy more of the same they already have. This is a function of changing styles,

---

Study Ten: Which Patterns* Consumers Say They Plan to Buy Next in Rank Order

1. Botanical designs
2. Stripes
3. Stone, marble, granite looks
4. Mini or small prints
5. Geometric/plaid
6. Natural textures
7. Abstract and watercolor effects
8. Fabric, material looks
   (defined as damask, moiré, silk)
9. Kids designs
10. Floral designs
11. Historic and architectural
12. Novelty, scenic and pictorial looks
13. Sports, thematic
14. Ethnic, cultural
15. Combination/blends of two or
    more designs

*Patterns defined as textiles, flooring, and wall-covering. N=500. Rodemann Patricia. © 1998. Study Ten. Thesis follow-up research project.

blending with what consumers already have to create a pleasing mix, and exposure to new ideas. How many buy what they originally intend or first set out to purchase? Think of recent examples in your life.

In home design, intentions and reality are pretty close. The higher the price point, the more apt a consumer is to get exactly what he or she wants. Consumers will switch to a close substitute or second choice when they cannot find what they had in mind; the selection does not appear to work as they had visualized; or they get "cold feet" and take a safer, "tried and true" approach. Sales or markdowns can and do sway decisions. Nearly sixty percent influence their spouse or others regarding the final outcome or decision. This can be agreement and affirmation, or disagreement—and result in an alternate selection.

Study Six: Pattern-Design Preferences Based on Gender Differences

Females:	Miniprints, florals, botanicals, fabric effects, natural textures, novelty
Males:	Light and dark wood finishes, faux/stone/marble, geometrics/plaids, architectural/historic motifs/themes, novelty designs, brushed metals

N=3,500 shown in rank order by gender. Rodemann, Patricia. © 1996. Study Six. Derived from general data compiled from The Rooms of America© I Survey.

Males rated most pattern designs lower than females, preferring solids, textures, and natural materials instead. Many times there is a love/hate relationship with pattern. She loves it, he hates it, and vice versa—statistically verifiable. Though we bring individual experiences (a personal context) to pattern judgment, men in general tend to vote similarly. In some cases, income, education, or ethnic background play a larger role than gender.

Study Six: Pattern-Design Preferences Based on Regional Differences

Northeast:	Miniprints, botanicals, florals, stripes, geometrics
Midwest:	Miniprints, botanicals, stone/faux effects, stripes, geometrics, novelty
South:	Stone/faux effects, miniprints, botanicals, fabric effects, natural textures, abstract/watercolor, stripes, florals, historic/architectural
West Coast:	Stone/faux effects, ethnic/cultural designs

N=3,500 shown in rank order by region. Rodemann, Patricia. © 1996. Study Six. Derived from general data compiled from The Rooms of America© I Survey.

Nationally, individual pattern-category rankings are similar in many instances. These individual regional profiles become quite pronounced statistically as one begins to examine the subtle differences by specific geographic subregions in terms of finish, style, rendition, color combinations, and income level.

Northeasterners tend to pursue traditional style and "sophisticated-understated mix" (eclectic) style with a conservative palette direction. The pattern selection is complemented by other product selections, such as tile and wood floors. Midwesterners show similar preferences to Northeasterners with some selections, but are more like West Coast residents with other selections. The Midwesterner tends to go for more earthy, basic looks, natural textures, faux/stone, and miniprints. The West Coast and Southern regions tend to vary the most. Southerners seem to place a higher priority on home decor. West Coast residents tend to have a very distinctive, more casual contemporary style. These regional pattern-design differences are highly dependent on *style* preferences. Residents of the Southwest are more apt to select Western designs; residents of the Pacific Northwest may be more apt to select "lodge-lake" style and novelty (pinecones, etc.) designs that complement the style. Although this may seem obvious, research now proves a statistical connection; but there are also exceptions to the rule. Many consumers will design theme rooms. Personal hobbies and traveling change the regional norms.

There are noticeable connections with local history and architecture as well as exterior home style. Fifties, sixties, and seventies vintage ranch-style homes are less likely to feature formal styles and patterns. And realtors will verify how difficult it is to sell a Spanish-style ranch home in an incongruous region. Though these are generalizations, they are based on solid large-scale research studies — with a touch of humor — and are not meant to be used for ironclad decision-making without further research and discussion.

By population density/market size, urban dwellers prefer a sophisticated mix of patterns — often in tonal or textural renditions. Suburbanites, small-town residents, and rural/country residents prefer

Study Six: Pattern-Design Preferences Based on Market Size

City/urban:	Large-scale florals, stone looks, print fabric (tapestry), abstract, architectural/historic/cultural
Suburban:	Small prints, botanical designs, stripes, geometric/plaids
Rural/country:	Miniprints, botanical designs, natural textures, novelty

N=3,500 In rank order by population size market. Rodemann, Patricia © 1996. Study Six. Derived from general data compiled from The Rooms of America © I Survey.

more organic designs—small or miniprints and botanicals (leaf, ivy, fruit, berries). Market size is less of a factor if the individual has had broad design exposure, or in cases where the individual travels frequently to shop in larger markets. Market size is a major factor in pattern and style selection when coupled with income, region, and/or occupation. The resident of rural Georgia is less likely to select a similar design to that of a resident of Atlanta. Based on region and similar incomes, that same rural Georgian is also less likely to select design combinations similar to those of a resident of rural Vermont. It has to do with cultural, geographic, and style considerations. They may both be watching cows graze, but the style of one rocking chair is Shaker and the other is a more rustic early American. It does argue for niche marketing to a very high degree. Cluster marketing is a reality in home decor and pattern/style selection. Though it is conceivable to fine-tune this mix by zip-code area, we are dealing with an ever changing mosaic of individuals.

Study Six: Pattern Design Preferences Based on Ethnic Heritage	
Caucasian:	Small/miniprint, stripe, florals, geometric prints
African American:	Faux/stone, print/textured fabric look, naturals, abstract/watercolor, stripes, florals, ethnic/cultural motifs
Hispanic American:	Faux/stone, geometric, architectural, ethnic/cultural, small print
Asian American:	Small/miniprint, botanical, faux/stone, natural textures, abstract, geometric prints, historic/cultural and architectural motifs

N=3,500 in rank order by ethnic background. Rodemann, Patricia. © 1996. Study Six. Derived from general data compiled from The Rooms of America © I Survey.

Some of the selection differences are subtle, and all groups agree on some things based on other demographics such as education, occupation, age, gender, and so on. However, page-by-page and style-by-style colors, finishes, and pattern selections can vary significantly. Specific design profiles emerge coupled with cultural context, regional and socioeconomic factors. In some cases, there are splits within a group—primarily Hispanic. *Hispanic* is a broad term that can be taken to mean Mexican, Spanish, Cuban, or Latin American in origin. Similarly, *Asian* can refer to Chinese, Japanese, Vietnamese, or Indonesian origin. There are probably differences between Italian, German, and British descendants as well. The Pantone Color Institute researches color preference internationally and has found both country/cultural differences and world color preferences that transcend boundaries.[1]

Our purpose in looking at ethnic background is related to giving the customer base the designs it prefers. With significant growth in other demographic groups versus Americans of Northern European origin, we will be seeing change in what is offered and accepted at market. I believe the changing American demographic mix is responsible for new eclectic designs and color palettes, and a rejuvenation of design. Why would a Vietnamese American entrepreneur select Queen Anne–style furniture? It is understandable culturally that African Americans would perhaps not rate country miniprints as highly, or that country farm or lodge-lake color palettes might appeal more to Norwegian Americans in Wisconsin than a Cuban family in Miami. It is a call to understand and delight in our multicultural diversity. Clearly, *assimilation factors* are also at work between the need to "belong" to a larger group, and the need to *assert one's cultural identity,* whether in an individual neighborhood or a larger region. Design is a sociological statement.

Heritage + education + income + region + occupation = pattern predisposition

Caucasian Americans tend to prefer country motifs, miniprints, and medium-finish woods, and seem to be moving to a mix of "'prairie" and casual nineties simplicity in their style orientation. African Americans favor greater pattern complexity, variety, and contrast; are more sophisticated in color use; and express a higher trend awareness in their design orientation. Hispanic Americans tend to prefer greater pattern simplicity, natural materials or looks, interesting metal finishes, and both brighter and more subtle color palettes. Asian Americans tend to be "power shoppers" with purpose and prefer botanical and natural themes and textures, and a variety of natural finishes and materials. Our research shows significant statistical differences in style selections as well. In a multicultural society, it is important to appreciate and offer pattern-design styles and mixes that different cultures and regions are comfortable designing with. It is also good business.

Study Six: Pattern-Design Preferences Based on Household Income Level	
Less than $35,000	Fabric looks, novelty designs, kids patterns
$35,000–$75,000	Miniprints, fabric looks, abstract, stripes, novelty, kids
Greater than $75,000	Botanical, stone, fabric, abstract, stripe, florals

N=3,500. Rodemann, Patricia. © 1996. Study Six.

Household income will naturally limit the rendition and availability of design selections in one's price range, but other factors are at work. There is a distinct correlation between a person's educational level and his or her household income and occupation. It is not always the case in the late nineties that higher educational levels, professional occupations, and income go hand-in-hand.

For example, the college French professor with a doctorate, on a very modest income, is likely to select entirely different pattern designs than the plumbing contractor with a high household income and no college debt. Additionally, in recent studies we have seen a move to simplify, downsize, and recycle. Younger age groups also are less enamored with fashion dictates, and tend to prefer natural looks and distressed effects. Their heritage mix and sometimes hand-me-down style combinations are referred to as "trash chic" or "shabby chic" in some quarters, or "treasured finds"—a source of pride. This is the bohemian version of the deliberate "sophisticated mix." Those with incomes below-$35,000 desire more than they can currently afford but they tend to also be less pro-pattern and prefer solids and textures, along with simpler color palettes. Novelty designs and character/kids patterns do a bit better with this group—often young and old households. In fabric looks, moiré-type designs and satin effects are perceived as higher end. There also are retirees in this group, making it more conservative. This under $35,000 household-income group includes stay-at-home moms, homemakers, retirees, and part-timers, which accounts for the higher rating of character/kids patterns.

In the $35,000–$75,000 income range, there is a higher interest level in more types of patterns and finishes, which tends also to reflect a middle-American suburban selection. The style of choice is country, leaning toward a more casual approach in a simpler color palette. The next higher-income group (more than $75,000) is more likely to favor "sophisticated eclectic blend," with traditional looks next. This group also gives the palette of navy, light blue, forest green, berry, oyster, and so on, and darker wood finishes a higher ranking. It is a "preppy" look. The higher-income group gives higher ratings to a much greater variety of patterns.

It should be noted the $75,000-plus income range level is 14.8 percent of the population based on U.S. Census data and the annual real median income in 1995 was $34,076.[2] Households in the $125,000 plus income range level constitute 7.3 percent of the population. It is important to pinpoint income-level differences for a designer's higher-end client base and to accomodate higher earning levels on both coasts, urban areas, and dual-income households. It is also important to consider a lower- to lower-middle-income— and very large—consumer base.

Study Six: Pattern-Design Preferences Based on Occupation

Professional/technical/managerial:	Miniprints, botanicals, faux/stone, fabric looks, natural
Service/blue collar/administrative:	Miniprints, botanicals, natural textures, novelty, kids
Homemakers, part-time, retirees:	Miniprints, fabric looks, kids

N=3,500 pattern types in rank order by occupation. Rodemann, Patricia. © 1996. Study Six.

Designs preferred in a higher income level are stripes, silks, damasks, faux/marble, and florals. Transitional and combinations of pattern designs also do well in this group. Younger high-income consumers were less apt to select the small prints and florals, and instead go for textural and natural looks. Historic, cultural, and architectural designs rated higher with this higher-income group. Increasingly a "clean" patternless, more exotic, textural look is emerging.

All three occupational groups were affected by two factors: 1) the rendition of a design (fine painterly quality vs. poor rendition), and 2) the caché associated with both the type of design and/or brand name. As discovered in thesis research, a cheap, simulated rendition scores poorly in both high and low income groups, and among professionals and laborers alike. *Similarly, a well-known, highly regarded brand-name design is better received when all other things are equal—including the design.* Higher-income professionals will rate a light small print on a dark-hued background higher than its reverse: the same design in darker hue on a white background. The opposite is true for blue-collar employees and retirees. Some of this tendency may be a function of smaller spaces and fewer windows in older homes; some of it may be exposure-based, or fear of making a design mistake. Similar findings came out of extensive color-research studies.

In general, professional/technical/managerial occupations tend to rate a broader range of designs and more diverse patterns and finishes higher than service/administrative/blue collar and support-staff occupations. Consistent with higher income levels is a more sophisticated style look with a neutral or traditional palette and natural materials. Homemakers/part-timers and retirees frequently have similar pattern perceptions to blue-collar/administrative/service employees or those with household incomes of more than $35,000; however, these groups part as different palettes, styles, finishes, and shopping plans are evaluated. In this scenario, retirees and homemakers mirror both the shopping-destination preference and some of the selections of professional/managerial consumers—perhaps based on prior experience and exposure.

It is apparent that there are regional differences. Retirees in Florida may have a very different design outlook than retirees in Idaho. Residents of Arizona, regardless of occupation, will have regional predispositions that transcend other demographic factors. *It is impossible to say which factor will be more significant in predisposing an individual to select one pattern design over another. In looking at groups of consumer ratings based on each demographic factor, we are able to derive profiles or pictures that may be compared with sales results or used for predictive modeling. Because pattern introduction/acceptance runs in cycles—like hemlines—it is important for the research process to be an ongoing one, and not opinion-driven. I see changes year to year. Typical product development and launch cycles do not always coincide with the "mood of the moment."*

Study Six: Pattern-Design Preferences Based on Educational Level

High school/two-year tech:	Miniprints; lower % ratings on all design types
College degree/postgraduate:	Miniprints, botanicals, faux/stone, fabric effects, natural textures, stripes, florals

N=3,500. Rodemann, Patricia. © 1996. Study Six.

Consistent with professional occupations and higher income, a higher education tends to predispose an individual to a greater variety and diversity of patterns, color palettes, and finishes. With higher educational levels (four-year college degree and/or postgraduate), tastes are bolder and more sophisticated. High-school graduates tend to take a more conservative decorating approach with more solid colors, fewer colors, and more neutrals. The differences become more noticeable by specific design styles, with college-educated consumers giving "country French," "neoclassic," or "Shaker" and patterns associated with

Study Six: Pattern-Design Preferences Based on Age

< age 35:	Faux/marble, moiré, wide stripes, narrow stripes, small prints
age 36–45:	Small prints, faux/marble, moiré, wide stripes, narrow stripes, small floral trail
age 46–55:	Small floral trail, miniprint, vertical silk
age 56–65:	Miniprint, medium-scale florals, damask, small floral, moiré

N=3,500. Rodemann, Patricia. © 1996. Study Six.

these styles higher ratings—perhaps because of increased awareness and understanding.

The youngest consumer group preferred botanicals, wide stripes, abstract stripes, tapestry, and paisley designs overall. The oldest group preferred damask stripes and prints; and the middle-aged groups split the difference. *And retirees of the 1980s and '90s will not necessarily predict the behavior of retirees of the future.* With the exception of small floral miniprints and patchwork, all highly rated pattern designs show a higher-educational-level consumer—regardless of age. What are the individual demographic profiles that go with each pattern-design type? What are the preferred patterns by style? Can we generalize that far? Which types of designs do consumers prefer overall? Does response vary among applications?

After reviewing hundreds of samples within each design category with thousands of consumers over more than a decade, we are able to make some generalizations in a Western contemporary cultural context from both small qualitative and nationally projectable data:

> *1) Each pattern design and each pattern grouping has its own semantic vocabulary—what I call "traits of meaning"—associated with it. 2) Certain renditions or pattern types are preferred within each category—nationally. Initially, I began my thesis studies in grayscale/neutrals across all types to eliminate color bias. Later, as I had sufficient numbers of both design samples and consumers, I evaluated designs in several color palettes. 3) If a pattern-design type rated highly and was well liked, results were consistent across several color palettes. If a pattern-design type rated poorly or mediocre, a "favored" color palette could cause the design to score higher than the other color renditions, but below what a truly preferred combination of pattern and color could do.*

Though each design and colorway has its own ratings and interpretations, I have distilled these responses from several thesis studies to assist our understanding, supplemented as needed by selective research data from the first large-scale study. Looking at each pattern category, we can arrive at a fuller understanding of pattern preference, pattern "meaning," and pattern "personality." We will look at behavior in later chapters. One would expect a consumer who rates traditional style highly to also rate traditional patterns highly. This is why we also evaluate pattern by style. It is important to look at many measures rather than to say, "Floral rates thus and therefore…" Context is everything. Within a particular shopper class, income class, or age group, one understands each pattern rating differently.

There are many ways to approach "pattern," pattern research, pattern-color combinations, and pattern classifications, and there are almost as many opinions. There are experimental approaches, personality/social psychology, retail, marketing, product- or industry-specific, interior versus exterior, and evolutionary/biological or fashion approaches. No single approach is right for everyone, just as pattern doesn't work the same way for everyone. Pattern research is an art rather than a science; it is always referential and contextual. As we look at pattern use, preference, and context through the various lenses of standard research methodologies, very interesting observations arise that transcend our preoccupation with "what's hot and what's not." Pattern research should

IHDG, Sunworthy Splash of Color

There is no doubt that region, age, gender, cultural heritage, occupation, and education inform our color, pattern, and style selections. Physiological, emotional, cognitive, and seasonal/climactic influences are also at work.

go far beyond preference alone to include utility/function and purpose. *Lifestyle will dictate function; lifestage will dictate the motivation; and the space itself will direct purpose.* It is all highly complex, but also fascinating; and ultimately, our results are very, very useful. Pattern effect, use, and preference are essential, because billions of marketing dollars are at stake, along with human functioning and well-being.

References

1. Pantone, Inc. 590 Commerce Boulevard, Carlstadt, N.J. 07072-3098.
2. U.S. Bureau of the Census. 1997. "Money income of households percent distribution, by income level, race, and Hispanic origin in constant (1995) dollars: 1970 to 1995," in *Statistical abstract of the United States,* 117th ed., no. 717, prepared by the Economics and Statistics Administration of the Bureau of the Census. Washington, D.C., 465.

CHAPTER 3

Pattern Language and Response

Looking at the consumer responses to pattern categories, we begin to see expectations, preferences, mental imagery, and contextual boundaries defined for us. Several years of thesis surveys and survey methodologies are represented to help enrich our understanding of common pattern categories. Often the pattern in and of itself is little more than decoration, art, and ornament. It has little ability to impact our spatial perception, mood, or even behavior until it moves into a full setting in myriad lighting conditions and different scale spaces, with other design mixes. Pattern selections are also sensitive to economics, weather conditions, and cultural and world events, in the same way color palettes are. What we have learned is how absolutely referential pattern types, renditions, and categories are, and what cognitive associations consumers are making. This is what we will explore in chapter 3.

FLORALS

Traditional floral design

Romantic floral design

From the first thesis study, I evaluated contemporary florals, traditional florals, Jacobean florals, floral stripes, stylized florals, random small floral trails, medium-scale floral designs, large cabbage roses and large-scale floral trails, abstract brushy florals, medallion-effect florals, Victorian oversize florals, and tonal floral designs, among others. With the floral-pattern category, much depends on the style and the scale. Some styles, such as traditional, Victorian, country French, and American country, tend to be associated historically with greater floral-pattern usage. My ongoing research supports this. Rendition, too, has become an important factor. In many cases, the more tonal and simpler the pattern rendition, the greater acceptance (less to take offense at). I believe this runs in cycles, much like color or fashion. The larger the scale of the design, the smaller the group of people the pattern appeals to. A great deal of this is related to potential usage, fear, or degree of sophistication. There may be evolutionary biological explanations, or lifestyle/behavioral factors at work. A fatigued individual probably is less likely to select a "busy" combination of florals. Perhaps in our distant past, busy florals in a setting of heavy vegetation concealed danger.

Because florals, natural textures, and botanic patterns derive more directly from natural inspiration, we also may find a different standard of acceptance than for modern geometric design types. These cues bear further research.

Semantic vocabulary: Traits of floral designs as perceived by consumers

Archives of Columbus Coated Fabrics, Div. Borden, Inc.

Contemporary floral (Study One)

Archives of Columbus Coated Fabrics, Div. Borden, Inc.

Traditional floral (Study One)

Thesis Study One: Contemporary

Ascending quality	67%
Simple (rendition)	62%
Busy (movement)	61%
Positive	52%
Orderly	52%

Based on 32 adjective pairs: responses > 50%.

Study One: Traditional Design

Would be comfortable with design on all four walls: 66% disagree or strongly disagree

Design would be appealing in different color: 58% disagree or strongly disagree

Thesis Study Two: Group of Floral Designs

Archives of Columbus Coated Fabrics, Div. Borden, Inc.

 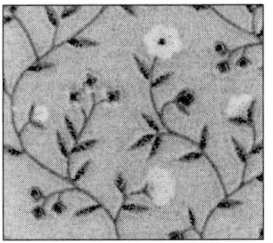 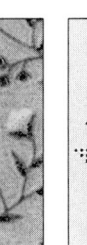 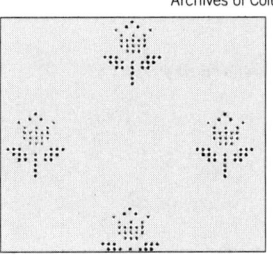 

Traditional design
Least liked

Small trail

Miniprint

Contemporary
Best liked

Study Two: Semantic vocabulary

Simple	59%
Hospitable	59%
Appealing	53%
Harmonious	53%
Relaxed	53%

Based on a selection of 66 adjectives;
responses > 50%.

Would be comfortable with any of these patterns on all four walls:

Yes:	70%
No:	24%
Maybe:	6%

Note: Language is relatively neutral to positive. Smaller-scale designs are preferred.

Likely to consider purchase of this pattern type for my home decor:

Study Ten

Floral patterns Medium-Large-scale	For Walls	For Borders	For Textiles/ Furniture	Rugs/Carpet/ Flooring
Major/heavy or Primary usage	9%	30%	36%	19%
Coordinate/some use	16%	31%	23%	19%
Very limited or Accent use only	75%	39%	41%	62%

© 1998, Patricia Rodemann. Study Ten, Thesis Follow-up.

Note: As the area and scale increase, the rating and applications decrease.

Where is a floral-pattern type most likely to be installed:

Study One: Contemporary		*Study Two: Group of Floral Designs*	
Home	48%	Restaurant	70%
Hotel	38%	Home	59%
Hospital	28%	Hotel	53%
Office	19%	Hospital	47%
None of the above	19%	Office	29%
Store/s	14%	All of these	18%
Church/religious	9%	Store	6%
School	4%	Church	6%
All of the above	4%	School	0%
		None of these	0%

Rodemann, Patricia. ©1991. Master's Thesis, The Ohio State University. Columbus, Ohio.

> Note: Restaurant, hotel, home, health-care applications—florals convey the "home" ambience.

Personal usage:

Study One: Contemporary

Would not install in own home: 66%

Feelings about design type:

Study One: Contemporary	*Study Two: Group of Floral Patterns*
Combined age groups:	41% like or strongly like
48% neutral on design	29% neutral

Comments	*Comments*
Okay in large space	Normal, common, neutral,
Shapes too large/too close together	comfortable, not too busy
Not my style	dislike because too many flowers
Not my taste; like, not for *my* home	moving sideways, diagonal, busy

Which floral-pattern rendition is most preferred and why:

Soft Contemporary:	*Small/Miniprints:*
Has nice overall effect	Not as much is happening
Casual feel	Orderly
Simple styling	Least distraction
Not overbearing	Nice overall background effect
Brushy, most pleasing	Not too busy

Style and pattern rendition:

Study Six: Floral Designs in Order of Importance by Primary Interior Style of Home

1. American country
2. Victorian-romantic
3. Traditional style
4. Sophisticated-mix style
5. Casual contemporary

Note: Style context associated with floral-design type. Country, Victorian, traditional styles are notably "pro-floral."

N=3,500. ©1996 Patricia Rodemann

Which consumer demographic prefers floral designs:

There is a greater acceptance of floral designs overall in Southern regions. Smaller-scale florals find additional acceptance in Northeastern and Midwestern markets; medium-scale florals in the Midwest. Small- and medium-scale florals tend to rate more highly in smaller and midsize population markets, with large-scale florals doing best in urban markets. From a gender standpoint, florals are preferred by females; for small-scale designs, nearly 2:1. There also is a correlation between scale and income, with small-scale florals appealing more to lower-income households, and income increasing to the highest levels for large-scale designs. Though there is a differing degree of sophistication evident with larger-scale designs, this is true for complex, newer color palettes and neutrals, but not necessarily for brighter palettes.

From an occupational standpoint, homemakers, part-time employees, and retirees are more apt to prefer small- and medium-scale designs; professional/managerial employees are more apt to prefer larger-scale florals. Younger households (under age 45) tend to select smaller-scale designs; medium- to larger-scale florals are selected more often by age 46–55 consumers. Consumers selecting floral patterns are more likely to have a college education.

Traits consumers prefer in floral designs:

Do	Don't
The right scale	Knock "em dead size—bigger than a human hand
Simple	But not so plain the design is boring
Not overbearing	You should not feel seasick in any setting
Not fussy	With tendrils, trails, buds, blooms, too many colors
Doesn't crawl	You should not feel suspicious of your wallpaper
Not involved	Tight, too realistic and pointy with lots of stuff
Orderly	Without seeing regimental blobs every 6 inches
Contemporary rendition, soft	But not too cutesy
Casual feel	But not so they're reading things into it, guessing
Brushy look, watercolor	But the spacing is critical between the repeat
Not too busy	Thirty florals in a 10" x 10" rooms is too much

GEOMETRICS/PLAIDS

York Wallcoverings, Carey Lind Houndstooth Collection

York Wallcoverings, Scottish Plaid

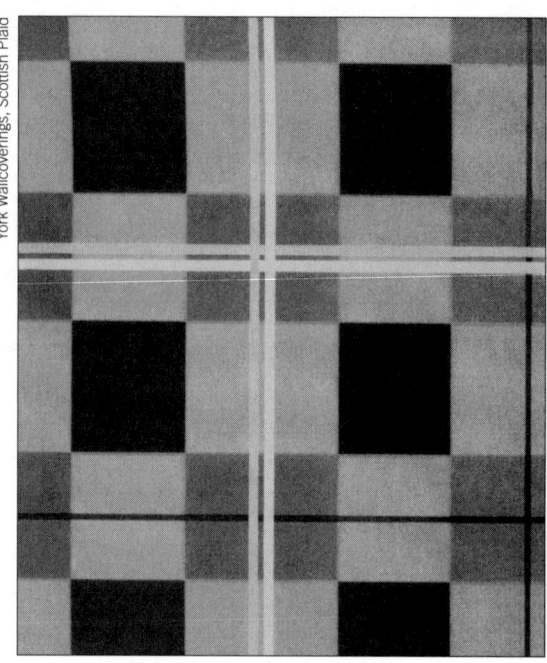

Soft plaid paired with other patterns adds warm appeal.

Rich hues add sense of quality, and plaid is both balanced and contextual.

In the first thesis study, I compared stripe and checkerboard designs within the geometric category. Subsequently, from study two onward, stripes became a separate category. For my thesis research, I evaluated checks, plaids, diagonals, diamonds, checkerboards, grids, ginghams, tartans, houndstooths, Campbells, herringbone, squares, and buffalo checks in as many color palettes. With the geometric category, it is imperative that we consider familiarity, context, and rendition, and product type/application such as flooring, fabric, laminate, or wall-covering. Flooring is the most expected and predictable application for this type of pattern design. Fabric is used in more limited quantity; therefore, some of the considerations we address may not be as critical as for either floor-covering (tile) or large-surface wall designs.

In this category and stripes, what works in fashion does not necessarily work in home decor. Expensive argyle socks may make the man, so we infer they will also "make" his bathroom or den in the same scale and color palette. A madras plaid that makes a gorgeous fabric does not always translate as well to wall-covering on all four walls and the ceiling. The pattern in context also tends to tie heavily with gender because we invariably carry internalized hierarchial relationships between visual images, memories, and cultural programming. Beyond matching issues, it becomes a question of degree: How much is too much? Our thresholds vary. A geometric flooring motif may be unsuitable for textiles or walls without adjustment in scale. A sharp-edged and contrasty rendition of geometric/plaid patterns may have optical characteristics to it. In general, softer renditions in less contrasty colors or with a textural component are preferred. In nature, tortoiseshells, snakeskin, honeycomb, and insect eyes in magnification reveal intricate geometric designs. This should tell us that believable color mixes, proper hue saturation, and context are critical design factors for geometrics. The more organic our geometrics—in fractal or natural designs—the higher the preference. The higher contrast, the greater the danger signal to us. In the hands of a talented professional, geometric designs can add tremendous warmth and a sense of familiarity.

Semantic vocabulary: Traits of geometric/plaid designs as perceived by consumers

Study One: Checkerboard

Noisy	81%
Unlivable	76%
Unappealing	71%
Awful	71%
Distracting	71%
Upsetting	71%
Annoying	66%
Tense	66%
Uncomfortable	62%
Disturbed	62%
Unhealthy	61%
Discordant	57%
Wearying	52%
Awful	71%

Based on 32 adjective pairs: responses > 50%.
Rodemann, Patricia. © 1991. Master's Thesis, The Ohio State University. Columbus, Ohio.

Archives of Columbus Coated Fabrics, Div. Borden, Inc.

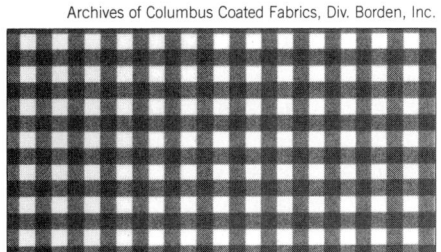

High-contrast checkerboard design (Study One)

There is a significant difference in response to familiar flannel-shirt plaids vs. the acuity patterns, as we note here.

It should be noted, the older the age group, the worse high-contrast designs fared. Positive to neutral responses in the youngest group, were often neutral to negative in the middle-aged group and negative to very negative for the elderly.

Study Two: Group of Geometric Designs

Archives of Columbus Coated Fabrics, Div. Borden, Inc.

Big blanket plaid design, least liked (Study Two)

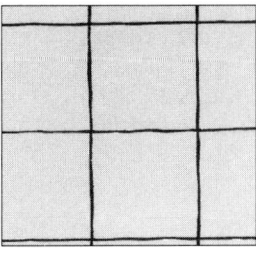

Checkerboard (Study Two)

Gingham (Study Two)

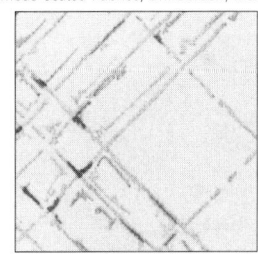

Diagonal/softness, most-liked (Study Two)

Study Two: Semantic Vocabulary

Orderly	65%
Directed	41%
Busy	40%
Annoying	35%
Repelling	29%
Uncomfortable	29%
Unexciting	29%
Simple	29%

Based on a selection of 66 adjectives: responses >25%.

Would be comfortable with any of these patterns on all four walls:

Yes:	24%
No:	76%
Maybe:	0%

Rodemann, Patricia. © 1991. Master's Thesis, The Ohio State University. Columbus, Ohio.

Note: Between studies one and two there are significant semantic differences "crossing the line" between rejection and acceptance. This is a finer line with the geometric-pattern category. The second group of geometrics offered far less contrast. An exciting Art Deco geometric may be ideal for a theater lobby, but not the 12' × 15' living room.

Most suitable product categories for this type of pattern:

Study Ten: Likely to consider purchase of this pattern type for my home decor:

Geometric/Plaid Patterns	For Walls	For Borders	For Textiles/ Furniture	Rugs/Carpet/ Flooring
Major/heavy or Primary usage	27%	23%	48%	18%
Coordinate/some	16%	24%	26%	16%
Very limited or Accent use only	57%	53%	26%	66%

N=500. © 1998, Patricia Rodemann. Study Ten, Thesis Follow-up.

Note: Upholstery fabric is the most expected and natural application for this type of design. But this fabric also is used in more limited quantities; therefore it is not as critical as for large-surface wall designs. A great deal depends on the skill of the designer, the contrast and *texture* of the design.

Where is a geometric-pattern type most likely to be installed:

Study One: Checkerboard

None of the above	38%
Hotel	28%
Home	28%
Store	24%
Office	19%
School	9%
Hospital	4%
Church/religious	0%
All of the above	0%

Rodemann, Patricia. © 1991. Master's Thesis, The Ohio State University. Columbus, Ohio.

Study Two: Group of Geometric Designs

Restaurant	70%
Home	47%
Hotel	41%
Office	47%
Store	47%
Hospital	24%
School	18%
All of these	6%
None of these	6%
Church/religious	0%

Consumers expect to see geometric types of design in commercial spaces—particularly in flooring design. At the same time, we need to be sensitive to nuances and effects in all applications.

Personal usage:

Study One: checkerboard

Would not install in own home: 76%

Feelings about design type:

Study One: checkerboard

Combined age groups: 61% dislike design

Comments:

Squares too close; too loud
Can't deal with this; makes me very tense
Gives me claustrophobia
Hurts my eyes and makes me feel sick
A smaller check would be okay; not for walls

Study Two: Group of Geometrics
59% dislike
29% strongly dislike

Comments:

Don't like the ones that radiate
Plainer is better, not too contrasty
Too distracting, bleah—I feel sick
Behind my eyes, see spots, too busy
Is bold and graphic, contemporary-like

Which geometric pattern rendition is most preferred and why:

Soft Diagonal Plaid:	*Diamond Motif:*
Used to have in home in red/white	Most soothing
Smooth and subtle	Not dramatic
Least distracting	Least distraction
Okay	Pleasant background effect
Not exciting	Not too busy

Style and pattern rendition:

Study Six: Geometric Designs in Order of Importance by Primary Interior Style of Home:

1. Traditional style
2. American country
3. Victorian-romantic
4. Sophisticated mix style
5. Casual contemporary

N=3,500. © 1996. Patricia Rodemann.

Consumers expect to pair plaids with country-club traditional looks, and with homespun American country-type designs. With other style categories, the differences between pattern renditions and types become quite pronounced. *The pattern-style connection is a strong one.*

Which consumer demographic prefers geometric/plaid designs:

Looking at three types of geometric designs: a small checker, a Scottish-look shirt plaid design and a graphic diamond, we found distinct differences in preference by demographic. All three designs were preferred by higher-educational-level consumers. The small checker— a simpler gingham-type motif—was better received among residents of smaller population markets, and among Southerners and Midwesterners. Females prefer the smaller scale (gingham) type of geometric 2:1 over males. The smallest geometric tends to appeal to two income groups: upper middle and lower income. Homemakers, part-time employees, and retirees are represented more than other occupational groups in rating this pattern type highly. This is most apt to be a middle-age consumer 36–45, and then 46–55. By contrast, both plaid designs and more graphic diamond motifs tend to be preferred by urban residents. Plaid design motifs are preferred by Midwestern, Western, and Southern consumers; graphic diamonds do better with Southern, Western and Northeastern residents. In both cases, males rate these types of geometrics higher for wall-surface coverings and females for textiles. Both design types—when medium to large in scale—are preferred by middle- to upper-middle income households with consumers under 36 years of age; though some of the plaid designs extend to the 36–45 age range.

Traits consumers prefer in geometric print/plaid designs:

Do	*Don't*
Low contrast; light touch	Attempt to recreate pop art for an aging population
Familiar	Overdo the clichés
Contemporary	Cross the line to another era
Not too busy	Forget the psycho-physical aspect
Simple	Use lots of colors, sharply crisscrossing everywhere
Less printed pattern	Go too dark, dense
Keep it subtle	Specify without seeing a bigger piece
Watch the scale	Forget the impact on walls or flooring
Diagonals better	Forget the edge-to-edge match
Watch spacing	Overlook the "closure" effect; vibration effect
Not hard-edged	Overlook the natural and textile origins

SMALL GRAPHIC DESIGNS/MINIPRINTS

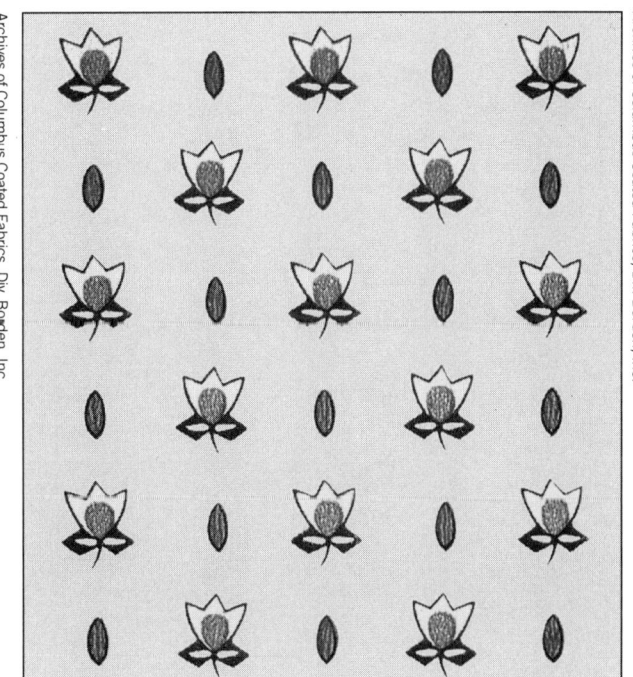

Archives of Columbus Coated Fabrics, Div. Borden, Inc.

Archives of Columbus Coated Fabrics, Div. Borden, Inc.

Miniprint design, country look background

Stylized miniprint design example

In examining the small-scale graphic or miniprint design, we must point out the wide variance in shape. A definition of this type of print puts the typical size at smaller than a quarter, and usually smaller than a dime for reference. These designs are almost always regimental, in that they repeat in a smaller range than other pattern types. I have researched Swiss dot, tiny stars, tulips, arrows, crosses, buds, fleur-de-lis, medallions, "ditsy dots," and foulards. In fashion, these prints make up neckties, socks, shorts, shirts, pajamas, girls' dresses, infant sleepers, ladies blouses, sleepwear, dresses, and similar articles of clothing. In home decor, this design type seems to have a specific context and is often used in smaller spaces when walls, countertops, or floors are involved. This is the "go with" piece of furniture or textile, because it can be used with other pattern types quite successfully. It is seldom a stand-alone pattern type. In commercial spaces the small graphic design is often wonderfully employed in upholstery for contract seating, in hospitality restrooms, or even in contract carpet in deeper hues with bolder borders of other pattern types. This versatile pattern type shows up in nature on a diamondback rattler, feathers, fur, insects (lady bug and butterfly wings), and in snowflakes. Perhaps our positive ratings connect with the latter and our negative responses to more insect-like designs, from a bioevolutionary viewpoint.

Semantic vocabulary: Traits of small graphic designs and miniprints as perceived by consumers

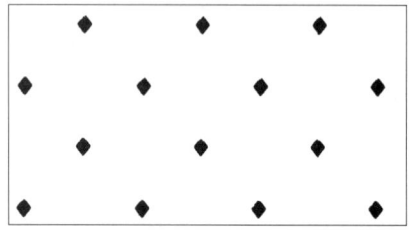

Tiny diamond print (Study One)

Archives of Columbus Coated Fabrics, Div. Borden, Inc.

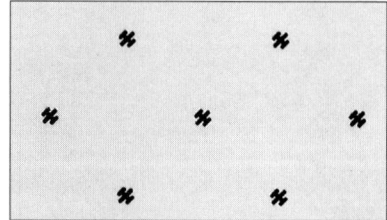

Small abstract shape design (Study One)

Study One: Tiny Diamond

Orderly	83%
Appealing	83%
Hospitable	83%
Familiar	83%
Comfortable	75%
Harmonious	75%
Rhythmic	75%
Pleasing	67%
Livable	66%

Based on 32 adjective pairs: responses > 50%.

Study One: Small Abstract Design

Would be comfortable with design on all four walls: 49% disagree or strongly disagree; 33% neutral

Design would be appealing in different color: 41% disagree; 41% agree

Rodemann, Patricia. © 1991. Master's Thesis, The Ohio State University. Columbus, Ohio.

Study Two: Group of Graphic Miniprint Designs[15]

Archives of Columbus Coated Fabrics, Div. Borden, Inc.

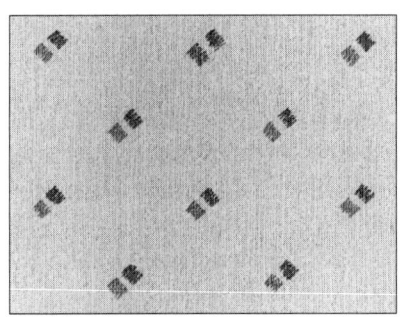

Square miniprint,
least liked (Study Two)

Medallion design
(Study Two)

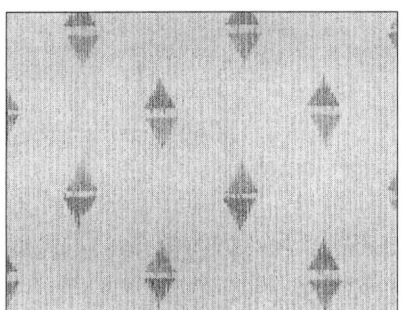

Flame and tiny diamond
graphic motif (Study Two)

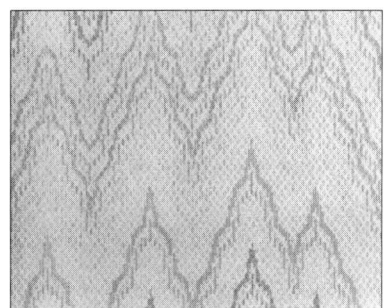

Chevron, most-liked
design type (Study Two)

Study Two: Semantic Vocabulary

Orderly	76%
Simple	53%
Appealing	47%
Livable	47%
Rhythmic	47%
Comfortable	47%
Pleasing	40%

Based on a selection of 66 adjectives:
responses >40%.

Would Be Comfortable with Any of These Patterns on All Four Walls:

Yes:	76%
No:	24%

Note: Consumers are largely favorable to this category of design in general terms. When shown dozens of specific designs, they become far "pickier," especially in the context of other more interesting patterns. In a framework of other types, the small graphic print is almost always selected in third or fourth place after the feature designs. It is often overlooked as boring, but pulls significant sales dollars in the right palettes.

Likely to consider purchase of this pattern type for my home decor:

Study Ten

Miniprint and small patterns	For Walls	For Borders	For Textiles/ Furniture	Rugs/Carpet/ Flooring
Major/heavy or Primary usage	33%	28%	39%	18%
Coordinate/some use	26%	32%	32%	16%
Very limited or Accent use only	41%	40%	29%	66%

N=500. ©1998, Patricia Rodemann. Study Ten, Thesis Follow-up

Note: There is a fairly high level of acceptance for the category in general. The more specific the small print design becomes, the narrower the audience and application.

Where is a small/miniprint pattern type most likely to be installed:

Study One: Diamond Miniprint

Home	83%
Hotel	83%
Office	75%
Hospital	50%
Store	50%
School	25%
Church/religious	16%
None of the above	0%
All of the above	0%

Study Two: Group of Small Prints

Home	70%
Hospital	59%
Hotel	53%
Office	35%
School	29%
All of these	29%
Restaurant	24%
Store	24%
Church/religious	12%
None of these	0%

Note: There is an almost universal application for this pattern type.

Personal usage:

Study One: Diamond Miniprint

would install in own home: 42%; no 42%; unsure 16%

Feelings about design type:

Study One: Diamond Miniprint

Combined age groups:50% neutral on design
41% strongly like

Comments:

Nonthreatening; not overbearing in scale
Prefer smaller prints and patterns
Simple, easy to coordinate
Scale too small; looks like bugs
Too distracting; moves on me (thick glasses)
Not ugly, but bothers me because of its motion

Study Two: Group of Small Patterns

65% like or strongly like;
29% neutral

Comments:

Soothing, light feeling, refreshing
Subtle, familiar, contemporary
Pleasing, feels homey, pretty effect
Seems overused, ordinary, and boring
Can't do anything with it like connecting
    the dots like other mini
Too many little "things"

Which small-print pattern rendition is most preferred and why:

Chevron Motif:

Light feeling, reminds of vacation
Shapes are familiar—like boats
Contemporary and clean look
More open quality
Other designs appear busy

Small Miniprints:

Decorative and lively look
Okay on lots of walls; not oppressive
Caught my eye but not distracting
Not so pronounced that it's first thing
your eyes go to

Style and pattern rendition:

Study Six: Small Print Designs in Order of Importance by Primary Interior Style of Home:

1. American country
2. Traditional style
3. Victorian-romantic
4. Casual contemporary
5. Sophisticated mix style

Note: Country and traditional styles favor miniprint designs the most; sophisticated styles the least.

N=3,500. ©1996. Patricia Rodemann.

Which consumer demographic prefers small-print designs:

Small-print or miniprint designs are most preferred by residents of small towns and suburbanites. Tiny-dot-cluster motifs are preferred by Southern and Midwestern consumers; tiny florals by Midwestern, West Coast, and Northeastern consumers; and small stylized shell designs by Southern and Northeastern consumers. Females prefer small-scale designs (in some cases, the floral types) 2:1 to males. This design type appeals largely to middle-income households; more abstract (dot cluster and shapes) appeal to higher-income households. The closer to defined florals, the more likely the tiny design will appeal to lower-middle-income range. Professional/managerial consumers are also more likely to find the abstract designs appealing; homemakers, part-timers, and retirees prefer the smaller floral miniprints; and service/blue collar/administrative consumers prefer shell-type designs. Interestingly, the more abstract small designs are preferred by the under-age-45 cohort; more defined designs are rated higher with over age 46. Abstract miniprints are preferred by college educated consumers; tiny florals and sharply defined designs by those with high-school backgrounds.

Small-print designs tend to be seen as simpler and easier to use. This type of pattern is more readily available at discount department stores, fabric stores, and home-center channels at affordable pricing in table wear, upholstered goods, accessories, and wall-coverings. In flooring, it is often used as part of an overall motif (carpet), or bordered by decorative trim.

Traits consumers prefer in small-print/graphic designs:

Do	Don't
A light feeling	Replicate fussy little designs over and over
Refreshing quality	Forget the importance of openness to this design
Newer shapes	Than Colonial, 70s minis, 60s daisies, shells
Familiar	Without being boring
Homey	But not odd little hairy, spikey shapes that look like they bite or sting
Differing values	Overlook the importance of background/motif
Orderly	But not regimented to distraction (squares/diamonds)
Enough spacing	But not a connect-the-dots effect, or too "floaterly"
Keep soft and intriguing	Don't get too hard-edged or photo-realistic
Use soothing tones	Overlook—especially in large spaces, open areas
Not too many things	Forget this pattern type is a "go with," not a "go from"

NATURAL TEXTURES

Archives of Columbus Coated Fabrics, Div. Borden, Inc.

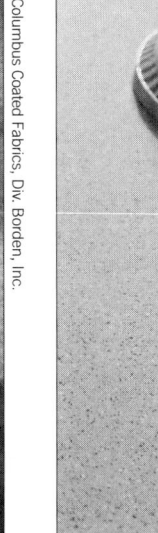

Formica Corporation

Faux marble wall surface design makes
a classic statement.

Finely rendered stone design laminate

Natural textures and simulations of natural textures are familiar to us as creatures of the earth. From the time we lived in caves and noticed the forest floor to the time we made huts and earthen homes, natural textures have formed our most basic and functional design materials. One would expect an innate familiarity and a different perception of the design patterns of natural textures. These designs are characterized by infinite variety, and regional and cultural qualities. As humankind developed, natural textures were considered crude—the stuff of peasant life—except for the finest, most precious of nature's gifts. Humankind became enamored with created, replicated, manufactured, and ornamented design—and even faux replications either for the fun of it, or when the real thing was not available. Faced with extinction, scarcity, and a different (preservation) ethic today, "natural" has again taken on a changed quality of meaning. I have researched suede, leather, hides, skins, faux-finish looks, real marbles, granite, stone, mica, alabaster, terrazzo, clay, combed-plaster effects, woods and wood grains, steel, iron, parchment, papyrus, cane, basket-weave effects, bamboo, and cloud-print effects. Though the natural-effects design type is most heavily used in contract installations, sophisticated consumers increasingly are again turning to these materials and looks for countertops, flooring, walls, and occasionally even printed and textured-fabric effects. Reptile skins, furs, and related looks are not included in these data or pattern groupings, even though I have researched these pattern types. Natural elements such as snowflakes, clouds, galaxies, aggregates, and even corpuscles may be composed of fractional dimensions—geometrically—which give them an infinite quality. These are known as fractal designs. In other words, a small portion gives us an inkling of the whole design. One school of thought holds that humans are inherently predisposed to these natural types of designs. In initial thesis studies, my goal was to arrive at basic characteristics and perceptions of "natural" versus "created." In subsequent studies, natural designs were segregated into multiple renditions and types within multiple product categories in multiple color palettes. Stones, metals, woods, and grasses were not grouped as one "natural" category, but segregated. This provided a very sophisticated and deep level of data when coupled with other demographics.

Semantic vocabulary: Traits of natural-texture designs as perceived by consumers

Archives of Columbus Coated Fabrics, Div. Borden, Inc.

Smooth alabaster design (Study One)

Archives of Columbus Coated Fabrics, Div. Borden, Inc.

Textural marble design (Study One)

Study One: Smooth Alabaster

Subdued	83%
Harmonious	66%
Relaxed	66%
Unexciting	66%
Serene	58%
Comfortable	58%
Quiet	58%
Calm	58%

Based on a selection of 66 adjectives.
Responses >50% shown here.

Study One: Textural Marble

Would be comfortable with design on all four walls: 91% agree (50%), or strongly agree (41%)

Design would be appealing in different color: 58% agree (33%), or strongly agree (25%)

Rodemann, Patricia. ©1991. Master's Thesis, The Ohio State University. Columbus, Ohio.

Study Two: Group of Natural-Texture Designs

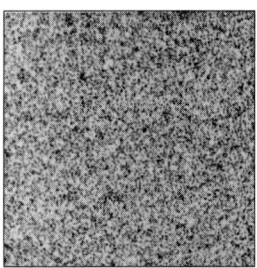
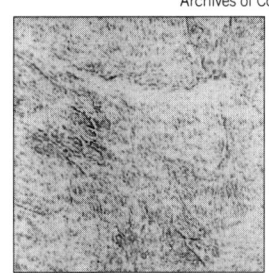
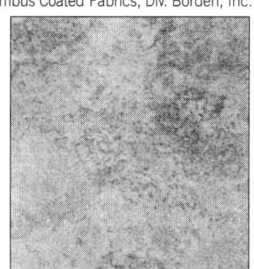

| Wood/woodgrain design, least liked (Study Two) | Fine, dense stone/granite design (Study Two) | Stucco/plaster-effect design (Study Two) | Leather/suede/skin/faux design effect, most liked (Study Two) |

Note: The "tighter" and "colder" the rendition (granite), the lower it was rated.

Study Two: Semantic Vocabulary

Appealing	59%
Comfortable	59%
Simple	59%
Restful	53%
Livable	53%
Calming	53%

Based on a selection of 66 adjectives. Responses >50% shown here.

Would Be Comfortable with Any of These Patterns on All Four Walls:

Yes:	76%
No:	24%

Rodemann, Patricia. © 1991. Master's Thesis, The Ohio State University. Columbus, Ohio.

Note: Natural textures are perceived as neutral to positive; usable and familiar anywhere.

Likely to consider purchase of this pattern type for my home decor:

Study Ten

Stone/Faux-look Pattern Design	For Walls	For Borders	For Textiles/ Furniture	Rugs/Carpet/ Flooring
Major/heavy or primary usage	45%	32%	23%	24%
Coordinate/some use	6%	8%	11%	13%
Very limited or accent use only	49%	60%	66%	63%

N=500. © 1998, Patricia Rodemann. Study Ten, Thesis Follow-up.

Note: Study Ten defines natural textures to include grasses, basket weave. Stone included marble and granite, plus faux looks.

Likely to consider purchase of this pattern type for my home decor:

Study Ten

Natural Patterns (Grass, Basketweave) and Products	For Walls	For Borders	For Textiles/ Furniture	Rugs/Carpet/ Flooring
Major/heavy or primary usage	32%	17%	32%	32%
Coordinate/some use	22%	17%	15%	13%
Very limited or accent use only	46%	66%	53%	55%

N=500. © 1998, Patricia Rodemann. Study Ten, Thesis Follow-up.

Where is a natural texture pattern type most likely to be installed:

Study One: Smooth Alabaster

Office	75%
Hospital	50%
Hotel	41%
Store	33%
Home	33%
School	16%
Church/religious	16%
None of the above	8%
All of the above	8%

Study Two: Group of Natural Textures

office	59%
hospital	53%
restaurant	47%
hotel	47%
store	47%
home	47%
all of these	29%
school	24%
church/relig.	18%
none of these	0%

Note: The natural-material look is most associated with commercial installations, though it increasingly is being used in the home — and especially at the higher end.

Personal usage:

Study One: Smooth Alabaster

Would not install in own home: 75%

Feelings about design type:

Study One: Smooth Alabaster

Combined age groups: 50% neutral on design; 25% dislike; 16% like lots; 9% unsure

Comments:

Would look good in the right place
Not emotionally moving
Okay, but not my personal taste
Don't like fake textures; go for real thing
Depressing, drab
Quiet, soothing—pleasing on large walls, floors
Other designs make me sick; this is healing

Study Two: Natural-Texture Group

47% like or strongly like; 18% neutral; 30% dislike; 5% unsure

Comments:

Simplest, subtle, usable anywhere
Subdued, yet visual interest
Has cold feeling to it, undefined
Simulated wood is never natural—imitations
    are contrived; awful
Peaceful, linear, little pattern
Open, light, more natural

Which natural texture/pattern rendition is most preferred and why:

Leather/Suede/Skin Effect:

Least obtrusive
Want to look more closely
Simplest, subtle, simplicity
Quite nice, restful
Not cold; not busy
Appears to have a "soft hand"

Style and pattern rendition:

Study Six: Natural Texture Designs in Order of Importance by Primary Interior Style of Home:

1. Sophisticated mix style
2. Casual contemporary
3. Victorian-romantic
4. Traditional style
5. American country

Note: The natural textures offer a wonderful "all styles go" opportunity to design around them. Consumers are inherently aware of this. Data indicate new approaches for the coming century.

N=3,500. © 1996. Patricia Rodemann.

Which consumer demographic prefers natural texture and stone designs:

There is a distinct correlation with "real" materials to higher household income, age, and higher educational levels. In general, there is an ever-growing trend toward authenticity in design selections, including pattern motifs and materials. Granite stone, multihued marbles, and woods are examples of such design types. Stone and complex textural renditions are preferred by urban residents; wood-finish designs in smaller markets—though there are sharp variations in the finish preferred. Western and Midwestern consumers seem to relate better to wood; Southern and Midwestern consumers to multihued marbles. Granite-type designs are also favored by Southerners, Midwesterners, and Westerners; and only the tiniest-flecked cooler granites are preferred by Northeasterners. Males tend to prefer granite/faux designs for walls; females prefer natural designs for textiles—but income plays a larger role. Higher-income households tend to prefer natural grass-cloth products and related renditions. In flooring, sisal and cork have made a comeback. All natural-inspired themes are favored by upper-middle-income consumer households. Homemakers, part-timers, and retirees place natural materials highly, as do professionals. The consumer for natural-stone-look designs is more likely to be college-educated. This audience also is more likely to fall within the 46–55 age range.

Traits consumers prefer in natural-texture designs:

Do	*Don't*
Simplest rendition	Do too many types in one material
Usable anywhere	But avoid the morgue effect or sauna feeling
Subtle surface interest	Get carried away and use everywhere
Peaceful	But it needs other design/color relief
Orderly feel	But watch the mix of designs
The real thing	Avoid poor imitations
Keep it light	Not heavy or dense
Contemporary rendition	Lose sight of texture and change in nature
Want to look closer	Use a synthetic, artificial-look finish
Warmth, timeless	Watch cold effect of stones; some woods are dated
Excellent reproductions	Not contrived renditions

TEXTILE EFFECTS

Damask stripe textile surface, a rich effect

Subtle background textile effect in neutral hues provides gentle surface interest.

"Textile effects" for our purposes are largely textural looks achieved by weave, finish, or design. Damasks, moirés, silks, burlaps, dobbies, plissé, seersucker, chenille, velvet, weaves, casements, tapestry, wool, linen, satin, cotton and Haitian cotton, corduroy, needlework, and flamestitch are all examples of textile effects I have examined. Printed textiles such as batiks, paisleys, and combination designs are excluded from this group; these have been examined in other categories. As with natural designs, textile effects have a quality of inherent familiarity—especially in a more organic, less processed form. The more formal renditions are associated with opulence, wealth, class, and a certain social status—a high historic-cultural meaning. Poor renditions and garish colors tend to be associated with imposters, "wanna-bes," specific objectives—like seduction—and less savvy or socially acceptable people. In this section, we will leave purple satin sheets, velvet paintings, and red-gold and black damask flocked wall-coverings up to the reader's imagination! For commercial use, hospitality and restaurant settings make the most significant use of textile effects for walls, upholstery, draperies and bedding, and flooring (custom carpet) designs. Health-care and office installations have also increasingly begun to include subtle, tonal variations of this design type. In the home, use of more formal satin, moiré, and watered silk looks have shifted to distressed, washed versions and aged effects with a timeless quality, less color and more tonal approaches. This new textural emphasis is most evident in upholstery, but has also extended to wall-covering looks, carpet, and other textiles. Diaphanous and shimmering fabric is as important as nubby texture today. It is an outcome of lifestyle and attitude changes. We want *real*. As web weavers, spiders are natural textile designers, but crosshatch and woven-effect visuals appear in many settings and objects, from leaves to cracked mud. Pearlescent seashells can have a moiré effect as even sand can appear like velvet in the right lighting. Our inspiration is natural, and we gravitate to this pattern type.

Semantic vocabulary: Traits of textile-effect designs as perceived by consumers

Archives of Columbus Coated
Fabrics, Div. Borden, Inc.

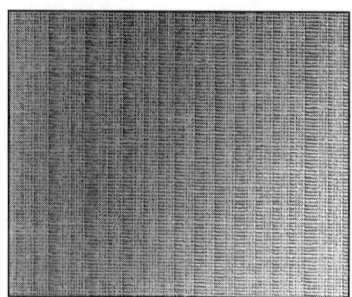

Woven effect textile (Study One)

Raw vertical silk effect (Study One)

Study One: Casement Weave

Orderly	100%
Harmonious	100%
Comfortable	100%
Quiet	100%
Familiar	100%
Relaxed	83%
Appealing	83%
Hospitable	83%
Harmonious	61%

Restful, rhythmic, pleasing, soothing, calming, nice = 75%

Based on 32 adjective pairs: responses >70%

Study One: Raw Vertical Silk

Would be comfortable with design on all four walls: 91% agree (41%), or strongly agree (50%)

Design would be appealing in different color: 58% agree or strongly agree; 33% neutral

Rodemann, Patricia. ©1991. Master's Thesis, The Ohio State University. Columbus, Ohio.

Study Two: Group of Textile-Effect Designs

Archives of Columbus Coated Fabrics, Div. Borden, Inc.

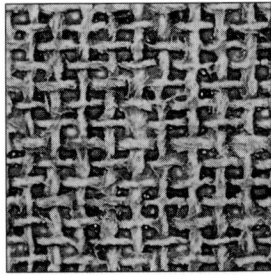   

| Burlap/coarse weave, least liked (Study Two) | Casement weave (Study Two) | Damask print (Study Two) | Vertical raw silk, most liked (Study Two) |

Study Two: Semantic Vocabulary

Orderly	65%
Simple	53%
Livable	53%
Hospitable	47%
Subdued	47%
Appealing	40%

Based on a selection of 66 adjectives: responses ≥ 40%.

Would Be Comfortable with Any of These Patterns on All Four Walls:

Yes:	65%
No:	35%

Rodemann, Patricia. © 1991. Master's Thesis, The Ohio State University. Columbus, Ohio.

Note: Largely favorable response to textiles, textile looks, and textile effects—even simulated for wall-surface treatments. The coarser the design, the lower the ranking.

Note: When the damask is also tonal, score increases to match moiré. This is not true of "woven looks," which can be perceived as dated. Though the casement rated higher "suitability," it does not indicate "excitement" or a "positively overwhelming" endorsement. Some said it was "safe."

Likely to consider purchase of this pattern type for my home decor:

Study Ten

Fabric Looks and Effect Patterns	For Walls	For Borders	For Textiles/ Furniture	Rugs/Carpet/ Flooring
Major/heavy or primary usage	22%	24%	41%	32%
Coordinate/some use	18%	11%	20%	12%
Very limited or accent use only	60%	65%	39%	72%

N=500. © 1998, Patricia Rodemann. Study Ten, Thesis Follow-up.
Study Ten: Defines category to include printed or woven textiles such as weaves, damasks, moirés, flamestitch.

Where is a textile-effect pattern type most likely to be installed:

Study One: Casement Weave		Study Two: Vertical Raw Silk	
Hotel	66%	Office	65%
Office	58%	Restaurant	47%
Hospital	50%	Store	47%
School	50%	Hotel	40%
Home	41%	Hospital	40%
Store	25%	Home	40%
Church/religious	25%	All of these	35%
All of the above	25%	School	18%
None of the above	0%	Church/religious	6%
		None of these	6%

Personal usage:

Study One: Textile

Would install in own home: 58%

Note: Though commercial applications remain strong, home emerges as a contender for this pattern type, with newer washed damasks and faded-tapestry looks commanding popular attention from younger consumers in textiles. Clichés such as black-and-gold or red-flocked fabric looks led to a backlash in wall-coverings, from which the market now appears to have recovered.

Feelings about design type:

Study One: Casement Weave

Combined age groups: 58% neutral on design; 33% strongly like

Comments:

Can see texture; has dimension
Neutral color; neutral pattern, workable, simple
Could take it or leave it
Unexciting, but easy to coordinate with
Too common, overused
Soothing and subtle

Study Two: Vertical Raw Silk

41% like or strongly like; 24% neutral

Comments:

All patterns in group are easy to live with and gentle on the eye
Familiar, exciting, pleasant, natural
Doesn't send me like some; static and consistent
They're ugly, just too much design

Which textile effect pattern rendition is most preferred and why:

Vertical Raw Silk:

Variegated, depth
Pleasant, quiet, gentle, simpler, airier, lighter
Simple yet there, elegant and neutral
Decorative, less busy
Has real fabric feel, inviting like comfortable clothing

Style and pattern rendition:

Study Six: Textile Effect Designs in Order of Importance by Primary Interior Style of Home:

1. Victorian romantic
2. Sophisticated mix style
3. Traditional style
4. Casual contemporary
5. American country

> Note: Textile/fabric looks are a great mixer, allowing both a dressing up or dressing down. Refer to newest "aged" formal fabrics with a softer hand, patina, and distressed textiles. This type of pattern goes casual or formal.

N=3,500. © 1996. Patricia Rodemann.

Which consumer demographic prefers textile-effect designs:

Textile-weave/finish designs appeal most to residents of larger population markets (urban) and upper middle to upper income households. Females are more likely to prefer these types of design in wall-covering and fabrics, whereas males only show a preference edge for woven design types for wall surfaces. All consumers who rate fabric looks highest are either homemakers or in professional/management positions. This consumer type tends to be under age 36 for woven looks and damask designs, and in the 46–55 age range for silks and moirés. In all cases this audience was more apt to have a college education. The biggest differences in pattern/fabric/finish preference related to region and style. Woven looks were preferred by Midwesterners and Northeasterners; damask types by Southerners and Westerners; silks by Westerners, Midwesterners, and Southerners; and moirés by Northeasterners and Southerners. This is a traveled and sophisticated audience, and consumers have learned to "break the rules" of formal/informal patterns to achieve the most workable effect.

Traits consumers prefer in textile-effect designs:

Do	*Don't*
Like comfy clothing	Necessarily replicate "clothes" on walls and chairs
Variegated surface	Forget the function and cleanability
Has visual depth to it	Not a flat, poorly printed version of a real textile
Airy, simple, quiet	Forget that sometimes less is really more
Less busy	Overlook amount of given design—chair, 9' sofa, wall
Gentle look	Plaid overprint on stripe multicolor with flamestitch and buttons
Casual elegance	Feel obligated to make silks, satins shiny—go matte
Avoid dense or fussy	Select designs perceived as dense, dark, and tight
Faded effects	Go so far it looks more moth-eaten or stained than gently aged
Textural interpretations	Forget the perceived "hand" of the design; is it stiff, crackly, or itchy?

STRIPES

Eisenhart Wallcoverings Co.

Richly hued masculine striped study

York Wallcoverings Co. Borders and Basics

Crisp stripe accents, leafy botanical design

There is much connotative meaning associated with the category of stripes. The referee wears black and white stripes. "He earned his stripes" (military advancement). Stripe designs speak of both law and order, and precision. Stripes indicate belonging: the Oxford-stripe shirt in the executive wing. The stripe tie, the polo shirt. We notice stripes. In interior spaces, stripes are a "go with" designs that offer a sense of geometric relief to florals and other design motifs, as well as pizzazz to otherwise sedate and simple naturals. Stripes can be subtle, amusing, or flamboyant. Stripes are frequently a transitional design used between larger spaces or in the presence of bigger design statements: as in a foyer, study, above/below a dining-room chair-rail, on side chairs. Occasionally a striped sofa will make a statement in and of itself. Stripes also have a fun and outdoorsy connotation, as in awnings, casual outdoor furniture, kids' rooms, and play areas. Consumers understand these intuitive meaings and have internalized the "pattern language." We are a noticeable tiger when wearing stripes; demanding respect for our prowess. I have examined horizontal and vertical stripes, pencil stripes, ticking stripes, narrow stripes, sponged stripes, embroidered stripes, embellished stripes, floral stripes, paisley stripes, medium stripes, variegated stripes, abstract stripes, watercolor stripes, botanical-fruit stripes, ribbon stripes, awning stripes, very wide stripes, designer stripes, menswear stripes, pinstripes, and many conceivable variations. In general, consumers prefer specific, easily identifiable style looks and feelings — country clubby, vacation home, little girl's room — to be associated with their stripes.

In contract design, stripes have a logical fit into office, hospitality, and other installations — often in a far more subtle rendition. In nature, beyond zebras and rows of trees seen from a distance there are many other examples of stripes. (We are attuned to stripes. A faint movement among patterns of trees (striped rows) or grasses put our early hunter-gatherer ancestors on alert.) Yellowjackets and bees carry warning stripes, tiny versions of the tiger. But often, nature's stripes are subtle — like ridges left in the sand from a retreating ocean, or layers of packed sediment that form rocky "striped" cliffs.

Semantic vocabulary: Traits of stripe designs as perceived by consumers

Archives of Columbus Coated Fabrics, Div. Borden, Inc.

Black-and-white high contrast ticking stripe (Study One)

Study One: Ticking Stripe

Would be comfortable with design on all four walls:
83% disagree or strongly disagree

Design would be appealing in different color:
58% disagree or strongly disagree

Rodemann, Patricia. ©1991. Master's Thesis, The Ohio State University. Columbus, Ohio.

Study Two: Group of Stripe Designs

Archives of Columbus Coated Fabrics, Div. Borden, Inc.

Broad stripe, least liked
(Study Two)

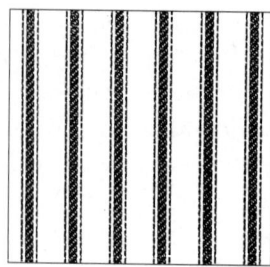

Ticking stripe (Study Two)

Narrow stripe (Study Two)

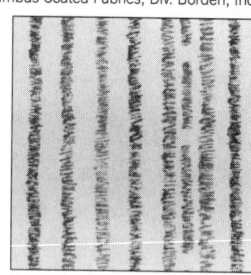

Free-form stripe, most
liked (Study Two)

Study Two: Semantic Vocabulary

Orderly	70%
Directed	40%
Simple	40%
Rhythmic	40%
Busy	35%
Unappealing	35%

Based on a selection of 66
adjectives: response >30%.

Would Be Comfortable with Any of These Patterns on All Four Walls:

Yes:	47%
No:	53%

Note: Stripes are perceived neutral to positively, but the potential for very negative visual-optical effects also needs consideration. The more variance from "typical" or "tonal," the smaller the audience appeal. This is fine if the producer/retailer is reaching the intended niche market. Stripes are highly contextual.

Likely to consider purchase of this pattern type for my home decor:

Study Ten

Striped Pattern Designs	For Walls	For Borders	For Textiles/ Furniture	Rugs/Carpet/ Flooring
Major/heavy or primary usage	45%	35%	52%	15%
Coordinate/some use	27%	16%	15%	11%
Very limited or accent use only	28%	49%	33%	74%

N=500. © 1998. Patricia Rodemann. Study Ten, Thesis Follow-up.

Where is a stripe pattern type most likely to be installed:

Study Two: Group of Stripe Designs

Restaurant	53%
Home	53%
Office	53%
Hotel	47%
Hospital	24%
School	24%
Store	18%
All of these	18%
Church	6%
None of these	0%

Note: There used to be "taboos" about using stripes in certain settings—such as healthcare—but this is not necessarily the case in the mind of the consumer. Many "restrictions" have lifted in contract.

Rodemann, Patricia. © 1991. Master's Thesis, The Ohio State University. Columbus, Ohio.

Personal usage:

Study One: Ticking Stripe

Would not install in own home: 83%

Feelings about design type:

Study One: Ticking Stripe

65% see afterimages with stripe design; 53% perceive movement

Comments:

I am claustrophobic; this pattern makes it worse—would sit by door
Wall-covering is too intense
Could not stay in room with it long; it moves
Neat and orderly; white walls are boring
Need visual relief like doors and windows
Need openness; less distracting

Study Two: Group of Stripe Patterns

26% like or strongly like; 29% neutral
41% dislike or strongly dislike; 6% unsure

Comments:

Is orderly
Comfortable, dressy looking, nice
The usual business patterns; could use with other designs
No real reaction one way or another
Too vertical, has optical effect, radiates—especially hate "A" (ticking)—drives me to distraction; it's confining
Too intense, too much "static" between stripes

Which stripe pattern rendition is most preferred and why:

Free-form:

Neat, crisp, simple, orderly
Most comfortable of the stripes
Pleasant, subdued, gentle, not busy, least discordant, neutral
Not so rigid, creative, artsy looking, expressive, fun
More artistic, less structured, restful
Non-threatening

Note: Preferred by under-47 age group; over 47 chose ticking for familiarity.

Style and pattern rendition:

Study Six: Stripe Designs in Order of Importance by Primary Interior Style of Home:

1. Traditional style
2. Sophisticated mix style
3. Victorian-romantic
4. Casual contemporary
5. American country

Note: Stripes clearly fit more with the traditional "polo club" look than with a simple, natural approach, which favors solids.

N=3,500. © 1996. Patricia Rodemann.

Which consumer demographic prefers stripe designs:

In most cases, stripe designs rate most highly with urban residents. Stripe consumers are most likely to be younger professionals with higher household incomes. It is important for this newest group of consumers to "belong" and to "arrive." Females, as well as consumers under age 36, are most likely to rate stripe designs highly. College-educated home owners are also more likely to rate stripe designs highly. Occupationally, professional/technical/manager career types and homemakers prefer this pattern type. As with textile looks, the biggest differences are by style and by region. Midwesterners and Southerners prefer narrow stripes, but Southerners also rate medium to wider stripes highly. Southerners, Westerners, and Midwesterners tended to prefer abstract design stripes more than Northeasterners.

Traits consumers prefer in stripe designs:

Do	Don't
Neatness in rendition	Select crooked or overlapping
Crisp	Be a slave to "sharp"
Creative	Forget alternate approaches
Orderly	Don't frustrate consumer by chopping it up
Consider subdued	Feel all stripes have to be regimented or same value/width
Watch contrast	Overdo the high contrast in great quantities
Simplicity	Forget the possible optical effects
Free-form, artistic	Forget younger customers who rate free-form higher
Make fun	Feel stripes have to be "office-ly" or militant
Watch the spacing	Don't go for the "closure effect"
Comfortable, familiar	Forget this look is easy to overkill
Good "bridge" pattern	Use without some visual relief
Consider tonal, natural	Overlook natural color palettes and inspiration

ABSTRACT/CONTEMPORARY/WATERCOLOR

Archives of Columbus Coated Fabrics, Div. Borden, Inc.

IHDG Imperial Home Decor Group

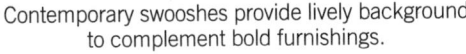

Contemporary swooshes provide lively background to complement bold furnishings.

Modern motif-gold script on black provides dramatic effect.

Abstract designs can take many forms. In one sense, the category encompasses contemporary renditions that do not fit easily into other categories. In another sense, this group can be artistic and organic in its own way. I have typically examined watercolor motifs, painted brushstrokes, squiggles, scribbles, splatters and splashes, swooshes, crayon, painted effects, "cloud" designs, swirls, modern designs, and impressionistic renditions of possible florals, possible gardens or scenes, loosely rendered, or vaguely recognizable shapes and forms. Many abstract designs are not only "softly" rendered, but done in pastels or paler versions of mid-tone colors. On occasion, island hues, 1960s brights, or primaries will pop up. A large manufacturer experimented with layered transparent washes of ink and softer-edge designs. But the design team may have been ahead of the market, or too contemporary for the time, when styles were largely traditional or country. The look is just now gaining wider appeal. Being first or leading-edge has a price. There are also issues of integration.

Consumers respond with surprise and positive attitudes of appreciative recognition to this design type. A reason for this may be our familiarity with the changing palette and canvas of the sky every morning and evening. The surface of water embodies a changing colorscape and character that would be best termed "abstract" were we to capture snapshots of it at any point throughout the day. Textile and wall-covering designs in this group bring to mind the way the wind shapes snow or sand. In the home, abstract designs are used for quilts, bedding, drapery, area rugs, upholstery, and wall-coverings. This design category fits specific styles and ages/eras of home building, as well as having regional specificity. In commercial interiors, there is a strong hospitality and secondary health-care application. Increasingly, the swirls and more graphic/symbolic motifs have found acceptance in upholstery design and, now, flooring design.

Semantic vocabulary: Traits of abstract/contemporary/watercolor designs as perceived by consumers

Examples of Abstract/Contemporary/Watercolor Designs:

Sunworthy

Mannington Mills

IHDG Imperial Home Decor Group

Gramercy Wallcoverings

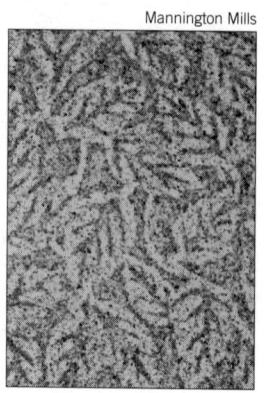

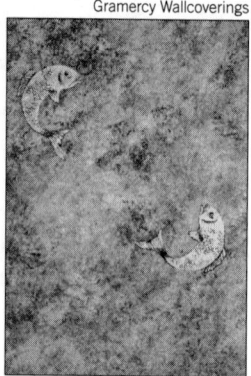

Abstract Wallcovering Design

Abstract Leaf Floorcovering Design

Brushstroke

Overall abstract motif

Key Words: Semantic Phrases

Appealing
Natural quality
Implies fresh air
Clean looking
Fun, playful
Simple
Pleasant
Relaxed feeling

Mentioned unaided by consumers.

Note: There is a playful quality to these designs consumers are wistful for. The need for "escape" drives ratings higher. Abstract designs have an escapist quality.

Note: Openness and mysterious space in these designs make them appealing. The "fussier" the rendition, the lower it rates.

Rodemann, Patricia. © 1991. Master's Thesis, The Ohio State University. Columbus, Ohio.

Highly likely to consider purchase of this pattern type for my home decor:

Study Ten

Abstract Pattern Motifs	For Walls	For Borders	For Textiles/ Furniture	Rugs/Carpet/ Flooring
Major/heavy or primary usage	27%	30%	28%	23%
Coordinate/some use	19%	19%	18%	11%
Very limited or accent use only	54%	51%	54%	66%

N=500. © 1998, Patricia Rodemann. Study Ten, Thesis Follow-up.

Style and pattern rendition:

Study Six: Abstract Designs in Order of Importance by Primary Interior Style of Home:

1. Sophisticated mix style
2. Casual contemporary
3. Traditional style
4. Victorian-romantic
5. American country

Note: Contemporary/abstract designs are seen as sophisticated, not country. An "abstract traditional" design might be an overall painterly dappled effect with gold fleur-de-lis overprint.

N=3,500. © 1996, Patricia Rodemann.

Which consumer demographic prefers abstract/contemporary/watercolor designs:

Abstract designs such as watercolors, leafy abstractions, colored swooshes and swirls have shown increasing appeal among consumers over the past ten years. All abstract designs seem to have greater preference among urban residents. Three regions—the South, Midwest and West Coast—were most apt to embrace abstract/watercolor and amorphic designs. This "fluid" design type rated most highly with females—in some cases higher than 2:1—though there were individual exceptions. Abstract designs also rated highest with upper middle to upper income households and college-educated consumers. Professional/management occupations and homemakers are more likely to prefer this design type. For abstract designs, age and style were the big divide. The more literal the rendition was, the more likely consumers were to be in the 46–55 age range; the more abstract fabric pattern renditions fared better with age 36–45 home owners, and under-age-36 consumers for wall surfaces. (Note: Higher household incomes, urban settings, and Southern/Western emphasis for abstract looks.)

BOTANICAL AND NATURAL

York Wallcoverings, Antonina Vella

York Wallcoverings, J. Chesterfield Studios York Traditions

Fresh leafy botanical design

Soft "documentary" botanical

Botanical designs encompass leaves, weeds, ferns and vines, ivy, apples, grapes, pears, lemons, watermelons, pineapples, berries, cherries, pussy willows, weeping willows, pine trees, shrubs, bamboo, pinecones, topiary, and combinations thereof.

Typically, botanical designs evaluated include fruits and often fall into the "combination" category, because they are paired with flowers and/or stripes. Botanical design is a veritable still life of nature's opulence rather than nature's simplicity, as I have addressed in the natural category. This group shows some particularly interesting interpretations from Dutch-master quality gravure printed and 6 color offset printed designs to brightly hued surface-print renditions of apples or other fruit fabric. In between, one might find ivy leaf upholstery in a tonal rendition distinguished by its texture, weave, or finish. In home decor, this pattern type is favorably regarded, but consumers are very picky about the rendition. It seems the botanical category has replaced the floral category as a more organic contemporary version for the late '90s. Herb tea packaging and even Caswell-Massey type soap wrappers inspire home decor.

Note: Leaf-design motifs scored higher with fabrics than wall-coverings. Hues are extremely important. Botanical designs for floor-coverings, wall-coverings, accent pillows, and textiles—as in beddings and tabletop linens—are growing in popularity. More open renditions are preferred to tighter, busier designs.

Consumers may say they like this category of design, but do not find the range of patterns to satisfy them as readily available as other types. Typically, the simpler the better, with a select few familiar designs—such as ivy—commanding huge interest. There is also a fatigue factor at work with this category—as with florals—which may not be as true of textile or natural-texture designs. How long can one live with large swirling banana leaves on the floor, weeping-willow-patterned foyer walls, a tropical-fruit medley on a comforter, or a pussy-willow powder room? For this reason, classic, artistic, or abstract interpretations may have greater longevity than novelty or literal renditions. Botanical borders, flannel bedding, abstract single-color overlapping leaf flooring, or occasional chairs and accent fabrics may be more appropriate applications than overblown, large-scale, still-life fruit scenes. In commercial design, botanical motifs tend to be more stylized in a smaller form—almost like a miniprint or overall design—or go to a grand scale for formal elegance in convention hotels or related settings. In nature, fruit is ripe only for so long; seasons change, even perennials die. Perhaps this is why we prefer more abstract renditions or use botanical designs in less heavily used or time-sensitive spaces, such as the formal dining room, or for placemats.

Semantic vocabulary: Traits of botanical designs as perceived by consumers

Examples of Botanical Designs:

Eisenhart Wallcoverings Co.

York Wallcoverings, J. Chesterfield Studios

York Wallcoverings, Antonina Vella

Botanical pattern design

Botanical border "accents"
architecture

Chapters Market Square

Fruit Salad Border

Key Words: Semantic Phrases
Natural feeling
Organic
Its own elegance
Can get too busy
Prefer light and contemporary versions
Open quality to leaf designs
Familiar
Artistic and painterly

Note: Consumers seem to be more critical about botanical traits than other design types. This may be due to real-life benchmarks.

*Mentioned unaided by consumers.

Rodemann, Patricia. ©1991. Master's Thesis, The Ohio State University. Columbus, Ohio.

Highly likely to consider purchase of this pattern type for my home decor:

Study Ten

Botanical Patterns	For Walls	For Borders	For Textiles/ Furniture	Rugs/Carpet/ Floorings
Major/heavy or primary usage	36%	54%	41%	27%
Coordinate/some	21%	20%	17%	11%
Very limited or accent use only	43%	26%	42%	62%

N=500. ©1998, Patricia Rodemann. Study Ten, Thesis Follow-up.

Style and pattern rendition:

Study Six: Botanical Designs in Order of Importance by Primary Interior Style of Home:
1. Traditional style
2. Victorian-romantic
3. American country
4. Casual contemporary
5. Sophisticated mix style

Note: Botanical interpretations vary widely. They tend to be perceived as pairing better with traditional, Shaker, Victorian styles than with casual and sophisticated looks—though neutral, tonal, more abstract renditions fare well in those styles.

N=3,500. ©1996, Patricia Rodemann.

Which consumer demographic prefers botanical designs:

Botanical designs vary widely in rendition from a "go with" leafy motif and a traditional fruit-and-berry print to a more sophisticated, widely spaced design. In general, leafy motifs and leaves coupled with fruit, grapes, or berries tends to rate higher in larger markets and suburban settings. The closer to a vine theme and smaller scale, the more apt a design will be preferred in a smaller market. Botanical designs are most preferred by the South and Northeast, except for more purely leafy designs, which are preferred by West Coast residents. Females are more apt to prefer botanical designs for fabric and walls, with a few specific exceptions; males tend to rate leafy designs higher for walls.

The "botanical" consumer is most apt to be a homemaker, then a professional, and college educated. There are age and style discrepancies by specific design type. Leafy, abstract, and similar design renditions are preferred by the under-age-36 consumers. As more specific design statements are introduced—berries, grapes, pears, fruits—the age level increases to 46–55 and then 56–65, respectively.

NOVELTY/PICTORIAL/SCENIC

York Wallcoverings, J. Chesterfield Studios, The Great Outdoors

York Wallcoverings, Carey Lind Houndstooth, volume 3

Ducks border novelty design   Fly-fishing theme walls and border

Novelty designs can cover the gamut from sports themes to library scenes to children's designs and animal themes. The scenic weeping-willow and antebellum mansion mural seen in countless funeral homes is a well-known cliché. Scenics and thematic designs are very familiar to us. Over the years I have examined pictorial 1890s newspaper-ad scenes, seashells, starfish, fish, leopard spots, lighthouses, boats, birds, dishes, houses, kitchen "pots and pans," horses, dogs, cats, maps, rainbows, balloons, angels, Disney characters, farm scenes, forest settings, seashore, jungle, spaceship, and more. Printed textiles and papers show the most diversity; but upholstery, flooring, laminate countertops and even ceiling tiles mimic these novelties. (Armstrong introduced a ceiling tile with a train border for pediatric health care use.)

Consumers typically embrace several pattern/symbolic designs each trend cycle, which are repeated, reiterated, and reinforced across several product categories. Licensing practices in the design arena today, coupled with large retail purchasers, contribute to this phenomenon. Thematic approaches then seize the imagination at a critical time, and the market moves from one retailer or one seasonal fad to a trend within the pattern cycle. Lions, tigers, leopards, zebras, and jungle themes might be one such pattern-design cluster coupled with batik, basketweave, and related natural-design motifs. Consumers are most apt to use thematic designs in specific rooms, such as a guest bathroom, family room, or child's bedroom. In commercial design, restaurants and retail are more apt to utilize themes, along with the entertainment industry—gaming, casinos, resort hotels—than other types of installations. The "horsey" lounge, the "golf club paradise," the "seafarer's buffet," "the Starship game room," the Egyptian casino, are all examples of novelty/pictorial designs. The earliest human decor—cave paintings of animals—may have had a symbolic-religious purpose, but in a sense it was a harbinger of the hunt-club motif. In nature, a great example of an imitator is the chameleon. Has humankind really come such a long way using design knockoffs to survive? *A key facet of the novelty/pictorial and scenic design category is its shorter lifespan.* For this reason, popular designs such as a sunflower theme are less apt to find their way from tabletop decor and bedding to flooring designs—except in area rugs. The more specific the theme/category becomes, the smaller the market appeal for longer term use products. Again, this is dependent on one's target niche. If your audience prefers lodge/lake and traditional designs, is male, and fits your specific demographic, small niches may yield good numbers at point of sale.

Semantic vocabulary: Traits of novelty/pictorial and scenic designs as perceived by consumers

Study One: Newsprint Design

Flashy	100%	Busy	91%
Familiar	83%	Noisy	91%
Tense	83%	Chaotic	83%
Complex	75%	Distracting	75%
Unlivable	75%	Uncomfortable	66%

Based on 32 adjective pairs: responses >65%.

Rodemann, Patricia. © 1991. Master's Thesis, The Ohio State University. Columbus, Ohio. Studies One through Five.

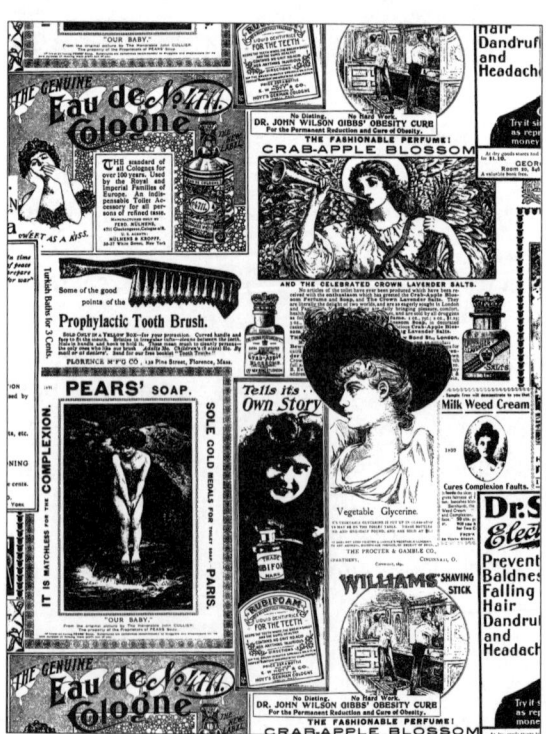

Note: Though 66% said this pattern was suitable for walls, 100% said they would not install in home, though many knew someone who had installed a similar design at some point in time. Though 66% said they disliked it; 25% were neutral and 8% liked the design. Fifty-eight percent said they would be uncomfortable with the pattern design on all four walls, and the same percent felt changing the color would have no impact on their rating. Themed designs are more apt to invoke love/hate responses.

Study One: Feelings about Design Type

Too busy, overbearing, confusing in small area
Don't like; it's outdated
Too graphic; maybe for a counter, bar, or Wendy's tables
Too much to have appeal, offensive to senses
Walls would be too much of a focal point
Like it for positive feel, okay for some settings
I like old-fashioned items, but more country designs
Way too much visual stimulation; prefer more subtle
Okay; nice for limited commercial uses—like restaurants

Where Is a Pictorial/Novelty Design Like This Most Likely to Be Installed?

Store/retail	41%
Home	25%
Hotel	16%
Hospital	0%
Office	0%

Likely to consider purchase of this pattern type for my home decor:

Study Ten

Novelty/Theme/Scenic Patterns	For Walls	For Borders	For Textiles/ Furniture	Rugs/Carpet/ Flooring
Major/heavy or primary usage	14%	23%	10%	8%
Coordinate/some use	12%	17%	16%	7%
Very limited or accent use only	74%	60%	74%	85%

N=500. © 1998, Patricia Rodemann. Study Ten, Thesis Follow-up.

Likely to consider purchase of this pattern type for my home decor:

Study Ten

Sports Patterns	For Walls	For Borders	For Textiles/ Furniture	Rugs/Carpet/ Flooring
Major/heavy or primary usage	14%	22%	11%	10%
Coordinate/some use	9%	10%	11%	11%
Very limited or accent use only	77%	68%	78%	79%

N=500. © 1998, Patricia Rodemann. Study Ten, Thesis Follow-up.

Likely to consider purchase of this pattern type for my home decor:

Study Ten

Kids Patterns	For Walls	For Borders	For Textiles/ Furniture	Rugs/Carpet/ Flooring
Major/heavy or primary usage	21%	36%	29%	16%
Coordinate/some	12%	11%	15%	11%
Very limited or accent use only	67%	53%	56%	73%

N=500. © 1998, Patricia Rodemann. Study Ten, Thesis Follow-up.

Examples of Novelty/Pictorial & Scenic Designs:

Lighthouse design

Menemsha seashell border

Tropical fish border

Southwestern novelty cactus border

Key Words: Semantic Phrases

Theme rooms
Like paint by numbers
Lots of possibilities
You can imagine the room
Easily tire of it
Okay for a year or two
Must be a quality rendition

*Mentioned unaided by consumers.

Note: positive responses upon viewing ranges of novelty type designs. Familiarity vs. boredom is a fine line.

Rodemann, Patricia. © 1991. Master's Thesis, The Ohio State University. Columbus, Ohio.

Style and pattern rendition:

Study Six: Novelty/Pictorial Designs in Order of Importance by Primary Interior Style of Home:

1. American country
2. Victorian-romantic
3. Traditional style
4. Casual contemporary
5. Sophisticated mix style

Note: American country favors novelty and scenic designs; Victorian sports/kids/characters could represent dolls, angels, teddy bears in lace dresses.

N=3,500. © 1996, Patricia Rodemann.

Which consumer demographic prefers novelty/scenic/theme designs:

There is a sharper difference between demographics for novelty/scenic/themed designs and other pattern categories. The closer to high quality painted murals, the higher the income level, occupation, and education. For all other novelty and themed designs, the consumer is less likely to be an urban highbrow type and more likely to enjoy the whimsy and charm of novelties. This consumer is more likely to enjoy crafts and home activities such as gardening. Examples of novelty designs are birds, cactus, kitchen utensils, teapots, fish, shells, patchwork, and so forth. In the '50s, '60s, and '70s, Wall-Tex wall coverings became well known for their pots-and-pans designs on a vinyl substrate for kitchen use. Even today, in most cases, the novelty design rates higher with smaller markets, smaller suburban areas, and country settings regardless of product type.

Depending on the design type, Southern and Midwestern residents typically rate novelties higher. "Birds" and bird designs tend to have better reception in the Northeast, whereas cactus or Western themes do better in the West. Theme designs are also highly gender-sensitive. In most cases, this is a lower- to lower-middle-income consumer in service/administrative/blue-collar positions or homemakers, part-timers, and self-employed. With the exception of more country-clubby golf, horse, and fish designs, this consumer is less likely to have a college background. There are also more pronouned ethnic and cultural preferences with thematic designs. Thematic designs are typically favored by two age groups: 36–45 and 46–55. As we move into sports themes, the demographics are somewhat more likely to favor a mid- to upper-middle-income consumer. Again, this is dependent on the theme and style.

HISTORIC/ARCHITECTURAL/ DOCUMENTARY DESIGNS

York Wallcoverings—Masculine

Rich Oriental design adds drama.

York Wallcoverings, Ronald Redding Maestro II

Architectural border adds historic touch.

This design type is highly recognizable in the popular neoclassic or Greco-Roman themes that were used to embellish textile borders, accent pillows, draperies, and furniture from the mid-1980s into the mid-1990s. The revival of egg and dart, acanthus leaf, fleur-de-lis, toile, swag and garland, rosettes, fretwork, Victoriana, William Morris, and Arts and Crafts motifs added sophistication to the post 1970s backlash that began in the "Neoclassic" postmodern mid-1980s. Oriental themes, Mission, Art Deco, Shaker, and Art Nouveau are showing signs of awakening interest along with their respective historic/architectural patterns and themes. Perceived as always classic, somewhat formal, and never out of style, historic patterns go through cycles of popular acceptance. The Renaissance was one such period of awakening when classical elements once again enjoyed prominence. Gothic and medieval themes are "flirted with" from time to time. The consumer market for these themes remains somewhat highbrow.

There are distinct sociocultural associations that affect perception and usage practices. African, Indian, and Latino preferences may differ sharply from European or American views of "historic" and "architectural" design. I have examined patterns and styles from each and all eras and types. Paisleys, flame motifs, lotus blossom, batik, and filigree are all examples with non-Western origins. In my recent research, I have also categorized styles by decades. Is 1950s revival a historic design movement? In a world culture with pop design exportable, and decorative arts museums doing retrospectives, I would argue for the "historic" moniker. The most common approaches for historic/architectural, ethnic, and cultural design motifs are formal, fun, or faithful to a theme. In commercial design, historic and architectural motifs tend to stay in the architecture and in accent, accessory, or border form with more subtle echoes in textile and wall patterns.

Semantic vocabulary: Traits of historic/architectural/documentary designs as perceived by consumers

Examples of Historic/Architectural/Documentary Designs:

York Wallcoverings- Ronald Redding Maestro II

Archives of Columbus Coated Fabrics, Div. Borden, Inc.

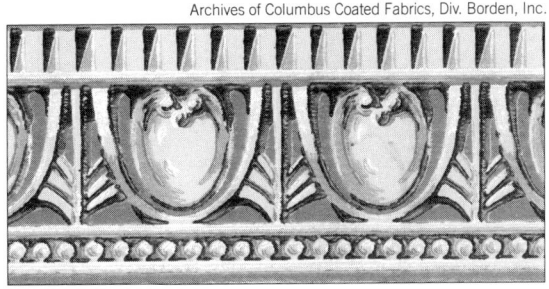

Architectural border

Historic architectural molding design

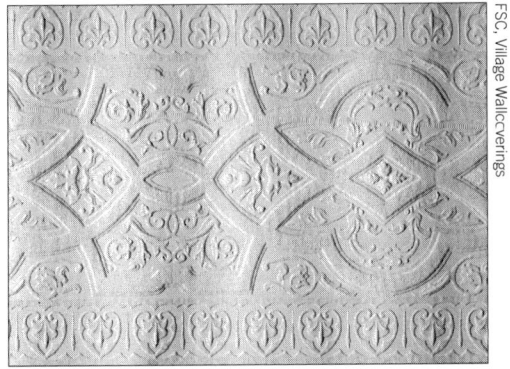

FSC, Village Wallcoverings

FSC, Waverly Wallcoverings

Border design in relief-historic, architectural character

Wall design in relief-historic, architectural character

Keywords: Semantic Vocabulary*

Very specific use
Need to know what you're doing
Awful in some settings; gorgeous in others
Sophisticated
Lots going on
Familiar, old-fashioned
Too complicated; like simpler, newer

Note: There is some wariness with historic/ethnic/cultural designs. This category inspires more love/hate thinking.

*Mentioned unaided by consumers.

Rodemann, Patricia. © 1991. Master's Thesis, The Ohio State University. Columbus, Ohio. Studies One through Five.

Likely to consider purchase of this pattern type for my home decor:

Study Ten

Historic/Architectural Pattern	For Walls	For Borders	For Textiles/ Furniture	Rugs/Carpet/ Flooring
Major/heavy or primary usage	18%	32%	14%	13%
Coordinate/some use	12%	12%	8%	7%
Very limited or accent use only	70%	56%	78%	80%

N=500. © 1998, Patricia Rodemann. Study Ten, Thesis Follow-up.

Likely to consider purchase of this pattern type for my home decor:

Study Ten

Stylized Ethnic/Cultural Pattern	For Walls	For Borders	For Textiles/ Furniture	Rugs/Carpet/ Flooring
Major/heavy or primary usage	11%	17%	18%	8%
Coordinate/some use	15%	19%	21%	14%
Very limited or accent use only	74%	64%	61%	78%

N=500. © 1998, Patricia Rodemann. Study Ten, Thesis Follow-up.

Style and pattern rendition:

Study Six: Historic/Architectural Designs in Order of Importance by Primary Interior Style of Home:

1 Victorian-romantic
2. Sophisticated mix style
3. Traditional style
4. Casual contemporary
5. American country

Note: Sophisticated customers are apt to mix ethnic/cultural designs with eclectic aplomb. Traditional customers opt for historic and architectural styles, whereas country lovers decidedly prefer less formal authenticity.

N=3,500. © 1996 Patricia Rodemann

Which consumer demographic prefers historic/cultural designs:

Looking at several types of historic/architectural/cultural design types—Greco-Roman, Chinoiserie, Indian Batik, French Toile, Arts and Crafts, Far Eastern Paisley, and Mediterranean—one sees common threads by demographic. With the exception of Mediterranean and Greco-Roman designs, most patterns are more likely to appeal to Southern and Northeastern home owners. The Mediterranean designs also appeal to West Coast residents. Simpler architectural themes and tonal designs appeal more to country and small-town residents; the rest to urban markets. Males rated Mediterranean, Batik, Arts and Crafts, some architectural and Chinoiserie motifs higher than females. In most cases, this type of design appeals to upper-middle-income households. Paisley and Arts and Crafts motifs appealed to an under-age-36 cohort; Batik and Mediterranean to a 46–55 age cohort, and the rest to the 56–65 age cohort. This pattern type appeals to professional/technical management employees with a college education. The richer, deeper hued, and more exotic, the more likely the audience is urban, high income, and professional. More tonal, lighter in value architectural designs may appeal to those with older homes to renovate/remodel. The Toile and the Chinoiserie may appeal to older audiences because of an affinity for previous popular cycles earlier in the century or a distinct favorite style correlation.

DESIGN MIXES/COMBINATIONS

York Wallcoverings: Antonina Vella Collection

Damask stripe hybrid design with classic border

Archives of Columbus Coated Fabrics, Div. Borden, Inc.

Historic textile design, floral stitch effect

A large percentage of the pattern designs can be considered hybrid combinations or mixes of design types. One would mistakenly think at first glance that this category is a catch-all. Within the mixed category we usually find designs that feature 50-50 of one common type or another; and certain looks predominate—especially by product type. In flooring designs, varieties of geometric and natural or architectural motifs prevail. In wall-coverings, one typically finds paisley stripe, fruit stripe, floral and fruit, stripe and abstract, and so on. Having researched many of these designs, I found that the groups also are usually close to the ratings of their respective categories. In textiles, hybrid designs are a significant and meaningful consideration, because one is able to achieve pattern, weave, and special finishes/in-line treatments all at once. A design that is both a plaid and a flamestitch and has special moiré-finish qualities offers a classic example.

Botanical still-life tapestries, puckered satin stripes with damask overlay, and sheared velvet/chenille multilevel designs all make this category challenging and interesting to research. Consumers seem to like this type of design complexity *in limited doses,* because it offers them options to play with. For this reason, upholstery that sets the theme/character of a space or adds an accent to other patterns is the most common use. For larger surface areas, wall borders, chair-rail design applications, accent wall applications, and smaller areas—stairwells, foyers, offices, powder rooms—seem to round out the wall surface category. In flooring, hybrid designs are often wood-strips framing tile, or more ornate borders on simpler design area rugs and carpets. The consumer who rates combination historic/cultural pattern rugs highly (oriental, Aubusson, tapestry) tends to be more sophisticated and design-oriented and has a higher household income. In commercial spaces, hybrid designs are most often seen in wayfinding: used as an accent design to notify of an elevator bank or to indicate a change in use/function of a space. Themed restaurants, hospitality/hotel and resort, and to a lesser degree, health-care providers are the biggest users of hybrid or mixed-design category. In office applications, the use is primarily in upholstery on a more subtle scale.

Our anthropological/ cultural/biological heritage predisposes us as humans to understand and relate to multiple-pattern design phenomena at the same time. Our brains are "wired" for not only multiple-pattern effects but changing light conditions, movement, and seasonal color. We can tell time by shadows; weather by visual cues; and seasons by leaves, bark, insects, and the coats of wild critters. Pattern perception is a hugely important faculty.

Semantic vocabulary: Traits of design mixes/combination designs as perceived by consumers

Examples of Design Mixes and Combination Designs:

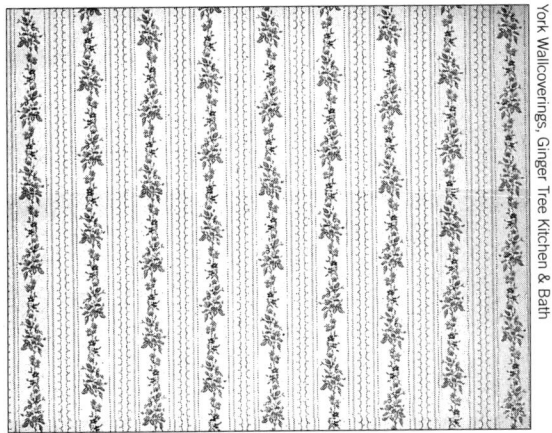

Floral stripe

Novelty golf, small-print stylized motif

Quilt-inspired geometric effect with florals and hearts-country

Damask stripe, richly hued classic textile effect

Key Words: Semantic Vocabulary

Complex

Lots of possibilities

More to work with

Too much going on

Flashy, kind of exciting

Good floor design; busy, hides the dirt

Note: This pattern type is more likely to be richly hued and/or textured.

Mentioned unaided by consumers

Rodemann, Patricia. ©1991. Master's Thesis, The Ohio State University. Columbus, Ohio. Studies One through Five.

Highly likely to consider purchase of this pattern type for my home decor:

Study Ten

Combination Pattern	For Walls	For Borders	For Textiles/ Furniture	Rugs/Carpet/ Flooring
Major/heavy or primary usage	7%	7%	14%	6%
Coordinate/some	8%	15%	20%	7%
Very limited or accent use only	85%	78%	66%	87%

N=500. © 1998, Patricia Rodemann. Study Ten, Thesis Follow-up.

Study Six: Combination Pattern Designs in Order of Importance by Primary Interior Style of Home:

1. Victorian-romantic
2. Traditional style
3. Sophisticated mix style
4. Mission/Arts and Crafts
5. Casual contemporary
6. American country

Study Six: N=3,500. © 1996 Patricia Rodemann

Note: Clearly, Victorian romantic, traditional style, and fabric hybrids pair well; whereas more woven/geometric type designs are better suited to Mission or other styles. This may seem self-evident, but to date has not been documented. A popular, high-scoring design type — such as a miniprint and floral — coupled with another can raise the overall score. Pair a similar floral with a poor-scoring geometric, and the overall score is lowered. Some designs seem less "natural" in one form or another, and this too, will affect the score (as in geometric types — walls vs. textiles vs. flooring).

Which consumer demographic prefers hybrid-mix pattern designs:

There are significant differences in suburban-type designs and urban-type designs. Satin flame-stitch patterns, damask stripes, and some geometrics appeal to urban residents; bordered designs, floral and miniprint stripes, floral and geometric-stripe type designs tend to appeal to suburban and smaller-town residents. Natural woven–geometric pairings appeal more to Midwestern and Southern audiences, satin flame-stitch designs to Southern and Western markets, and bordered inset designs to Northeastern audiences. The gender difference is also apparent, as males rate geometric-type designs more highly. The consumer who prefers hybrid/combination designs is slightly more apt to have some college education. There are many other factors to examine in response to each of these designs, which we will not address here. Taken together, a picture begins to emerge of who "belongs" to which designs and vice versa. It is like piecing together a horoscope from characteristics of star constellations, with leading traits corresponding to the lead design.

Though pattern preference does remain highly individualistic, there are certain overriding characteristics common to pattern categories and renditions. It is clear there are broader social, historic, cultural, demographic, and geographic connections.

CHAPTER 4

Perception Psychology: How Our Eyes and Brain Process Pattern

Typically, pattern-design research is concentrated primarily in the following areas: industry oriented to product introductions with a goal of greater sales and profits; artists and craftspeople concerned with the art and ego of it; neurology, the medical science of the brain/nervous system and its disorders; psychiatrists of the 1920s and 1930s who used pattern (and inkblot tests) to uncover our deepest secrets. The Gestalt psychologists sought to understand our perception of lines, shapes, patterns. Ophthalmology studies the anatomy, functions, pathology, and treatment of the eye; pattern is used as a diagnostic tool. Environmental psychology examines the effects of acoustics, space, light, crowding, and other environmental factors on behavior. The interior design and architectural professions use pattern design beyond decorative purposes: to indicate status and create an image, to invite specific behaviors, or to distinguish the function of different areas within a larger space. Biologists examine our evolutionary natural heritage, while anthropologists examine patterns we created and left behind.

Why is it important to examine pattern in a perceptual-psychological view? In a very broad sense, we are dealing with complex pattern images throughout our lives and this sensory information, coupled with cognitive impressions, comprises an adult's entire perceptual experience.

Our visual systems are sophisticated tools, allowing feedback from the environment to be fed to and filtered by our brains. The classic question goes like this: You are sitting in a blue room. Is the blue actually on the walls, or is it in your eyes or brain? Is color a phenomenon of physics, light waves, vibrations? Or is it understood in terms of our perceptual makeup between the eye/brain and how we process visual information? In this chapter, we will look at perceptual illusions in light of some of my pattern-research findings, as well as from psychological angles. We will examine new neurological brain science findings, and findings from other disciplines.

Perception psychologists developed several tools to measure and explain various eye/brain processing phenomena. Many of these early tests began with line length, convergence, and optical/perceptual phenomena such as afterimage, contrast magnitude, perceived color change, and perceived depth. We call the process that goes on in our minds "perception," when we process color, pattern, shape, light, and textural cues from the environment around us and try to make sense of it. Our brains make inferences about shading, proportions, spatial enclosures, and other qualities based on this input. Perspective illusions explored by Italian Renaissance masters are one example of early interest in perception. Dutch eighteenth-century trompe l'oeil paintings are another example. The Dutch graphic artist M. C. Escher is well known for his repetitious geometric patterns, spatial illusions, impossible structures, and optical effects, which have become exceptionally popular again in recent years.[1]

Many perception studies of perceptual illusions have been undertaken. More than two hundred illusions have been documented and more than 1,000 research articles have been written, illustrating the enormous popularity of the subject. Many of these illusions are grouped by the phenomena they appear to produce: for example, the phenomenon of mentally connecting the dots is referred to as "closure," where four dots are perceived as vertices of a square. One consumer looking at a wall-covering design said, "I would go crazy with this pattern trying to connect the dots." Another consumer told of a grandchild who did just that: connected the miniprint dots with an ink pen on grandma's sofa fabric.

"Closure" explains our innate propensity to "fill in the gaps" of what is missing visually to make sense of an incomplete image. We humans, it seems, have an urge to "connect the dots." Remember popular children's drawing games with numbered dots? Some pattern designs have a quality all their own that invite the same behavior. When exposed to a room full of dot patterns—such as a familiar acoustical ceiling tile—for any length of time, visual, psychological, and physiological side effects begin to act. Much of the time we tune it out. But the patient on his/her back in traction is probably the first "victim" that comes to mind.

Research shows a high degree of correlation between visual acuity and tolerance to certain types of patterns. Those with glasses, contact lenses, or other visual aids are quite likely to find unpleasant pattern designs that are tiny, regimented, closely spaced, or directional because they create a perception of movement or trigger afterimages.

The Gestaltists suggested that shapes, forms, and patterns take precedence over the individual lines or dots used to create them. It's not the components that produce the effect, but how we perceive some type of "attractive force" among the components. This is why elements near each other seem to be perceived as a group. The greater the distance, the less the "attractive" force.

We have seen this in responses to many pattern designs. The tighter the spacing and the more regimental the design, the more apt it is to produce this type of phenomenon, but this perception is also contrast dependent. Consumers repeatedly give these types of designs lower reviews for this very reason. If the design is a softer hue or more broken rendition, or the spacing appears less obvious, the design rates much higher. Tonal designs in a painterly rendering will mitigate this effect. If a design is too widely spaced—as in brushstrokes on a white background—the distraction is more apt to be related to a desire to pull the design together or adjust the scale. Consumers are intensely sensitive and aware of these phenomena, though it may not always be overt.

Examples of closure effect:

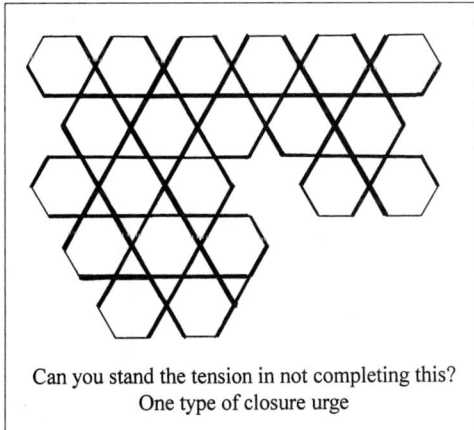

Can you stand the tension in not completing this?
One type of closure urge

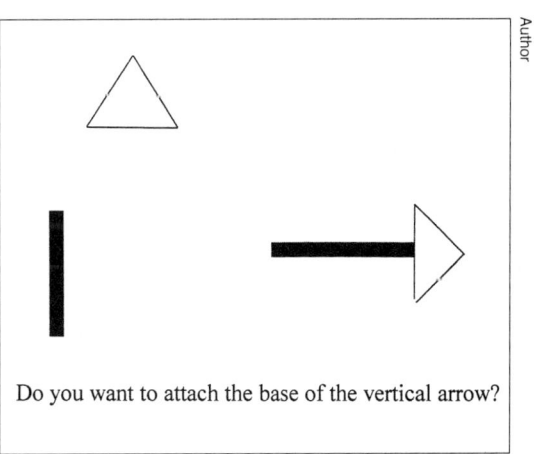

Do you want to attach the base of the vertical arrow?

Closure effect illustrations

There are examples of "good gestalts," which means only a few lines are sufficient to form organized perceptions.[2]

According to the Gestaltists, "Our perceptions of the everyday world are also organized actively into coherent wholes."[3] These principles of perception include the *"principle of similarity,* where equal and similar elements form groups or wholes ... *the principle of proximity,* where elements that are proximal or close together tend to be grouped. ... The *principle of closure* refers to our tendency to fill in or complete the missing parts of a configuration to make it perceptually complete."[4]

Common illusions such as a person, an animal, or a familiar object presented in component parts are used to assess the integrity of the right hemisphere of the brain. If there is poor performance, there may

Illusions

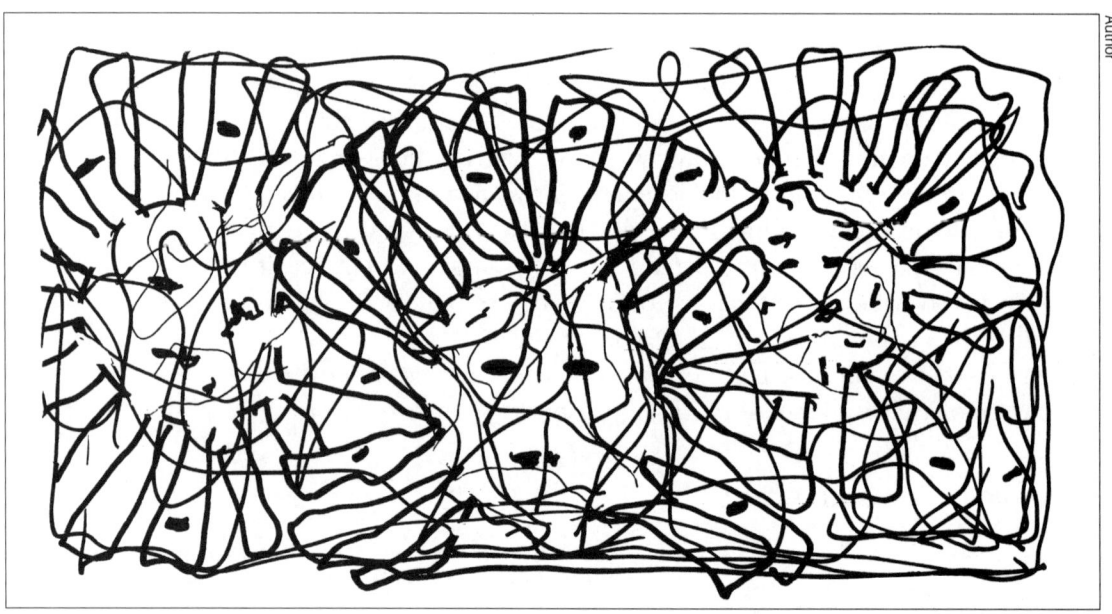

Faces in abstract design

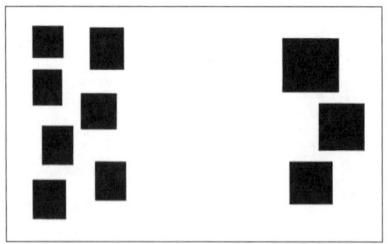

Principle of proximity

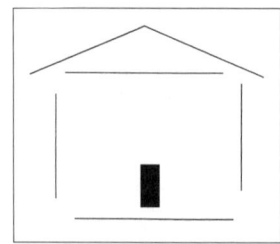

Closure

Do you see squares or a grid?

Examples of illusions:

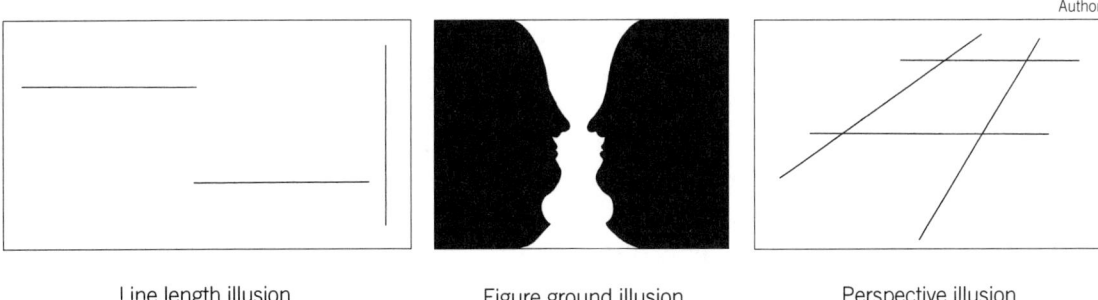

Author

Line length illusion   Figure ground illusion   Perspective illusion

have been some impairment to a portion of the brain. Though many other factors are also involved, the illusion is one diagnostic tool.

Then there are the *properties of figure and ground.* "When two areas share a common boundary, the figure is the distinct shape with clearly defined edges. The ground is what is left over, forming the background."[5] Some of these figure-ground properties state that the figure is perceived as a "thing" versus the ground, which is perceived as a "substance"; that the ground continues behind the figure; that the figure seems closer; and that the figure is more dominant and appears brighter than the ground. "Our tendency to organize perceptions leads to a perceptual or psychological environment that is often very different from the physical one."[6] In some sense, the Gestaltists were identifying neuro-biological coding, which references our earlier instinctual heritage: the fight-or-flight response. Pattern perception on a higher level introduces emotion and memory, but the underlying response mechanism remains intact.

Escher created some wonderful illusional figure-ground compositions and other designs that have been used on neckties and art pieces. A common illusion, figure-ground is seen most often in flooring design. Any illusionary effects are lessened if the hues are complementary, the edges less sharp, and the texture "soft." The angular images pervasive in architecture and design of the developed world are reinforced and interpreted early in life, so processing the images becomes automatic and unconscious. Cultural conditioning is also at work in perceptual phenomena.

In well-known line illusions such as the horizontal-vertical illusion, we realize that what we see physically and perceive psychologically don't correspond with one another. When we react to environmental cues this way, we may in fact be responding to something different psychologically than what exists physically. "In visual perception, you prime yourself to see an object when you only have part of the picture," said Stephen Kosslyn, a psychologist a Harvard University.[7] Kosslyn suggests people can fool themselves by their mind's eye.

Line illusions may be implied by stripe designs. Professional designers sometimes react with anger at the mere suggestion that their selection might present a problem and refuse to look at the data or discount it altogether. But our DNA may predispose us to respond to different pattern types differently.

Consumers often fail to look at larger samples of their selection before committing a substantial investment. Another common practice is to make a selection based on context, familiarity, and intent rather than practicality and exposure. An example of this is the mother who associated stripes with male designs, red/white/blue with boy's themes, and "good/patriotic/moral" with the palette and pattern. The pattern design had a very active component in the spacing of the stripes and the contrast. Unfortunately, the child also suffered attention deficit disorder; and though not many direct studies have been done, there is enough related research to suggest an alternate design selection.

In addition to line length illusions, there are perspective illusions, area illusions, direction and shape illusions, size, distance, and depth illusions. Working in plan view and with elevations and sample boards does not give the full effect of computer simulation. And computer simulation is not foolproof. Believable virtual reality is not accessible to all yet. Pattern designs can enhance perspective illusions. A faux-marble stripe wall design in a hotel corridor can make it seem like a very long walk to the turn at the end of the hall in a perspective-type illusion. Photographs often conceal or reveal size, distance, or depth illusions. In a professional kitchen-advertising photo, the distance between the counter top of an island and the countertop behind it appeared to be no more than six inches. Designers who master illusions are important allies to residents of small apartments or cubicle offices. The 1970s solution of mirrors everywhere to enlarge a space often compounds the problem. A Chicago advertising agency mixed glass, reflective steel surface, and mirror on the facade of their suite. The suite did not have typical doorknobs or levers, creating a dilemma for visitors unaccustomed to the visual game. It was very difficult to determine which panel was actually the office entrance. Visitors arriving in the hallway with reflective surfaces opposite the office suite had to stop and think not only which image was real but also how to keep from making a fool of themselves. The faux-marble patterns used in the space were reflected, making the opposite wall appear to be solid.

Depth illusions are particularly problematic for a visually impaired population. An elderly woman carefully lifted her leg to step down in what was actually a depth illusion created by a darker shadowed stripe in the rug. Although it was amusing to her grandchildren and made them giggle, it was, in fact, a "put down" for a woman trying to maintain independence and dignity. (We will not address more serious pathologies of perception in this section.)

Perception psychologists have also studied contrast. Again, reality and perception differ. Two color/contrast illusions demonstrate the importance of contrast. For example: "*Simultaneous color contrast* means that the appearance of a color can be changed because of another color that is present at the same time. ... *Successive color contrast* means that the appearance of a color can be changed because of another color that is presented beforehand. ... *Negative afterimage* is a term that is often used as a substitute for successive color contrast, but negative afterimages also include black and white afterimages. The term makes sense because it is an image that appears afterwards, and it is the opposite, or the negative, of the original image. In special cases these afterimages may persist for hours and even days."[8]

I first noted the difference in perception of afterimages in studies one and two between pattern types. As a result of these findings, I installed and applied the geometric checkerboard and the ticking stripe to an entire wall in each of two comparable graphic design/quick copy office settings to see if behavior could be affected by design. Because these were graphic art settings, exceptionally graphic designs or artwork were not out of the ordinary. These patterns were from product collections in the marketplace, similar to many others. This constituted study three. For study three I used a different methodology. This involved behavior mapping with common task behaviors listed, observed, and recorded unnoticed for three months before installation, throughout installation of the pattern designs, and after the designs came down. I also used a hidden video camera to record behavior once the designs were installed. After project completion, questionnaires were sent to staff and customers.

Study four was a postoccupancy evaluation of a music practice hall connected to a performing arts center. An acoustic wall that had been installed (specified by a famous architect) featured a tightly spaced dot pattern that reportedly drove people wild. An on-site visit took place and performers were interviewed individually. Faculty and conductors were interviewed by mail and telephone. The findings for this pattern type illustrate what we have observed in the Gestalt phenomena. There may be more than one illusion at work. Following are examples of pattern-perception-induced behaviors in a behavioral map.

Example of a behavioral map*

Behavioral Map
Date:
Time of Day:
Duration of Observation:

Range of Behaviors Observed:	Subject One	Subject Two	Etc. (Staff/Customer)
1. Subject approximate age:			
2. Subject gender:			
3. Glasses/visual correction:			
4. Enter room from outside:			
5. Enter room from other area:			
6. Notice wall (floor, etc.) with pattern:			
7. Task at copier (other):			
8. Look at task exclusively (avoidance or fixation):			
9. Glance to right or left (observant):			
10. Stare blankly at wall (floor/other):			
11. Engage others in conversation:			
12. Are engaged by others in conversation:			
13. Proceed through space to other task area; no notice of environment:			
14. Proceed through space to other task area; glance at surroundings:			
15. Proceed through space to other task area; notice/respond to stimuli:			
16. Make comment about environment:			
17. Make comment on pattern (wall/floor, etc.):			
18. Wait on work in process:			
19. Leave work to be performed by others:			
20. Stand in center area and converse (no nonverbal notice of environment):			
21. Stand in center area and converse (obvious nonverbal notice of environment):			
22. Length of time in area of subject (minutes):			

*May be scored on rating scale, frequency, total count/% etc. I used a checkmark tally system—behavior occurs spontaneously and is fast-moving.

Rodemann, Patricia. ©1991. The Ohio State University. Masters thesis.

Note: Behavior maps are useful tools when a specific behavior is desired or the design or marketing professional wishes to arrive at what is actually happening. This methodology is most widely employed in package goods and retail—for traffic patterns, planogramming of merchandise, and positioning fixtures. The methodology is time consuming and expensive to implement. It is seldom used strictly for pattern design or color research, which tends to the more academic and theoretical.

Perception of afterimages:[10]

Comparison of pattern types

"I see afterimages when I close my eyes after viewing this design."

Study One:	Floral	Geometric	Graphic	Texture	Textile	Novelty
Strongly disagree	0%	0%	0%	33%	41%	0%
Disagree	33%	8%	16%	66%	50%	33%
Neutral	15%	8%	25%	0%	8%	8%
Agree	50%	33%	41%	0%	0%	58%
Strongly agree	0%	50%	16%	0%	0%	0%

Rodemann, Patricia. © 1991. The Ohio State University. Masters thesis.

Perception of movement:

Comparison

"The pattern appears to move."

Study One:	Floral	Geometric	Graphic	Texture	Textile	Novelty
Strongly disagree	16%	8%	0%	25%	16%	0%
Disagree	25%	8%	33%	58%	66%	25%
Neutral	25%	0%	8%	8%	16%	16%
Agree	33%	16%	50%	8%	0%	50%
Strongly agree	0%	66%	8%	0%	0%	8%

Study One Pattern	*Study Three Patterns*		*Study Four Pattern*

Archives of Columbus Coated Fabrics, Div. Borden, Inc.

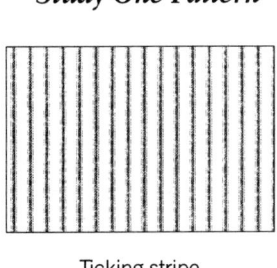

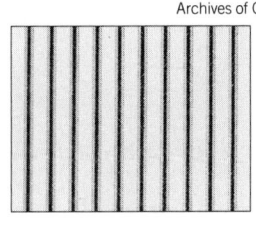

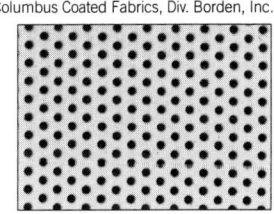

Ticking stripe	Checkerboard (Study Three)	Ticking stripe (Study Three)	Acoustic dot (Study Four)
Consumers: Afterimages: 33% agree 50% strongly agree	**Staff:** Afterimages: 75% agree or strongly agree	**Staff:** Afterimages: 100% unsure*	**Performers:** Afterimages: 21% not sure* 58% agree or strongly agree
Movement: 16% agree 66% strongly agree	**Movement:** 100% agree or strongly agree	**Movement:** 100% agree or strongly agree	**Movement:** 86% agree or strongly agree

*Claim effect is wavelike or wavering

Study Two Group of Geometric Patterns

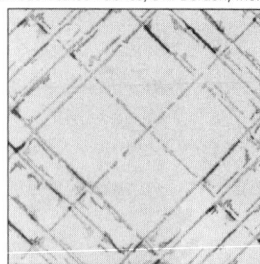

| Gingham (Study Two) | Blanket plaid (Study Two) | Check (Study Two) | Diagonal/soft rendition plaid (Study Two) |

See afterimages:
65% yes; 35% no

Perceive movement:
65% yes; 35% no

Study Two Group of Stripe Patterns

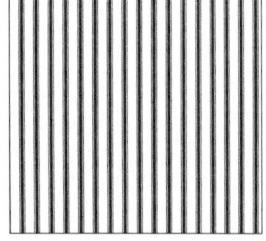

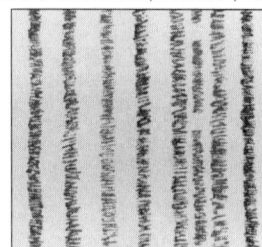

| Ticking stripe (Study Two) | Broad stripe (Study Two) | Narrow stripe (Study Two) | Free-form stripe (Study Two) |

See afterimages:
yes 47%; no 53%

Perceive movement:
yes 53%; no 47%

Examples of Installation: A Tale of Two Performing Arts Centers

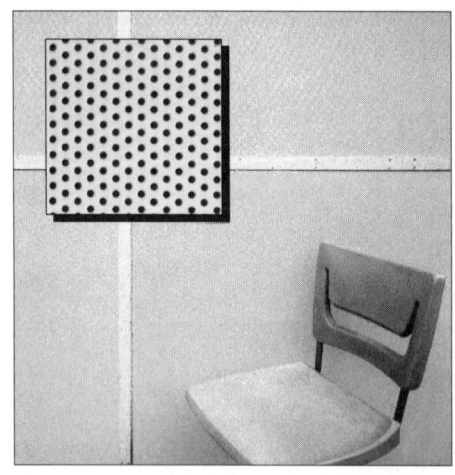

Walls of music rehearsal room (Study Four)
Close-up of acoustic wall.

Carpeting of public area (Study Four)

We look at *constancy,* which implies that "objects seem to stay the same though the representations on the retina *change,*" and *illusions,* which indicate that "objects look quite different though the representations on the retina stay the *same.*"[9]

What this means is that the properties of the object remain the same even though our image of those objects may change. For example: I am holding a coffee cup full of coffee. My image of the object itself will change based upon location, lighting, heat, mood, and other considerations. Constancy perception extends beyond the physical characteristics of objects to our psychological perception of them. Constancy studies on size, shape, and brightness extend to color, motion, bending, position, and existency. From a distance a house looks symmetrical. Up close, at the bottom of an angled driveway against cloud movement, the dormers and roofline may appear to be tilting. In one case, the illusion was so pronounced that it prompted the father of a young couple to recommend a structural engineer. In pattern perception, our movement in the environment in relation to the pattern itself comes into question versus the perception of a flat, constant experimental approach of a floor, wall, or object. A long drive on a hot summer afternoon on a road surface with horizontal stripes can create the illusion of a walk through an airport connection between terminals.

"Size constancy means that an object seems to stay the same size despite changes in its distance.... Brightness constancy means that an object seems to stay the same brightness despite changes in the amount of light falling on it. ... Shape constancy means that an object seems to stay the same shape despite changes in its orientation. Position constancy means that an object seems to stay in the same place, despite the body's movement relative to that object."[10]

The contrast theory of brightness constancy assumes observers judge the intensity of illumination in comparison with other objects. The observer considers perceptual cues in judging illumination. Those cues are shadows, slant, position, and shape.

Contrast is the first thing that attracts us, causes us to take notice of the environment, whether we are talking about art, architecture, or product design. Similarly, bright lighting—especially accent spotlights—commands more attention than dim lighting, which is why we use focused lighting in museums and galleries, and halogen spots in jewelry stores. High contrast is also used for signage to attract the attention of commuters and pedestrians. In most cases, high-contrast designs score lower for home use; however, these designs do have their place. When the mood called for is "lively," "bistro," "action-oriented," "fun," "attention getting," "exciting," and/or image-making, higher contrast is a plus. A fashion analogy is the "spectator pump"—look at those legs!

In addition to the constancy notion is the aspect of movement or implied movement. Because our human condition is an active one, our eyes never remain in a fixed position. Some have suggested that all our movements change our perceptions. "There is also evidence that motion perception is an extremely basic aspect of vision ... *motion perception* is so basic that it can be found in organisms that lack other visual skills."[13]

In the case of the acoustic dot pattern, not only did the walls exhibit a bad "closure" Gestalt, but the vibrational effect of implicit movement led to the perception of waving motion. Coupled with the movement of the performers playing musical instruments, the subliminal flicker of fluorescent lighting and reading black notes on white pages, the effect was almost unbearable to some — with physiological repercussions. These phenomena are unintentional side effects most self-respecting professionals abhor and seek to eliminate or change once the "accident" becomes apparent. There is no room for professional arrogance.

Apparent or illusory movement is another type of perceptual "error." *Autokinesis* was first noted by astronomers who perceived that the stars they were watching moved. *"Induced movement* occurs when a visual frame of reference moves in one direction and produces the illusion that a stationary target is moving in the opposite direction. ... *Stroboscopic movement* is the illusion of movement produced by a rapid pattern of stimulation of different parts of the retina. ... *Movement aftereffects* occur when you have been looking at a continuous movement and then look at another surface; that surface will seem to move in the opposite direction."[12]

Driving past rows of dark tree trunks in bright winter sunlight can trigger an unpleasant effect, as can riding in a train and visually fixating on stationary objects. Strobe lights at discos, intense flashing lights at retail sales, and airport runways all serve very different purposes. Several op-art patterns create movement effects: a swirling illusion where static high-contrast circular shapes are closely spaced and appear to be revolving inward, or a static pattern of alternating-width stripes that appears to vibrate. Illusions have become very popular. There are plenty of optical theories to explain these experiences. One theory is that the elements that create the illusion cause the eyes to look in the wrong place. This is known as the eye-movement theory.

The disturbing effect one perceives from looking at parallel lines or rays may be because of small eye movements that shift repeated lines upon the retina. The receptors respond to this on-and-off-again stimulus as they would to a flickering light. It is important to avoid this type of effect in architecture.

Later theories and explanations involving eye movements were replaced by other ideas such as that of fatigue. Fatigue is closely allied to the overload theory, which is a neurological view. *Our neuro-optic channels are "set" to detect specific and changing light levels, colors, patterns, shapes, and movements.* Any excess or unusual stimulus may instigate our primitive and very useful warning system. One cannot study perception and illusion without an adequate understanding of the physiology of vision. "Each retina contains about 125 million rods and 5.5 million cones; yet as counted with the light microscope, only 1,000,000 optic nerve fibers lead from the retina to the brain. Thus, an average of about 125 rods and 5 cones converge on each optic nerve fiber."[13]

Guyton describes how ganglion cells are excited by light intensity, especially a change in intensity and the adaptation effect of neurons in the visual chain. In the design arena, this has specific implications. "If a person looks at a blank wall, only a few neurons of the primary visual cortex will be stimulated ... by the time the visual signal is recorded in the primary visual cortex, it is concerned mainly with the contrasts in the visual scene rather than with the flat areas. At each point in the visual scene where there is a change from dark to light or light to dark, the corresponding area of the primary visual cortex becomes stimulated."[14] Guyton further explains how the neurons are arranged in columns, and how specific neurons are stimulated only by lines or borders of specific lengths. "In analyzing information, the brain depends to a great extent on 'patterns' of stimulation. ... For instance, a square is detected as a square regardless of its position or angle of rotation in the visual field. ... Beautiful examples of the ability of the brain to process information for determination of patterns have been discovered in relation to the visual system. Certainly [lines drawn on a sheet of paper] do not represent the actual picture of the person, but they do give the visual cortex the same pattern of contrasts that one's own visual system would give."[15] One can address binocular vision, saccadic, and vestibular eye movements, principles of optics or mechanisms of accomodation to account for some of the "perceptual errors" or illusion effects discussed earlier.

The physiology and spacing of the eye may account for a better understanding of depth perception. How might this work? "Since the receptive fields we have been discussing appear to be adapted for stimulation by different features of objects, eg. movement, bars or edges, the cells belonging to them have been called feature detectors ... it should be clear how exceedingly naive it is to think that anything resembling a 'picture' of the visual world is formed in the brain. Any representation of the world may be thought of as a pattern of cell firings in many different places and at many different times. This pattern is probably related to features of the world in a highly abstract way."[16]

It is certainly true that the patterns specified by the design team or purchased by the consumer have broader implications than merely decorative. Beyond the random or organizing firings of cells, the visual perception of patterns is an amazing thing. But how far might the nondecorative implications go, and what are potentially more serious consequences?

Psycho-physical responses to and effects of pattern

In the course of many studies, I have found some pronounced responses to certain types of patterns, which can best be described as "psycho-physical." In simple terms, we have a physical response based on what we are seeing. Some people are more prone to eye strain, motion sickness, and migraines. Others have shorter attention spans, are easily distracted, or are more readily agitated. There are about 2.5 million cases of confirmed epilepsy in the United States. About 3–5% of these are highly photosensitive, meaning that specific environmental stimuli have the potential to cause a seizure. It is estimated that 1 individual in 10,000 is photosensitive without suffering epilepsy.[17] All of the previous conditions have been linked with a higher degree of pattern sensitivity, which may actually be a trigger factor. Neurologists have found that *82% of migraine sufferers will experience a migraine after looking at certain types of pattern stimulus*—most notably stripe gratings. Neurologically, different areas of the brain are stimulated differently by different pattern designs and color combinations.[18] The response to pattern is more pronounced for some types of people than others. Brain surgeons have documented the ability to produce hallucinations or seizures when regions of the brain are stimulated to cause persistent visual images. Could pattern do this? Wilkins has suggested a neurological basis for visual discomfort[19] related to migraine sufferers and has reported on visually induced seizures. Soso researched pattern-sensitive epilepsy, based on spatial frequency selective response to stripes, or gratings, as they are termed by the neurologists.[20] Other neurologists interviewed confirmed that in addition to migraine patients, schizophrenics and Parkinsons patients have a greater sensitivity to verticality, wavy patterns, or flickering lights. The postoccupancy evaluation of a site with an acoustic dot pattern revealed not only a high degree of perceived "wave motion" but reports of visual fatigue, distraction, and even feelings of nausea. The subjects were healthy, young, talented college music students who practiced in the room for extended periods of time. It was something the architect never intended. In studies one and two, visual correction may have played a role as well. Subjects with glasses, bifocals, and trifocals were significantly more sensitive to the objectionable patterns, as were those with physical conditions such as migraines or motion sickness.

Pattern-induced responses have been studied by psychologists, neurologists, and ophthalmologists. Research measures of visual/neural acuity utilize both a grid or checkerboard pattern and a visual angle. "The human visual system is optimally sensitive to striped patterns with the properties used in our study. Identical patterns elicit epileptiform discharges in patients with pattern-sensitive epilepsy. Visual cortex neurons probably mediate aspects of pattern sensitivity."[21]

Under the test conditions of studies three and four, there were additional changes in behavior. Research subjects were unaware they were being monitored. The average amount of time spent in each space was 6 minutes pre-test. During the three months of the test pattern; the amount of time dropped from 6 minutes to 4.79 minutes in site A; and grew to 8.33 minutes with about 2.5 minutes of that time spent in other areas of site B away from the patterns. Post-test, the amount of time spent on site was an 8.4-minute average—both sites with an over-all increase in waiting behavior.

Floor plans showing the positioning of the test and test condition results:[22]

Author

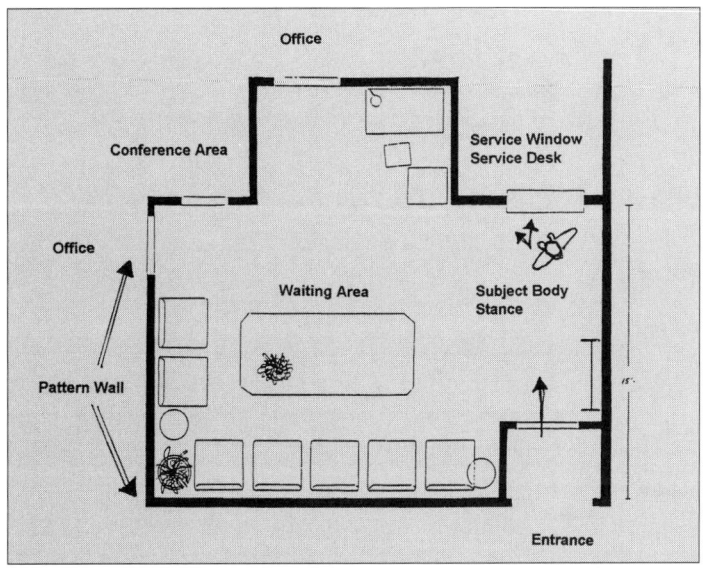

Checkerboard pattern floor-plan positioning site A (Study Three)

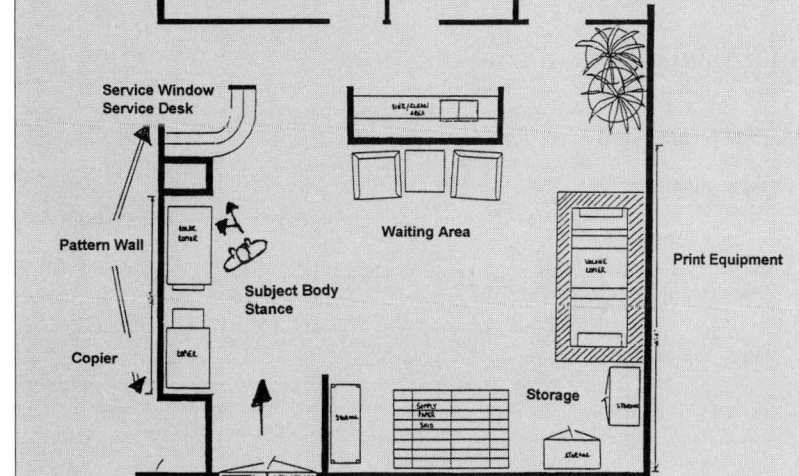

Stripe pattern floor-plan positioning site B (Study Three)

Attention arousal:

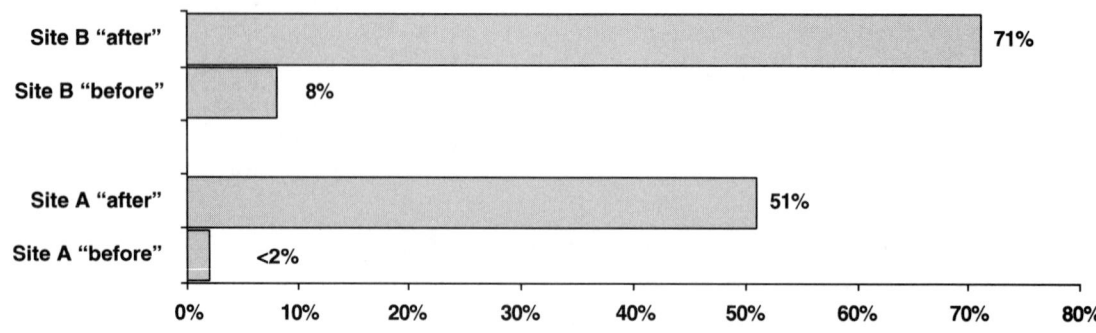

N=74 customers. Behavior observed: Notice of wall increases dramatically. Patterns have the ability to "grab attention" as subjects enter room. Videotape footage shows quick glances, turned heads, or thoughtful gazes (versus 20% in post-test).

Task Behavior Focused—To Point of Avoidance

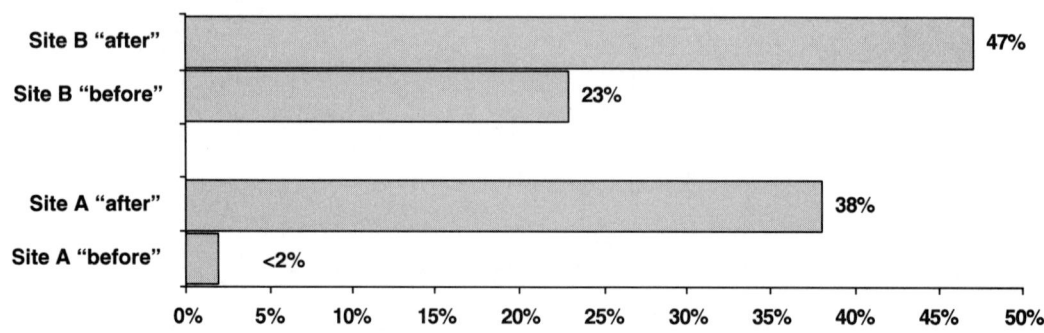

N=74 customers. Behavior observed: Subjects engaged in specific task behaviors with body-stance orientation highly focused on task to the point of near avoidance of space/other subjects. Task behavior took on exclusive orientation with a "tightness" of motion.

Engaging others in conversation

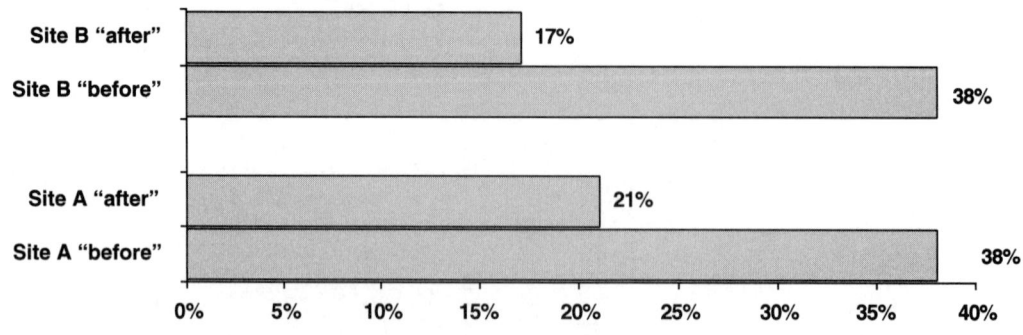

N=74 customers. Behavior observed: Both sites show a significant drop in subjects inviting comment or initiating conversation. There do not appear to be any other corresponding factors for the less social behavior. Subjects are more likely to drop work off and leave quickly.

Are engaged by staff in conversation

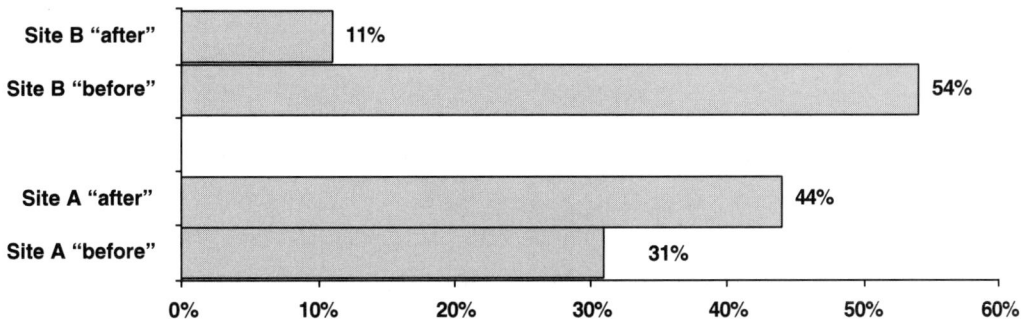

N=74 customers. Behavior observed: Site B staffers appear to avoid center area, which was confirmed in post-test interviews. Conversations initiated show a 43% decline. In site A, concerned staffers institute more conversations, as subject/customer-initiated conversation declines.

Proceed through space to other task areas/peripheral awareness

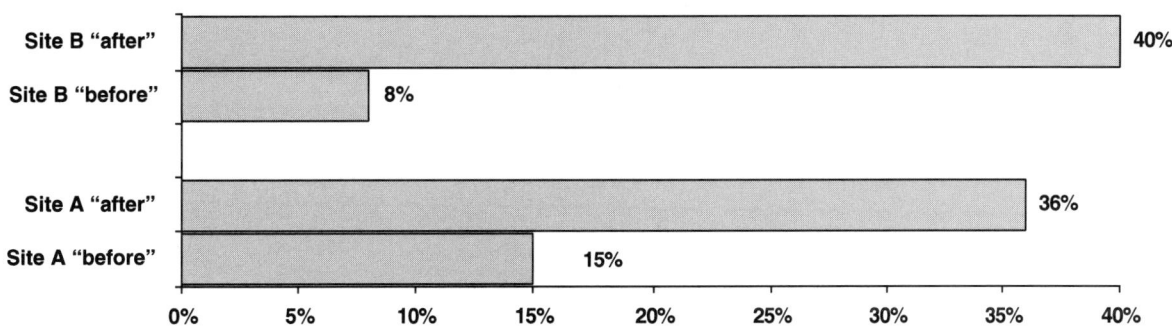

N=74 customers. Behavior observed: Behavior noted as "glancing around"—head and eye motion increases in the presence of both patterns.

Social behavior: Stand in proximity to pattern and converse

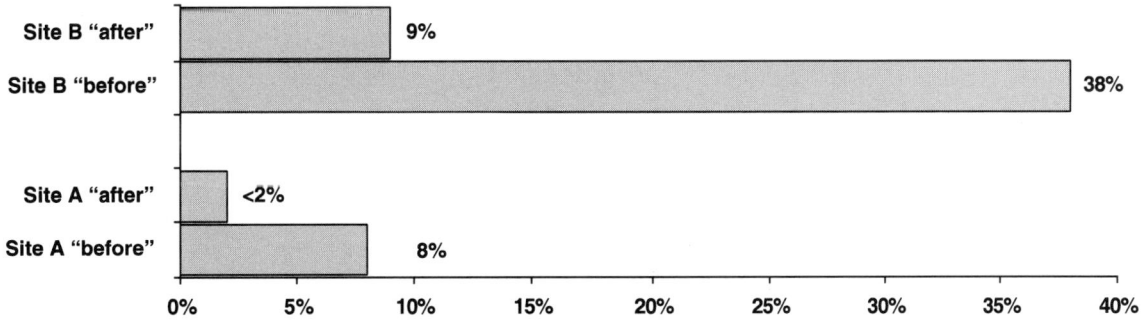

N=74 customers. Behavior observed: Conversations in the open area have dropped between 8% and 29%. An increase in workload might be a consideration; however, with subject moving to other areas, pattern may be implicated. (The site B pattern is in closer proximity to the copier.)

Wait on Work in Process

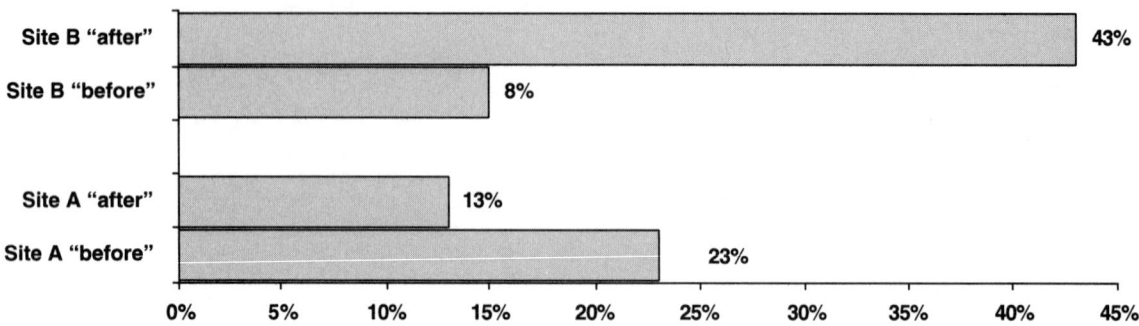

N=74 customers. Behavior observed: Variation in site A and site B design may impact response. Local/seasonal increase in workload may account for site variations. Site A customers do not have the time to wait; site B customers have to have it now. Waiting subjects were recorded on videotape biting their nails, exhibiting rapid head movement, adjusting their garments, fidgeting, and quickly flipping through magazines without pausing more than a few seconds per page. This behavior was not exhibited in the pre- or post-test conditions.

	Site A Check	Site B Stripe	Postoccupancy Site Dot	
Distracting	25% somewhat 50% significantly	25% somewhat 75% significantly	36% somewhat 43% significantly	(vs. soothing)
Busy	100% significantly	100% significantly	36% somewhat 50% significantly	(vs. calming)
Moving	25% somewhat 50% significantly	100% significantly	64% somewhat 36% significantly	(vs. stationary)
Vibrating	50% neutral* 25% significantly	100% significantly	50% somewhat 29% significantly	(vs. graphic)
Overbearing	50% somewhat 25% significantly	25% neutral 75% significantly	29% somewhat 43% significantly	(vs. simple)
Wearying	50% somewhat 25% significantly	25% somewhat 75% significantly	21% somewhat 58% significantly	(vs. refreshing)
Disruptive	50% somewhat 25% significantly	25% somewhat 75% significantly	36% somewhat 58% significantly	(vs. comfortable)
	N=74.		N=14 student/performers.	

*Write in comments: prefer to call it "popping."

Health-related factors:

	Staff		Subjects/Users	
	Site A	**Site B**	**Site A & B**	**Postoccupancy Site**
Age	25% age 25–29 25% age 30–34 25% age 50–54 25% age 55–59	50% age 25–29 50% age 40–44	33.5 average	50% <20 average age
Gender	50/50	100% female	20% male/ 40% female	43% male/ 57% female
Glasses	50%	100%	60% yes	
Motion sickness	none	75%	30% said yes	36% said yes
Medication				
Heart	12%	none	none	none
Arthritis	no	12%	none	none
Epilepsy	none	none	none	none
Migraines	none	none	10% said yes	14% said yes
Amount of time in space		20% several times/day 20% weekly 60% monthly		50% several times/day 29% several times/week 21% several times/month

Do you (staff) behave differently with the ___ pattern up?

25% yes—simply don't look, avoid it;   75% said no change
25% spend less time in the area;   75% said no change
12% notice it more; 25% notice it less after the first few days

Have you noticed a difference in the way customers behave?

25% of site A staffers said yes; 25% of site B staffers said yes.
Observed behavior: 12% spend less time as a result; 38% notice design more and
comments are made about the design.

Have you noticed a difference in the way co-workers behave?

25% of site B staffers said yes; 0% of site A staffers said yes.
Observed behavior: 38% notice it more and comment about it.

Fifty percent of the site A staffers could envision the checkerboard pattern in a restaurant setting and 25% in a retail setting. None of the site B staffers could envision the stripe in any commercial or home setting. None of the staffers at either site would be comfortable with the pattern on all four walls. Eighty-six percent of the performers in the post-occupancy site said they would not be/are not comfortable.

In the post-test case, we interviewed subjects and probed pattern-memory recall. Many had a good sense of recall and responded in a similar fashion as the staffers on the semantic portion, though not quite as negatively with time factored in as an additional variable.

One study to test recall and recognition found that *visual images exist in long-term memory, but are less detailed and less specific than the original patterns.* Recall varies because of the emotion/event connected with the visual image and the presence of other stimuli. As color, movement, sound, and dimension are added, recall increases. One subject remembered in vivid detail, from very early childhood, the scenic pattern in a Southern home—from the willow trees to the people in the scene—because it was associated with a specific emotional memory: the birth of a sibling.

These studies involved adult subjects. Activities and exposure to sensory stimuli are critical in brain development of children from birth to age three. It has been documented that infants deprived of sensory stimuli suffer. "Dr. Juliann M. Paolicchi, a pediatric neurologist and director of Children's Hospital Epilepsy Center, said there is a proliferation of neurons before birth-newborns are equipped with about 100 billion brain cells. These neurons are produced in the central brain and migrate to the outer brain, or cortex. Any damage to the brain at this stage can be devastating. Each neuron can produce as many as 15,000 synapses. By age three, the majority have been produced, and a child's brain has about twice as many synapses as it will ever need. Between ages three and six, excess synapses are discarded in a sort of mental pruning. Experiences define the brain during this time."[23] *There is no question that the designed environment can impact a developing infant/child. Color and pattern are part of this complex equation with interaction, touch, smell, and hearing integral in development.*

Pattern studies in infant/child development point to developing adaptability or a tempering mechanism in pattern exposure over time. A study that manipulated the black-and-white contrast of an achromatic checkerboard pattern evaluated the effects on four-month-old fixations during repeated presentations. Two findings emerged: that high contrast elicited more fixation than low contrast, and that decreasing response increments occurred between trials one and two. We have seen some of this effect between the initial installation of the test patterns and the time of their removal on video footage with the staff. The

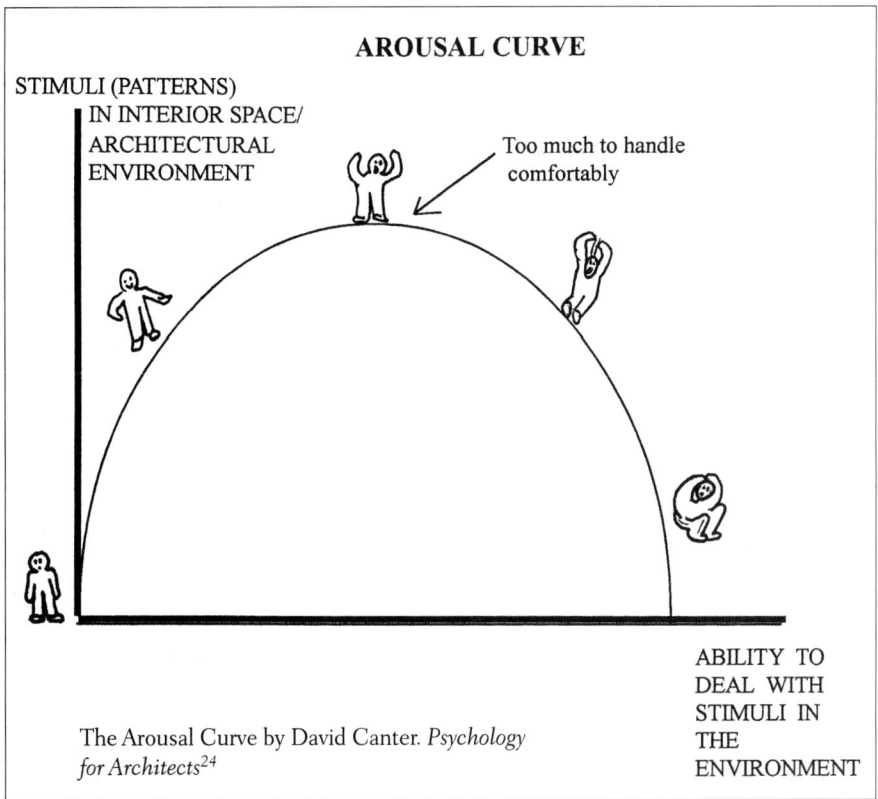

AROUSAL CURVE

STIMULI (PATTERNS)
IN INTERIOR SPACE/
ARCHITECTURAL
ENVIRONMENT

Too much to handle
comfortably

ABILITY TO
DEAL WITH
STIMULI IN
THE
ENVIRONMENT

The Arousal Curve by David Canter. *Psychology
for Architects*[24]

question remains: At what point does avoidance behavior become accli-
mation—or does it? Customers to sites A and B continued to be cog-
nizant of the design. There seemed to be a post-test "relief factor" at
work, perhaps on an unconscious level. More research needs to be conducted in a variety of sites, colors, situations in actual settings and test
simulations.

The key difference in pattern types and behavior remains the "individual comfort level." Canter has proposed this response via what he
termed the "arousal curve." Individuals each arrive at a point when the
stimulation level simply becomes "too much." This level varies depending on age, prior exposure to the situation, physiological and psychological factors.

Much of the pyschological and neurological research involves
experimental test conditions. From the viewpoint of an evolutionary
biologist, to a degree, we are at all times living, working, residing in "test
conditions" of a sort. The design team seldom thinks in these terms.
And it may very well be that an austere, unnatural synthetic-technical
environment is not optimal for human functioning. The response to
pattern stimuli and environmental cues must be examined from all
angles and disciplines, for coherence and applied understanding. Each

discipline will arrive at its own theoretical conclusions that are valid until the next set of hypotheses and experimentation reveal something different. "Visual theorists also would agree that seeing is a constructive process, one in which the brain has to carry out complex activities (sometimes called computations) to decide which interpretation to adopt of the ambiguous visual input. "Computation" implies that the brain acts to form a symbolic representation of the visual world, with a mapping (in the mathematical sense) of certain aspects of that world onto elements in the brain."[25]

Neurobiologist Semir Zeki proposed that "the concept of functional specialization in the visual cortex, which supposes that color, form, motion and possibly other attributes of the visible world are processed separately…and different areas of the brain show functional specialization." Using positron emission tomography (PET), which measures increases in regional cerebral blood flow when people perform specific tasks, researchers arrived at some interesting findings. "We found that when normal-seeing humans view a Land color Mondrian (abstract painting with no recognizable objects), the highest increase in regional cerebral blood flow occurs in a structure named the fusiform gyrus (referred to as cortical area V4 in humans). The results are very different when subjects view a pattern of moving black and white squares: the highest blood flow then occurs in a more lateral area, quite separate from V4, (which we call human V5). This demonstration of the separation of motion and color processing constitutes direct evidence that functional specialization is also a feature of the human visual cortex…and adjoining areas V1 and V2 must be distributing signals to different areas of the cortex."[26]

It is apparent that different visual stimuli (patterns) not only result in different behaviors, perceptions, and semantic responses but also different areas of the brain being stimulated and a potentially different recall sequence—making sense of the phenomenon and attributing it with meaning in perspective—and that this occurs most of the time, in a rapid and unconscious fashion.

The perceptual phenomenon goes beyond the theoretical in two additional case histories. The first example is named the "astigmatism shirt" and is manufactured by a men's clothing company of various striped fabrics, including pinstripes and other types of narrow ticking designs. The stripes are blue and white, rather than the black and white explored in the research. In addition to reports of cross-eyes are incidences of nausea and headaches from seamstresses/shirtmakers working on these types of pattern. In interviews with staff and management, it became apparent that the combination of pattern, close proximity, and movement all combined to cause the first symptom of eye strain and fatigue.

Jared Schneidman Design

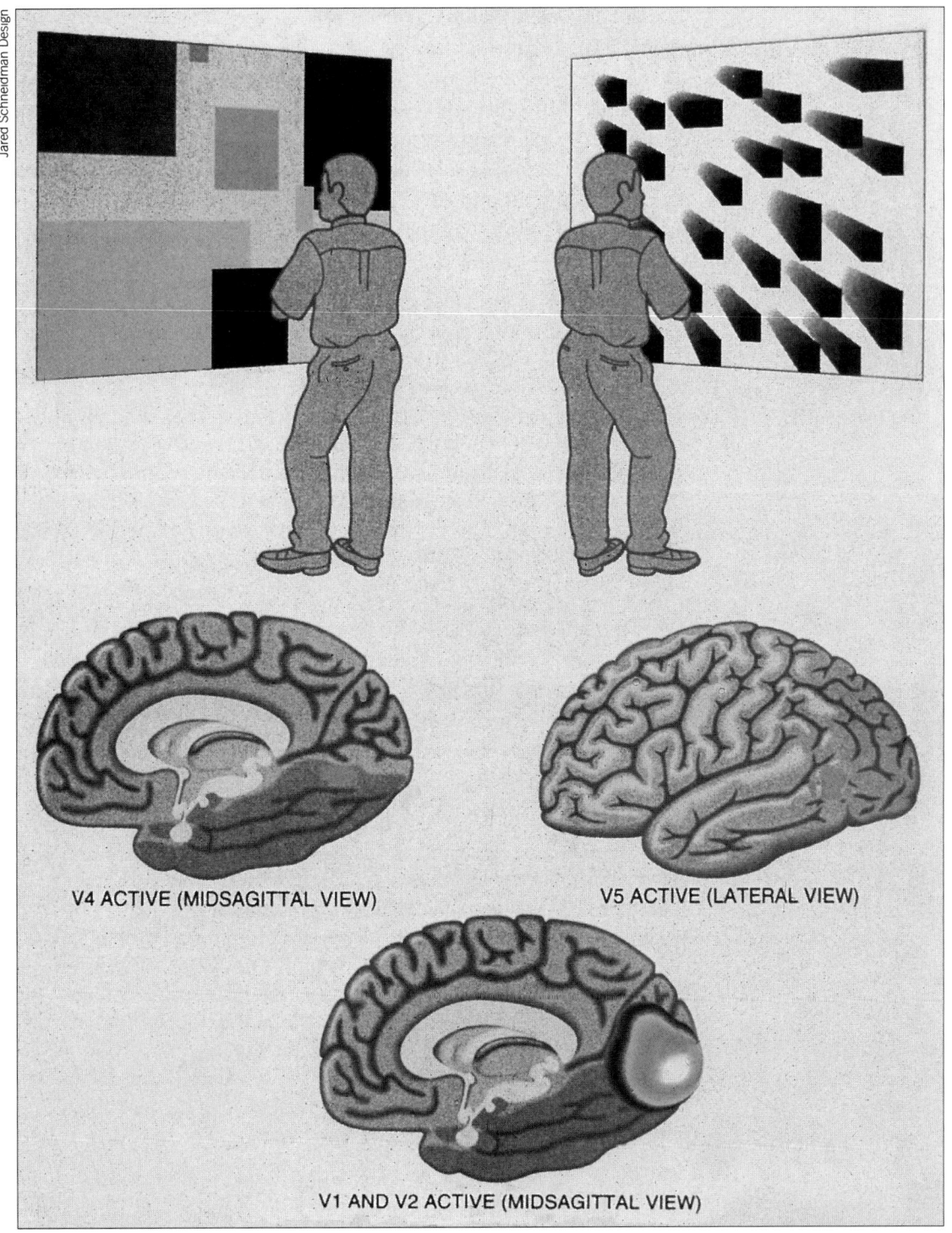

V4 ACTIVE (MIDSAGITTAL VIEW)   V5 ACTIVE (LATERAL VIEW)

V1 AND V2 ACTIVE (MIDSAGITTAL VIEW)

Different areas of the Brain "on Design." Dissimilar images stimulate different regions of the visual cortex. A brightly colored Mondrian causes area V4 to become highly active, as shown by tests of regional cerebral blood flow. Black-and-white moving images trigger activity in area V5. Both types of images lead to activity in areas V1 and V2, which have less specialized functions, and distribute signals to other cortical areas.

The second example comes from a large state goverment building with performing facilities. Outside the auditorium is a particularly striking geometric-patterned carpet, custom designed for the site by a well-known architectural firm. The contrast and pattern shapes combined with a smaller scale lead to a sensation of movement, whether a subject is sitting in the lobby or walking across the floor. Again, distance appears to be critical; and in this instance, the introduction of varied lighting and/or reading material causes the eyes to have difficulty focusing.

"Even when the term 'perception' is meant in its literal sense, it may cover differing aspects of behavior. Traditionally, 'perception' has been used for a whole class of processes, at one extreme bordering on sensation and, at the other, on concept-formation. When academic psychologists talk of perception they tend more often to refer to processes that are more nearly sensory; whereas when anthropologists employ the term, they more often refer to processes bordering on cognition. And even within experimental psychology, the term 'perception' has been variously employed."[27] Perception and response to pattern design is a complex subject within the context of each discipline.

Finally, we need not overlook the apparent reason behind the use of pattern, namely looking good/looking better or *"visual esthetic interest"* that is *"perceptually rewarding."*[28] Looking good is derived from the context of the individual and his/her behavior. It is cultural and highly subjective. It links with memories and past associations formed from birth on. According to Kosslyn:

Vision is not a simple process but rather a linking together of subsystems that process specific aspects of vision. Edges, contour, color, depth of field and a variety of other features are examined separately. ... The eyes send visual information to two higher subsystems of the brain for analysis. They are often referred to as the "what" system and the "where" system. ... The "what" system, in the temporal lobe, contains cells that are tuned for specific shapes and colors. ... The "where" system, in the parietal lobe, contains cells that are tuned to fire when objects are in different locations. ... When cells in the "what" and "where" systems are stimulated, they may combine their signals in yet a higher subsystem where associative memories are stored.[29]

At some time we will likely arrive at images that specific individuals find intensely pleasurable—and measurable in some scientific fashion. At this point, the role of the designer may shift to one of behaviorist.

It is the intersection of neurology, ophthalmology, biology, psychiatry, psychology-experimental, environmental, behavioral, cognitive with the design professions that can bring a truly valuable new approach to that which inspires, uplifts, delights, and expresses our sense of self: the patterns, colors, shapes, and textures in our lives, homes, and working environments. As creatures we are so intimately connected with the environment around us. Within the last one hundred years, we have "come inside" from a largely rural occupational base, to spending more than 95% of our time indoors interacting with an electronic environment rather than the natural world. We spend some 86,000 hours in the workplace alone over an average lifespan in a 43-year career (age 22–65)—and that is just the 40-hour-a-week crowd! It behooves us to understand the implications of these new, ever more synthetic structural creations (the built environment) on our bodies, brains, and emotions. The way we approach building design, lighting, color, and pattern selection is not so simple anymore.

References

1. M. C. Escher Web site: http://lonestar.texas.net/ªEscher or Cordon Art BV PlO. Box 101, 3740 AC The Netherlands.
2. Hothersall, David. 1990. *History of psychology,* New York: McGraw-Hill.
3. Ibid.
4. Ibid.
5. Matlin, Margaret. 1983. *Perception.* Boston: Allyn & Bacon.
6. Hothersall, David. 1990. *History of Psychology,* New York: McGraw-Hill.
7. Blakeslee, Sandra. 1993. Seeing and Imagining. *The New York Times,* 31 March.
8. Matlin, Margaret. 1983. *Perception.* Boston: Allyn & Bacon.
9. Matlin, Margaret. 1983. *Perception.* Boston: Allyn & Bacon.
10. Ibid.
11. Ibid.
12. Ibid.
13. Guyton, Arthur. 1987. *Basic neuroscience: anatomy and physiology.* Philadelphia: W.B. Saunders Company.
14. Ibid.
15. Ibid.
16. Kaufman, Lloyd. 1974. *Sight and mind,* New York: Oxford University Press.
17. Epilepsy Foundation of America, 4351 Garden City Drive, Landover Maryland 20785.
18. Restak, Richard. 1979. *The brain: The last frontier.* New York: Warner Books.
19. Wilkins, A., I. Nimmo-Smith, and A. Tait, et al. 1984. Neurological basis for visual discomfort. *Brain* 107: 989–1017.
20. Soso, M. J., E. Lettich, and J. H. Belgum. 1980. Pattern-sensitive epilepsy I: A demonstration of a spatial frequency selective epileptic response to gratings. *Epilepsia* 21: 301-312.
21. Marcus, Dawn. Migraine and stripe-induced visual discomfort. *Archives of Neurology* 46: 1129–32.
22. Rodemann, Patricia. © 1991. The Ohio State University. Masters thesis.
23. Paolicchi, Juliann. 1997. Children thrive when challenged early. *The Columbus Dispatch,* 11 May, section C.

24. Canter, David. 1974. *Psychology for architects*. London: Applied Science Publishers.
25. Crick, Francis, and Christof Koch. 1992. The problem of consciousness. *Scientific American* (September): 153–59.
26. Zeki, Semir. 1992. The visual image in mind and brain. *Scientific American* (September): 69–76.
27. Segall, Marshall, D. T. Campbell, and M. J. Herskovits. 1966. *The influence of culture on visual perception*. Indianapolis; New York: The Bobbs-Merrill Company.
28. Hochberg, Julian. 1978. *Perception*. Englewood Cliffs, N.J.: Prentice-Hall.
29. Blakeslee, Sandra. 1993. Seeing and Imagining. *The New York Times*, 31 March.

CHAPTER 5

Psychological Effects of Pattern Design and Our Cultural Perceptions

Cognitive psychologists explain that we process all information in terms of a hierarchy of connections and meanings. The information is contextual and referential, conditioned by our environment and memory, and experientially based. At the same time we are dealing with broader sociocultural (and economic) associations. For this reason "pattern" is never seen in isolation. This is problematic in that not all humans are born with equal exposure to a stimulus-rich environment. Impoverished children without access to the broader natural world and/or other rich visual/spatial stimuli may not make the same connections and develop as quickly or fully as their more privileged counterparts.[1] And yet, the pervasiveness of media in our lives teaches associations many would otherwise not have access to on a global level, reinforcing any design clichés.

Repeated exposure to the interiors, patterns, colors, fashion trends makes these connections hard to escape. How much we adapt to these usage cues and make identification with our own lives remains to be seen.

Degree of media influence on decorating approach

Influenced by advertising: Prefer brand names

Watch television shows on home decorating and remodeling

Rely on home-decorating magazines for my ideas

Visit builders' show houses and take home-decorating tours
  (public-relations events)

My research shows who each of these consumer types are more likely to be. The magazine reader tends to be female, professional, and younger with a college degree. Two income groups are represented in the magazine-influenced group: both a mid-range and a high-income household. The television viewer tends to be a younger male, in a smaller market from a slightly lower- to lower-middle-income household. The show-house visitor tends to live in larger markets, live on the West Coast, be in an upper-middle-income household range, and have a college degree. The show-house visitor tends to be under age 36, and then age 46–55. I have also found that consumers select designs that fit them personally and that the interior environment is an unselfconscious extension/projection of oneself.

This has big implications for the home-building market. According to the National Association of Home Builders, consumers increasingly are looking for feelings like a sense of spaciousness, openness in layout, elbow room but also privacy, natural light, unique features, textures, and garden vistas.[2] How do these "feelings" translate into pattern designs and selections?

Consumers are using similar semantic language in evaluating patterns. They increasingly are selecting looks that blend with their own eclectic style, with less rigidity to their approach and less distinctive pattern renditions in looser interpretations. The consumer of today appreciates classics as much as new takes on historic and cultural designs and does not follow rules but opts for what works with their lifestyle. It is important to understand what those life-style interests and behaviors are. Increasingly, there is a recognition that pattern designs are not a statement in and of themselves but long-term, "bridge looks" between styles, color palettes, and trends. As we move into a new century, there is also an appreciation for looks of the past several decades. Throughout all of my research of the past decade, I have found that consumers are keenly sensitive to patterns, styles, and colors perceived as "dated." Whether this is a function of marketing, media, or some innate predisposition to change is up for debate. One thing is clear: There is a profound relationship between the culture, the political/economic/social climate, the arts, retail environments, and the consumer design expression and selection. Pattern design is often a mirror of the moment.

Moving from a home context to a commercial setting, many of the same observations apply. On a tangible, immediately applicable level, you want to make people feel "warm" and "at home" in your hotel. If you want them to perceive your environment as welcoming and at the same time somewhat sophisticated, which pattern design will you select? To which we might ask: Who is the clientele and what is the price point? "Warm" might translate into color palette—siennas; roses; creams; aged, washed golds. "At home" might mean some self-service features. "Welcoming" could be the use of oak, maple, and medium-toned wood finishes. "Sophisticated" speaks to a limited use of pattern and greater use of textural and tonal elements. We perceive the use of design as high end or low end, common or special.

If you are designing a lawyer's office that handles criminal cases, your approach may well be a no-nonsense look: tonal stripes, faux-stone looks, simple geometrics, stylized designs and textures. The courtroom might feature finely rendered granite designs—which people describe as cold, expensive, formal, unapproachable and rigid—along with formidable dark woods. Many of these selections are the product of both learning and understanding the cultural mores of the context. We call upon this cognitive system naturally, intuitively, and instinctively. In evaluating which types of pattern design consumers find most suitable to different types of space, I found some exciting differences in what consumers and specifiers had to say.

Specifiers were easily able to manipulate the elements of design to create the image desired by the client, and to break the rules on occasion, which unwittingly caused cognitive dissonance in less creative, less receptive consumers.

Context is everything. Let's address pattern in a number of settings and situations in light of our research.

Consumers rated several pattern types as suitable for the home environment. Small prints were rated highest, with floral designs close behind. Stripe designs were expected. Fabric looks and textures/embossings (moiré, damask, etc.) were very popular. Novelty or pictorial designs were rated somewhat lower overall because of their theming. But this vocabulary and rating hierarchy varies significantly by room and product, company, retailer, and brand image. Thus, a child's room *might* be more apt to feature novelty designs; a kitchen, a sunrise design; a dining room, botanic designs; a study, geometric or architectural looks.

Home environment

Suitability of Each Pattern Type for the Home Environment:			Home Owners Likelihood to Purchase This Pattern Type:	
	Study One[a]	Study Two[a]	Study Ten[b]	
Graphic miniprints	83%	70%	30%	Prefer smaller scale, less regimental
Floral designs	48%	59%	23%	Prefer less hard-edge interpretations
Botanical designs			43%	Prefer lighter and more sophisticated renditions
Stripe designs	–	53%	37%	Prefer a contextual interpretation
Fabric looks	41%	40%	26%	Prefer embossed, lighter tonals
Natural textures	33%	40%	28%	Prefer real naturals with warmth
Stone/faux looks			31%	Prefer warmer, softer look, and the "real thing" as budget allows
Geometrics/plaids	28%	47%	29%	Prefer medium to larger scale, "softer"
Pictorial/novelty	25%	–	14%	Prefer painterly renditions
Abstract designs			27%	Prefer sophisticated interpretations
Historic/architectural			19%	Prefer authentic rendition for today's context; usually for borders only
Ethnic/cultural/stylized			13%	Prefer as an accent element
Combinations			8%	Prefer in limited use

[a]Rodemann, Patricia. © 1991. Master's Thesis, The Ohio State University. Columbus, Ohio. Studies One through Five.
*% reflects home owners likely to consider purchasing this pattern type for the home
[b]N=500. Rodemann, Patricia. © 1998. Study Ten. Thesis ,
follow-up research project

Botanical designs encompass leaves, herbs, fruit, berries, vegetables.
Printed/textured fabric looks encompass moiré, silk, damask, tapestry effects, strie, seersucker, chenille.
Geometric designs encompass plaids, checks, gingham, tartan, diamond.
Pictorial, graphic, and novelty prints encompass animals, ducks, dishes, newsprint, repeating shapes/motifs.
Abstract/watercolor designs encompass free-form colors, shapes, and derivative contemporary watercolor versions.
Architectural and historic motifs encompass classic themes such as fretwork, scrollwork, fleur-de-lis.
Ethnic/cultural prints encompass stylized sunrise motif, flame, fan, paisley, batik, Indian, Oriental.

Other factors enter into the psychological "meanings" of pattern in addition to income, occupation, education, or a regional matrix overlaid upon the national (general) data. Descriptive phrases to convey meanings of the home are: comfort haven, a castle or fortress, a place of

Degree of pattern use by product type for home decor:

Study Ten

Degree of Pattern use	For Walls	For Borders	For Textiles/ Furniture	Rugs/Carpet/ Flooring
Major/heavy or Primary usage	13%	54%	49%	18%
Coordinate/some	43%	33%	41%	39%
Very limited or accent use only	44%	13%	10%	45%

N=500. ©1998, Patricia Rodemann. Study Ten, Thesis Follow-up.

High likelihood to consider use of pattern in this room

Study Ten

1. Bathroom	43%
2. Child bedroom	41%
3. Master bedroom	39%
4. Kitchen	32%
5. Family room	26%
6. Dining room	24%
7. Study/den	22%
8. Foyer/hall	20%
9. Living room	10%
10. Other — foyer, laundry, exercise	7%

N=500. ©1998, Patricia Rodemann. Study Ten, Thesis Follow-up

refuge or escape, an active, fun family center, an extension of self, a place to eat and sleep, and so on. How the home is perceived points not only to its function, but to individual traits and attitudes of the consumer and the types of pattern they will select. As we have seen, the *design styles (traditional, contemporary, etc.) consumers choose are also indicative of the pattern types and renditions ("Jacobean" floral, "abstract" watercolor) they are likely to select.* It is enormously complex if predictive modeling is to be employed, because we are also dealing with a changing market and changing conditions. The statistician-planner must also be a designer, behavioral expert, sociologist, economist, and crystal ball gazer.

In an attempt to understand how consumers can be grouped by design approaches, in study six I employed additional statistical analysis of my now 15-volume database. From this I arrived at five distinct consumer types: 1) savvy consumers for whom design is a big priority;

2) consumers who are ready to make big changes in their more conventional home-design style; 3) do-it-yourselfers who value comfort and mix design types freely; 4) adaptable rearrangers with budget constraints and a practical approach; and 5) the image-conscious decorator-dependent consumer.

The *savvy* consumers, for whom design is a priority, are confident about their design expertise. They like to make an impact and tend to select more sophisticated blends or traditional styles. The *conventional* consumers are ready to make changes today, do not have strong convictions about how their home should look, and tend to decorate in country or basic style mixes. This group is more apt to be classified as lower middle income. The *do-it-yourselfers* mix colors, fabrics, and textures and pride themselves on getting the right look and keeping it that way. They compare prices and values, and tend to span the top five or six major styles more narrowly interpreted from casual contemporary to traditional. The *adaptable rearrangers* approach design from a stance of flexibility but must keep the larger elements of their decor the same because of budget constraints. This group selects economic changes that allow for a maximum impact affordably. Their styles tend to romantic Victorian and country looks. The *image-conscious, decorator-dependent* consumer likes to keep up with trends and styles, but not at the expense of perennially good taste. They shop to find the "right" look, and value both traditional and eclectic sophistication in styles. The evaluation of distinct consumer types is not perfect, and will vary by age, economic conditions, and with specific product types. People do not approach all design decisions the same or consider them with the same importance.

In general, how this impacts pattern selection is very interesting. From a familiarity and usage standpoint, *image-conscious* consumers, who rely on decorator/designer advice, are comfortable negotiating selections and mixes of florals, geometrics, abstract designs, marble/stone patterns, historic architectural looks, ethnic/cultural designs, natural textures, fabric looks/embossings, and stripes. This group rates all the above design types higher. The *conventional* consumers tend to adopt novelty or pictorial theme designs that are more easy to decorate with and around, ie., the family room with billiard table, game-room ambience, and giant television may have a sports border and male-influence pattern/color/texture selection. This group also buys into botanical designs—leaves, trees, grasses, fruit, berries, and related natural representations. The *savvy* group, for whom decorating is a priority, tend to buy into smaller prints, solid embosses, and sport/character prints. (For example, this group is more likely to feature a small foulard print, fabric look, and/or a horse border in the study/home office.)

Turning our attention to commercial settings, we find consumers' perceptions carry over and are interpreted in different ways.

Commercial Environments

York Wallcoverings, Studio Source, volume I

Hotel/hospitality installation

Color, pattern design, and product appearance used to be the "pretty pictures" part of the design business. Now, making the selection or recommendation is only half of the story. There are questions of flammability, toxicity, indoor air quality, and more, in addition to the daily maintenance concerns and critical issues of life-cycle performance and recycling. Essentially, in the commercial interior, there are two main design goals: appearance and performance/protection. Business managers would add a third goal: bottom-line efficiency or financial return. For hospitality, health care, retail, and restaurant businesses it is the perception, look, and "feeling" of a space that attracts customers to begin with; and it is the performance, updating, and maintenance of that space that keeps them coming back—coupled with the price, service, and products offered. Design theme is integral to setting a tone and conveying an image. Maintenance keeps it that way until its time for renovation, which is done within a much shorter time frame than in the past to stay competitive. Flexibility is more important with mergers, acquisitions, spin-offs, and both changing corporate functions and changing personnel needs.

A great deal depends on the budget allocated to the products and finishes—from floor to ceiling. Often, the least-expensive initial option winds up costing a lot more over time. And other times, in an attempt to design an architecturally sound "bullet-proof" long-term space, we sacrifice aesthetics, functionality, and the recognition that human creatures are attuned to change and periodic updates. The point is simple: Pattern design within the context of the overall interior cannot be viewed in isolation—especially in the commercial environment.

Hotel/hospitality environments

Hospital/health-care environments

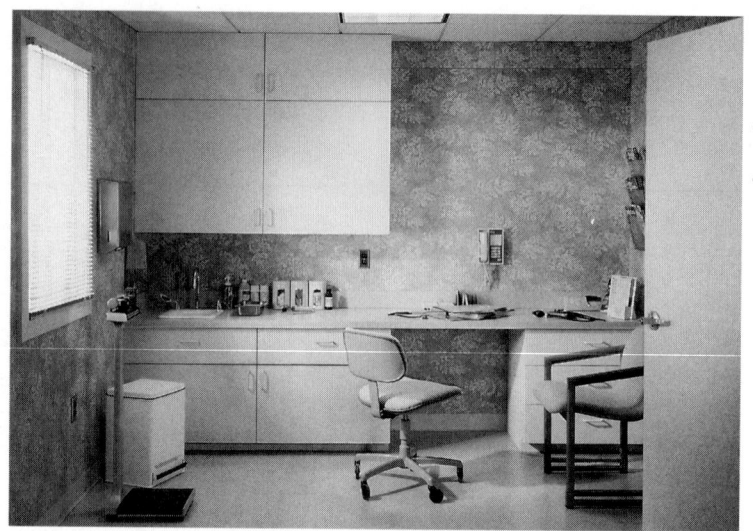

York Wallcoverings, Carey Lind Commercial

Perceived Suitability of Pattern Type for Hotel Environments by Consumers

Pattern Type	Study One	Study Two	Other Findings
Graphic miniprints	83%	53%	Prefer more sophisticated designs
Fabric looks	66%	40%	Prefer more traditional designs
Natural textures	41%	47%	Prefer more authentic designs
Floral designs	38%	53%	Prefer less gender specific designs
Stripe designs	-	47%	Prefer designs with less contrast/movement
Geometrics/plaids	28%	41%	Prefer bolder scale/multiple coloration
Pictorial/novelty	16%		Prefer limit to accessories, borders, etc.

Rodemann, Patricia. © 1991. Master's Thesis, The Ohio State University. Columbus, Ohio. Studies One through Five.

Fabric looks and natural textures are more important in the hospitality environment than in the home environment, because of their association with formal or contract settings. Consumers associate larger-scale damask and damask-stripe designs with hotel and banquet settings. But, hospitality settings cover a range of situations from budget hotel (Motel Six) to midpriced chains, convention hotels, those oriented to business travelers, suite concepts (Embassy Suites), resort destinations, family hotels, condo and extended-stay hotels, luxury hotels to the bed-and-breakfast inns. Within these distinctions are several looks oriented to their respective customer types. In these situations, it is most advantageous to research design palettes and combinations and mock rooms with the planned versus actual customer type before a large-scale investment is undertaken. Function also is a significant factor, with entirely different cleanability, flammability, and replacement standards than for home usage.

Hospital/health-care environments

Perceived Suitability of Pattern Design for Health-care Environments by Consumers

Pattern Type	Study One	Study Two	Other Findings
Graphic miniprints	50%	59%	Prefer larger scale, lower contrast
Natural textures	50%	53%	Prefer authenticity, "positive" color
Fabric looks	50%	40%	Prefer familiarity, but not too formal
Floral designs	28%	47%	Prefer less gender type-casting, fussiness
Stripe designs	––	24%	Prefer use not be in patient rooms, spacing
Geometrics/plaids	4%	24%	Prefer in some contexts, not others
Pictorial/novelty	–	–	Prefer more subtle theming approach, art

Rodemann, Patricia. © 1991. Master's Thesis, The Ohio State University. Columbus, Ohio. Studies One through Five.

The health-care environment has its own demands beyond looking good and performing functionally. There are many activity areas within the space: ambulatory care, corridors, nursing areas, offices, exam and treatment rooms, lobbies, nurseries, recovery, surgical, patient rooms, dining and waiting rooms. If we extend our consideration to specific populations such as pediatric, psychiatric, or elderly people, we introduce yet another set of variables with different pattern criteria. The importance of color, pattern, and visual stimulation in infant/child development cannot be overlooked. Earlier studies[3] showing that infants cry more in the presence of the color yellow need to be extended to pattern studies. Commonly accepted information today is anecdotal, or not widespread outside the realms of child development/ neuropsychology. In elderly populations, as the physiology of vision changes, pattern perception does too. In studies one and two, we noted how some designs were perceived as fuzzy, color perceptions were incorrect, and familiarity/past associations played a much greater role. *Several conditions are responsive to pattern exposure.* These are: migraines, motion sickness, epilepsy, certain visual corrections, conditions requiring medication that may predispose individual to sensitivity, alcohol or drug use (anesthesia), advanced age, dementia/mental instabilities to which we add Parkinson's disease, lesions in the brain, stroke, and developmental disabilities. Some pattern-sensitive individuals may also react more to odors, light or noise, washcloth, ice pack, heating pad on the head, or eating ice cream. In a neurological study of migraine sufferers, Soso and Marcus reported, "Many subjects who found the striped patterns aversive reported, after testing, prior experience of stripe-induced discomfort involving looking at escalator treads, ironing striped shirts, or looking at miniblinds, striped wallpaper, or paneling.

"Also in three migraineurs, migraine symptoms were induced within several hours of stripe viewing: scotoma in one and headache in the others. Eighty-two percent of the 38 subjects with migraine headaches demonstrated stripe aversion. Of the remaining 64 subjects (those with non-migraine headaches and those with non-headaches), only 6.2 percent evidenced stripe discomfort."[4]

This stripe discomfort can extend to other interior pattern cues and may include visual aura, flashing lights, and seeing stars as part of the migraine phenomena. This is most certainly an unintended effect when the design team submits selections to the building/owner operator. It casts yet another net of responsibility over our commercial design selections.

Office environment

York Wallcoverings, Carey Lind Commercial

Office installation

Perceived Suitability of Pattern Design for Office Environments by Consumers

Pattern Type	Study One	Study Two	Other Findings
Graphic miniprints	75%	35%	Prefer "non-home" designs
Stripe designs	–	53%	Prefer contextual or textural/tonal
Floral designs	19%	29%	Prefer sophisticated statements
Fabric looks	58%	65%	Prefer authenticity, quality
Natural textures	75%	59%	Prefer authenticity, open quality
Geometrics/plaids	19%	47%	Prefer bolder scale, historic context
Pictorial/novelty	0%	–	Prefer only in specific types of office

Rodemann, Patricia. © 1991. Master's Thesis, The Ohio State University. Columbus, Ohio. Studies One through Five.

During the past 100 years, America has moved from a largely agricultural society to a predominantly industrial one. Even the industrial age rapidly turned into a technological and service-oriented era. Less than 100 years ago, we did not have electricity or cars, or commute to offices on the scale we do today. On cold mornings, we stoked the fire and shivered while we milked the cows. In the 1920s and 1930s we rode trolleys from nearby neighborhoods and in the 1940s we took automobiles for Sunday drives.

To place it in perspective, even as recently as the 1950s, 4 million of us worked in agriculture (<3 million today), 5.7 million worked in manufacturing (<21 million today), and 4.5 million of us worked in service industries (>38 million today). In the 1950s, 5 million held professional white-collar office jobs, compared with 13 million in the 1970s and 24.5 million today. Commercial office design did not experience a renaissance until the 1940s.[5]

Today, not only have the percentages changed, but the majority of Americans hold service-oriented, technical and professional positions. We have moved indoors. While positions such as doctor, lawyer, banker, storekeeper, and innkeeper have been around since before the 1700s, the meaning of "indoors" and those roles and requirements have changed significantly since then. We have found statistically significant differences in pattern, color, and style selections based on the consumer's occupation. This changes as trends change in both workplace and home.

The U.S. Census bureau estimates that 117,342,000 (1996) of us are going to work every day.[6] Where does that leave the average American? If we estimate a 40-hour work week for 50 weeks of the year, the American is spending some 2,000 hours in the workplace each year. In a 43-year career (assuming age 22–65), the worker spends 86,000 hours in the workplace. For the 60-hour-a-week workaholic that's 129,000 hours. Office design, whether small, in-home, or extending to thousands is here in a big way. We have shown that 70 percent of all professional interior design projects involve office spaces.

For publicly traded companies, in addition to the product mix, public perception often impacts stock price. Bigger and better office towers were built over the 1960s, 1970s, and 1980s as older structures were razed to make way for the tallest, the fastest up, the biggest, the most prominent architect designed, and the glitziest or most technologically advanced. The theory was that productivity could be enhanced and the office interior easily redesigned for growth and decline within the corporate setting. This certainly fit well into the 1970s and 1980s, as many corporations played the acquisitions and spin-off games.

Concern for the worker took many forms through this time period. Ergonomics, or a keen interest in the relationship of the human body to furniture and vice versa, led to explosive growth in the office-furniture systems industry. Ergonomics and industrial design even extended to better truck-seat design with improved technologies of an air pump and sophisticated new materials. The ergonomics issue is back with concern about carpal tunnel syndrome in individuals who spend a great deal of time operating a computer. Concern about other health issues—radiation from computer terminals, airborne chemicals, or noise levels—are all interior-design issues that have become topics of popular interest within the last few years. The concept that a healthy, happy worker performs better is proven in reduced occupational health-care costs.

Reduced cost and increased productivity are serious issues. The growth of the facilities-design profession within the past ten years is an outgrowth of where we have come in such a short time frame. The employee is the subject of many studies. The facility is measured in square-foot costs and utility costs—and in the case of a resort hotel, how much more money can be turned by serving cocktails in the lobby/piano bar, formerly a wide-open welcome space.

To illustrate this new seriousness, the chief facilities manager of a major computer instruments company spoke about what is known as "speed space." Some fields—such as sales—do not require a lavish office setup because many of the staff travel rather extensively. Speed space was designed to support a phone and laptop computer with just enough privacy to allow client-contact calls. Other areas of the interior—such as engineering—offer private spaces off "think tank" group areas. It clearly shows how seriously the interior is taken into consideration for the large-scale corporate endeavor. It is not the whim of the chief executive alone that drives the look. Productivity is profitable. Product design is a productivity and profitability issue. And within product design is pattern design.

Beyond and integrated with design is a movement to improve indoor air quality and performance, and recycle building materials such as carpeting. These are related issues that come under the moniker "the green interior." Many claim the drive to energy-efficient buildings with fixed windows and an assortment of synthetic interior materials and machines has resulted in unhealthy interior air quality. The majority of indoor pollutants can be controlled by improved HVAC/ventilation systems and a bake-out period where interior materials are allowed to "off-gas" before occupants move in. This is just another sign that we are spending more and more time in the work environment and are concerned about its effects on our lives. The recycling movement is oriented around reclaiming materials, not contributing to the waste stream, and reducing or eliminating toxins. This has led to an explosion of efforts that directly affect the texture, pattern, and color of interior materials: new dye stuffs, new compositions, new performance requirements, different surface treatments, and a deepening respect for the natural environment in use of natural materials and environmentally friendly substitutes. With each new issue and discovery, our attention becomes more tightly focused on our "work selves." Currently, the press is heavily focused on Wall Street, retail sales, housing starts, economic indicators, global economy, and downsizing. Design issues are secondary in the macro environment, primary in the micro environment.

But how we approach design—and pattern—is also a function of whether we are addressing new construction or renovation. According to the U.S. Department of Commerce, $25.2 billion of new nonresidential construction spending is on office strucures alone, out of a total nonresidential 1996 estimate of $140.7 billion. Renovation may be quite costly, depending on the extent of the project. It is estimated that renovation (additions and alterations) represents a $46 billion market (1993).[7] The decorative aspects of interior renovation offer a significant opportunity to address pattern context. How many times have you visited a commercial building when you knew right away what year the wall-covering went in and when you looked at the flooring, you remembered the popular colors of that decade? If it was a dentist or doctor's office, you probably also wondered what year he or she bought the drill or exam-room furniture. If it was a bank, you probably wondered how much they had kept up with the almost fast-food atmosphere of retail banking today. *For many commercial settings, including offices, image is everything. Image sells. Image defines us to ourselves and to each other. And pattern design is as important in image as any other design variable.*

Let's talk about credibility as it relates to design. A bankruptcy counseling service with a lavish interior will probably not make the customer feel comfortable about restructuring debt payment. The office with cool white fluorescents, metal shelving, and vinyl chairs portrays a very different picture from the salon with white damask walls, aubusson carpeting, and pink velvet *bergère* chairs. Whether the visitor is discussing mousetraps, embalming, ball bearings, or weight loss, it is important to set a mood that creates the right corporate image for the business at hand. We know this design language. It is imprinted on us in cognitive associations. And it affects performance, perception, and outcomes.

Barring the very large architectural project, many of America's offices are smaller spaces in medium-size commercial buildings with tenant leases or privately held buildings such as clinics, attorney's offices, ad agencies, or small warehouses. Selections are code dependent and subject to manufacturer's offer as much as they are cost and personality sensitive. There likely are as many dated, dismal, and cluttered sites as their opposites, which grace the pages of trade magazines in well-lit splendor. Regardless of installation size, a new consideration has emerged with respect to pattern design. With many workers spending more time in front of computer screens, it is important for the walls to offer visual relief. From a color and finish standpoint, avoid glare and use complementary colors to the screen in softer, nonjarring palettes. Strong patterns are not advised where visual acuity is essential. The worker's horizon lines and visual angles should be examined relative to patterned carpets and window treatments. The solution of an off-white, high-tech cubicle may not promote optimum comfort or productivity. In large spaces, we also need to consider vistas and horizon lines that calm us.

Most consumers found florals fine for home office use, followed by hotel installations and hospitals. Geometrics drew a mixed review. For limited-time areas such as waiting spaces and to draw attention (or to make a "cozy" home office), many felt geometrics could be used—but preferably not for their own commercial office setting. This applied to plaids, stripes, checkerboards, and grids, and was highly context sensitive. Graphic patterns were well received if they were more masculine chevrons, arrows, diagonals, or diamonds, but not ditsy dots or tiny florals. Natural-texture patterns were described as relaxed and soothing—though granite types were thought to be "cold." Poor renditions of woods—as in paneling—provoked a very negative response; good renditions were thought to be "alright." Material, print, or fabric looks and solid or tonal embossings and weaves were well received as restful and nice. If the product was quite dark or had a dense quality to it, it was not as highly ranked. The benchmark for acceptance is whether a design could be used on all four walls or only for an accent wall or chair, and whether the subject faced the design, viewed it peripherally side to side, or it was behind them. The pictorial or novelty/scenic design type was ranked as only suitable for retail, restaurant, or specialty office settings, which often employ custom design.

In today's complex web of office settings, it becomes important to understand how much the interior design contributes both positively and negatively to productivity and performance. Color and pattern are important in the commercial setting. Health-care offices are becoming homier. Legal offices have always had an air of efficiency, stability, and old money. Bank offices are becoming more like conservative fast-food establishments, with drive-up banking and instant money in a nod to convenience. Corporate offices are updating to conform to rapid change and high technology. And home offices are increasing, with electronic data links becoming the new reality. It all adds up to one thing: For the next decade and beyond, the office interior environment and the pattern design selections that define it are very, very important.

Retail environment

Retail installation, Pick 'N Save (Prescott's Supermarkets, Inc.) West Bend, Wisconsin. Zimmerman Design Group, Milwaukee. Design shows focus on product, product packaging, purpose.

Mannington Commercial

Perceived Suitability of Pattern Design for Retail Environments by Consumers

Pattern Type	Study One	Study Two	Other Findings
Graphic miniprints	50%	24%	Prefer bolder, more graphic, less textural
Stripe designs	–	18%	Prefer in context: golf, polo, sports etc.
Floral designs	14%	6%	Prefer in context: high gender connect
Fabric looks	25%	47%	Prefer recognizable, traditional origins
Natural textures	33%	47%	Prefer plasters, stuccos, stones to faux wood
Geometrics/plaids	24%	47%	Prefer larger scale, more sophisticated
Pictorial/novelty	41%	–	Prefer cohesive theme; logical connect

Rodemann, Patricia. © 1991. Master's Thesis, The Ohio State University. Columbus, Ohio. Studies One through Five.

The retail environment is hard to typecast because it represents so many diverse channels, agendas, product, and price levels. Whether we are talking about the local hardware store, the discounter, the specialty retailer, the boutique, department store, outlet, catalog, or Web site, much is image dependent beyond the product itself. We do have statistics on who shops where for what, when, how much they are planning to spend by demographic, their favorite place to shop, and why; but that will not serve our purposes here. The primary function of the design is the retail purpose itself. In general, consumers are highly sensitive to the context in which they find their products, whether it be fashion footwear, power equipment, produce, or lingerie.

This is no secret to manufacturers of packaged goods or to the retailers themselves. Retail-design professionals routinely cite statistics to support changes in floor-surfacing materials, turn per endcap, sales by shelf position, traffic patterns, and position of cash registers to combat theft, or what is known as "shrinkage." Color, graphic design, and pattern are exceptionally important in product design. Recently, Kleenex and Puffs both launched patterned tissue cartons oriented around typical designs in the home. The package became a marketing campaign. Presumably, pattern is quite significant in which box a consumer grabs off the shelf. Design wins over function: The appearance of my tissue dispenser is more important than my runny nose. The typical rule for pattern in retail is that it not upstage product but do everything possible to support the message and overall sales ambience. When we consider pattern, we must also consider shopping behavior relative to decorating products for the home. Study six began to evaluate behavior types, destinations, shopping versus buying, and purchase approaches. This effort was later expanded to include specific products, retailer perceptions, preferences, and a host of related considerations. There are distinctly different customer demographics and behaviors by retail channel. But in the time-pressed environment in which we currently find ourselves, method, efficiency, and value are equally important. Consumers tend to premeditate larger purchases and pre-shop. For the physical trip to the retailer, they often become planners and jugglers, fitting many objectives into each trip. Sometimes a "hit and run" approach is indicated with speed/convenience uppermost. Savvy consumers with the means to buy top-quality products will often break "the rules" of visiting the typical premium store to go to an off-price seller. The difference between the much sought "power shopper" and the "comparison shopper" is one of "best available" versus "best value." Into this arena, we introduce pattern selection. The power shopper, who shops as recreation and who shops until he or she finds exactly the "right thing," tends to embrace most patterns with the exception of abstract/watercolor designs. The impulse shopper is captured by graphic/novelty designs, sport/character/kids designs, abstract watercolor, and naturals both marble and stone.

Through benchmarking of this and related questions, I have been tracking changes in shopping behavior and retail preferences over the past several years. This is a dynamic market; with a continuous influx of younger consumers and new retail venues, it has been instructive to watch.

Restaurant settings

Restaurant setting

Perceived Suitability of Pattern Design for Restaurant/Dining Environments by Consumers

Pattern Type	Study Two	Other Findings
Graphic miniprints	24%	Prefer a more subtle background look
Stripe designs	53%	Prefer hybrid design stripes, richer hues
Floral designs	70%	Prefer familiarity; excellent rendition, color
Fabric looks	47%	Prefer elegant traditionals, less dated approaches
Natural textures	47%	Prefer stuccos, woods, leathers to granites; warmth
Geometrics/plaids	70%	Prefer bistro look, tile effect, diamonds, clubby look
Pictorial/novelty	–	Prefer artistic, recognizable themes

Rodemann, Patricia. © 1991. Master's Thesis, The Ohio State University. Columbus, Ohio. Studies One through Five.

Like other commercial settings, restaurants represent a multitude of types, sizes, and price levels, not to mention menus. Restaurateurs have long recognized that ambience and image are as important as menu in creating a theme, which must be supported by service. The distinction is between eating out and dining, between fast food and convenience, all coupled with taste and trends in food. The consumer is notably fickle when it comes to restaurants and venues. A recent survey by the U.S.

Bureau of the Census showed an annual expenditure on food away from home to be $1.7 billion.[8] It is estimated that, on a per-capita level, households headed by those age 45–54 spent an average of $2,245 in 1995. Many sources document that the average individual over 8 years of age eats more than four meals away from home weekly.

Consumers understand and expect clichés in restaurant design. Whether it is a diner done in 1950s retro, a hamburger joint, a Mexican eatery, a Chinese restaurant, or a seafood chain, one can be sure the decor will reinforce the character of the menu and the experience. Restaurants have short lives. It is estimated that 80% fail or change themes/hands within five years. It is a highly competitive environment subject to discretionary income and consumer whims.

For one part of study two, we asked consumers about seating preference using a scale model and a square table with four chairs. This example featured papered walls. Consumers viewed the scale model and slides that more closely approximated a real setting. Everything was to 1" scale. Chair A was placed with its back to the door; chair B faced a neutral-hued plain wall; chair C faced the doorway; and chair D faced the patterned wall with its back to the neutral, plain wall. The room approximated a typical 10' x 12' dining room/area size, though the room was not defined to serve a specific purpose. After viewing the model, subjects selected a seat and expressed their feelings about the selection. In addition to the questionnaire, key-word analysis of interview transcriptions revealed similar responses to other methodology. Subjects were fascinated with the model, preferring it to the slides, and lifted it, looked through the doorway, peering at the room from different angles, expressing surprise at the impact of the room and the pattern in this form. A more timely method would be to use computer simulation, which can uncover many of the same findings/issues.

Presumably in a restaurant situation, many other factors must be taken into consideration—where there is seating availability, who selects the first seat, how many are in the party, and so on. Our purpose for the model and seat selection was strictly pattern related—to come to a new understanding of interaction, perception, and understanding before going to full-scale setup in study three. No doubt, there are potential psychological issues here as well. One consumer noted that it is sad not to be able to review all design selections in this form as revealing as the exercise turned out to be, and laughed, adding that it took only two days to decide on the last major pattern purchase after *months* of shopping.

Many of the comments consumers made are applicable not only to dining areas, but to guest rooms, patient rooms, and offices. This is

Study two: chair position selected relative to patterned surface

You have just entered this room. Where will you sit?

Pattern	Chair A Back to door	Chair B Face plain wall	Chair C Face door	Chair D Face pattern full on; plain wall to back
Traditional floral	6%	41%	53%	0%
Checkerboard	6%	82%	6%	6%
Ticking stripe	6%	40%	35%	18%
Tiny diamond*	24%	12%	35%	24%
Marble	12%	53%	24%	6%
Casement weave	6%	40%	18%	35%

*Subject did not select an individual chair because, "I would want to connect the dots. It would drive me batty."
Rodemann, Patricia. © 1991. Master's Thesis, The Ohio State University. Columbus, Ohio. Studies One through Five.

Chair A, back to door

Chair B, facing plain wall

Chair C, facing door

Chair D, facing pattern full on; back to plain wall

Why? Chair A: Back to Door

Traditional floral	Would be close to the door.
Checkerboard	Would be close to the door, could turn chair and face out.
Ticking stripe	I am claustrophobic, pattern makes it worse; I prefer to sit close to the door.
Tiny diamond	Can see all the walls, but am close to the door, appealing view.
Marble	To see all walls, natural, brings outdoors in.
Casement weave	Near door, have a full view.

Why? Chair B: Facing Neutral Plain Wall

Traditional floral	Pattern is too busy, uncomfortable to look at, righthanded, door affords spatial relief, not disruptive, wall in front of chair open, paper is too busy, too busy.
Checkerboard	See multiples, I would get sick otherwise, less distraction, soothing, plain is better, wall too contrasty, hurts my eyes, see less of it, calming, not to get whacked out looking at it.
Ticking stripe	It's soothing, visual relief, the wall-covering is too intense, I don't know if I could stay in this room very long—it moves.
Tiny diamond	Would connect the dots and make squares; don't want to see the pattern.
Marble	To face the open wall, would have to be sitting in B to enjoy wall without wall-covering, don't like this wall, plain wall is more quiet, pattern unappealing to me.
Casement weave	Not as dark, I would like to have warmth wrap around me, distracting, exhausting, too drab, need to break up pattern—important to see blank wall, so I don't have to look at patterned walls.

Why? Chair C: Facing Toward Open Door

Traditional floral	Very open, door is visible, most variety, nothing behind me, the view relieves the closed-in feeling, like the plain wall against the pattern.
Checkerboard	To see out the door.
Ticking stripe	Door breaks pattern, can see outside, more openness, less distracting.
Tiny diamond	Diversity of options, can see pattern and wall—it's open, there is nothing offensive here.
Marble	Like the contrast with the white wall, need view of exterior, a getaway, facing the door view with a blank wall is nice and open.
Casement weave	Like to see both the wall and door, doorway breaks up wall, need to have a view outside room with this type of pattern.

Why? Chair D: Facing Patterned Wall

Traditional floral	No one selected this option.
Checkerboard	Like pattern on all sides.
Ticking stripe	The white wall is boring, this is neat and orderly.
Tiny diamond	Back to white wall, like pattern, could sit here comfortably, can see out doorway and also relax with this pattern.
Marble	Can see both the door and the patterns.
Casement weave	No break in design, soothing, comfortable with this design and seats, contrast not needed, it's relaxing.

highly instructional. Simulations of flooring patterns are often approximated with the "old mirror trick," as a colleague calls it, to reveal any potential problems with a design. The mirror held at right angles creates a "vista" or horizon effect. Unfortunately, this is not always accurate or available yet with computer simulations. Effects also do not always appear working with smaller product swatches and samples until the product is installed. High-contrast, closely spaced tile-flooring installations and, on occasion, custom carpeting can have optical or unpleasant movement effects. Patterns in upholstery do not often exhibit the same traits because of their texture and limited surface area.

The more open spaces in restaurants, often broken by partitions, artwork, props, and other paraphernalia, are perhaps the best antidote to unfortunate outcomes. One colleague, aware of the research study, related how she had visited a Chinese restaurant with her spouse. They were seated in a dark alcove with a bolder geometric carpet motif before them that appeared to be popping and moving. It had recently been installed, and one could still smell the adhesive. The spouse suddenly jumped up, feeling claustrophobic and ready to have a panic attack. They had to leave at once. An otherwise calm and healthy professional, he attributed the effect to the flooring design and the faint odor, and had never before or since had such a profound response.

Educational settings

Ivy Tech State College, Fort Wayne, Indiana, Susan Parish designer, MSKTD & Associates. Educational setting shows outstanding use of natural materials, finishes, and patterns.

Mannington Commercial

Perceived Suitability of Pattern Design for Educational Environments by Consumers

Pattern Type	Study One	Study Two	Other Findings
Graphic miniprints	25%	29%	Prefer textural, tonal renditions
Stripe designs	–	24%	Prefer bolder graphic versions or textured
Floral designs	4%	0%	Prefer not to use this design type
Fabric looks	50%	18%	Prefer more typical weaves and textures
Natural textures	16%	24%	Prefer smoother stone, quality woods, colored granite speckle effects
Geometrics/plaids	9%	18%	Prefer larger scale, simpler hues, lighter
Pictorial/novelty	–%	–	Prefer to accomplish via murals, paint

Rodemann, Patricia. © 1991. Master's Thesis, The Ohio State University. Columbus, Ohio. Studies One through Five.

The educational environment covers a broad range of instructional settings, from libraries, private colleges, elementary schools, palatial high schools to community training centers and universities. The most important function *is function.* Architectural materials are the most significant design feature, and often serve as design in and of themselves. Architects—especially from the Bauhaus school feel this is how all design should be. Budgets may be tight, and color is often the only tool in addition to natural textures employed in these settings. As educational settings continue to upgrade electronically, it is important to consider design factors such as lighting, glare, and color in tandem with the natural patterns of wood, concrete block, VCT (vinyl composition tile floor), laminates, and steel. Given a choice, consumers opt for other finishes over block; and whereas graffiti and maintenance is a concern, a school should not inspire semantic connections like those of a prison.

Another aspect of the educational setting is the educational level of the consumer in rating preference for each pattern design type. Designed correctly, educational and institutional settings show a lively, creative, and exciting mix of finish, material, color, and pattern. Good design moves beyond mere longevity to a sense of timeless classic quality.

Consumers rated patterns differently based on their educational level. For those with four-year college degrees and/or post-graduate work, all pattern design types rated considerably higher, except for novelty or thematic designs, which rated equal to those with a high school education. The top-ranked pattern design type for the college graduate was a marble/faux stone look; for high school graduates, it was a miniprint. The lowest-rated design types for the high school educated were ethnic and cultural, such as paisleys, Chinoserie, and so forth.

The more significant differences may be accounted for by exposure to other cultures, historic time periods, sociocultural influences, income level, and availability of design types at different price points and retail destinations. Presumably, if one is designing a higher-education setting, one would want to consider these differences; or if one's audience prefers a simpler design and lifestyle.

Religious settings

Cherub tonal wallcovering—bridal lounge

York Wallcoverings, Antonina Vella

Perceived Suitability of Pattern Design for Spiritual Environments by Consumers

Pattern Type	Study One	Study Two	Other Findings
Graphic miniprints	83%	70%	Prefer tonal and textural small prints
Stripe designs	–	53%	Prefer textured and tonal stripes (i.e., moiré)
Floral designs	48%	59%	Prefer textured, tonal, and traditional
Fabric looks	41%	40%	Prefer vertical silks, more formal looks
Natural textures	33%	40%	Prefer authenticity, woods
Geometrics/plaids	28%	47%	Prefer larger scale, traditional renditions
Pictorial/novelty	25%		Prefer symbolic, artistic, murals, themes

Rodemann, Patricia. © 1991. Master's Thesis, The Ohio State University. Columbus, Ohio. Studies One through Five.

Americans, more than many citizens of the world, attend religious services and visit places of worship for services, community activities, and diverse types of outreach programs. Increasingly, in these ecumenical and multicultural times, religious settings are becoming multifunctional with training/teaching classrooms, musical and dramatic performance spaces, food service, places for homeless and the temporarily displaced during weather, catastrophes, or other crises. From private offices and counseling areas to larger public spaces, the religious setting takes on both a symbolic and a practical role in the community. That role is to inspire, uplift, embrace, coach, counsel, heal, teach, feed, and distribute charity. This is where baptisms, rites of passage, weddings, and memorials are held. The sense of connection, warmth, and familiarity is important outside and within the community. As highly individual as each denomination, faith, and group may be, there are common perceptions about design. The worship space itself is often focused, with minimal distractions. Lighting plays a key role. Adjacent and public areas usually begin to introduce a similar sense of design to that found in hospitality settings. This is how the pattern-design ratings and comments begin to make sense. It reinforces the cognitive connections made earlier in our lives and the imprint of culture upon our American psyche.

Public areas/galleries, airports, governmental buildings

Public/transportation space. Pattern contributes to excitement, product enhancement, and sense of quality.

Perceived Suitability of Pattern Design for Public Environments by Consumers

Pattern Type	Other Findings
Graphic miniprints	Prefer tonal and textural small prints
Stripe designs	Prefer textured and tonal stripes (i.e., moiré)
Floral designs	Prefer textured, tonal, and traditional
Fabric looks	Prefer vertical silks, more formal or background looks
Natural textures	Prefer authenticity, woods, stone
Geometrics/plaids	Prefer larger scale, traditional renditions
Pictorial/novelty	Prefer symbolic, artistic, murals, themes

Rodemann, Patricia. © 1991. Master's Thesis, The Ohio State University. Columbus, Ohio. Studies One through Five.

In most cases, public areas are transitory places that people are passing through. And that is usually the case except for the long wait that can take place in line, between hearings, at the airport, during intermission, before the performance, or awaiting sentencing. The experience of buying a car—as in our dealership photo—is enhanced by the interior ambience. Public space should be viewed in the same sense as a retail space—as a service environment. Appearances vary dramatically in public settings: from the most bare bones and fake wood paneling with orange vinyl and metal chairs to sleek international style gray, steel, and red accents and lavish historic restorations with mahogany paneling, gilded dome ceiling, damask, and red leather. Purpose, image, function, and service convey behavioral and perceptual cues. Message is as important as function for these sites. Given photos of designed spaces—minus the furniture—consumers find it easy to judge and fit "the envelope" to the role. The pattern must match the role and the image. Consumers expect the cues to fit. Neurobiologists tell us the more memorable the event taking place in the space, the more likely they will be to remember the details— pleasant and unpleasant. In this sense, pattern forms yet another association in the memory bank of the players.

References

1. Healy, Jane. 1991. *Endangered minds: why our children don't think.* New York: Simon & Shuster.

2. *What today's home buyers want.* 1996. National Association of Home Builders and Fulton Research, Washington, D.C.

3. Wagner, Carleton. Color Communications Inc. (formerly Color Research Institute), 4000 West Filmore Street, Chicago, Illinois 60624.

4. Soso, M. J., and Dawn Marcus. 1989. Migraine and stripe-induced visual discomfort. *Archives of Neurology* 46: 1129–32.

5. Statistical Abstracts.

6. U.S. Bureau of Labor Statistics. 1997. "Employment status of the civilian population 1950 to 1996," Bulletin 2307, no. 619, in *Statistical abstract of the United States,* 117th ed., prepared by the Economics and Statistics Administration of the Bureau of the Census in cooperation with the Bureau of Labor Statistics, Washington, D.C., 397.

7. U.S. Bureau of the Census. 1997. "Expenditures by residential property owners for improvements, maintenance and repairs, 1980, by type of property and activity," Current Construction Reports Series C50, in *Statistical abstract of the United States,* 117th ed., no. 1208, prepared by the Economics and Statistics Administration of the Bureau of the Census, Washington, D.C., 729.

8. U.S. Bureau of the Census. 1997. "Average annual expenditures of all consumer units," in *Statistical abstract of the United States,* 117th ed., no. 715: 464.

CHAPTER 6

Cultural, Historic, and Environmental Nuances of Pattern

S ince the beginnings of recorded history, humans have enhanced the surfaces of the interior environment with paintings, frescoes, murals, epics, tapestries, and intricately woven rugs, tiles, and textiles. Let's look far back to the historic evolution of pattern, and how influential specific themes and motifs have been and still are today. The ability and urge to create apart from instinct—(like a spider spinning a web)—distinguishes human beings from animals. Philosophers claim creatorship is a trait of *imago dei,* or being in the image of God. "Along with providing immeasurable joy to its creators, art's great purposes have been to assist men to come to terms with their environments and to realize self-reproduction and self-liberation. Art takes its place along with science, for example, in the civilizing of humanity... art is a skillful and imaginative process of expression that historically has led to the creation of objects capable of producing an aesthetic response."[1]

Our prehistoric ancestors peered at the sun through the changing patterns of light and shadow cast by trees, grasses, and shrubs. Anthropologists verify the profound influence of the natural environment: from the feathers, fur, and species of the animal kingdom to flowers, leaves, buds, and berries of abundant vegetation; rocks, earth, sea, insect, and sky—all depicted in garments; sand and cave paintings; textiles, jewelry, household objects; architecture, and monu-

133

ments. Many of the early cave paintings from Lascaux and Altimira are dated to 20,000 B.C. A recent discovery of cave paintings found in Algeria documented twelve superimposed layers of depictions of wild sheep and other figures. Researchers believe the act of painting filled a ceremonial function more important than the artwork itself.[2] Indigenous cultures from Bedouin tent peoples to Egyptian and Greco-Roman citizens used pattern design for religious purposes, for historical record keeping, as well as for status enhancement and symbolic ornamentation. By 7,000 B.C., pottery and metalwork routinely displayed pattern design; and by 3,000 B.C., people were actively engaged in making bricks and planning the great pyramids.

Other cultures—Aborigine, Eskimo, Mayan, Nomadic, African tribal, Viking, Celtic—have all used pattern as both ornament and symbol. The symbolic aspect to pattern cannot be overlooked. Think of a well-known pattern of today in sports: The referee wears a black-and-white-striped jersey. Or the common Ralston Purina checkerboard logo — which, though highly recognizable, is not usually affiliated with the red-and-white check tablecloth of your local Italian eatery. There is history behind pattern, but also individual and collective meaning—and *emotion*.

For many cultures of the world, pattern is not taken lightly. Principles of Feng Shui from China teach the "right" and "wrong" patterns and symbols to invoke good chi and to promote positive energy, good fortune, health, and prosperous outcomes. It is generally thought that eight-sided trigrams deflect evil influences; the square symbolizes the earth, justice, and authority; the circle stands for wealth; and the octagon is auspicious and rights many wrongs. Other pattern motifs are derived from elements of nature. Water ripples suggest wealth and heavenly blessings, clouds and scroll motions mean heavenly blessings and wisdom, flowers symbolize wealth, and fruit stand for luck. Fish or fish-scale design for the Feng Shui practioner means success; for early Christians, it symbolized Christianity.

Fish motifs in current use

Village Designs

Tropical fish border, realistic rendition

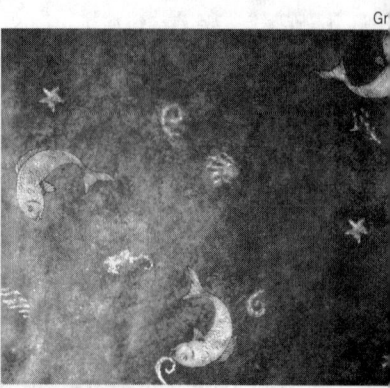

Gr

Historic-abstract rendering of fish and g

When we imbue pure forms with meaning, we arrive at the symbolic nature of pattern. The red cross carries a very specific meaning of charity in time of distress; the heart symbolizes love. Pineapples are symbols of fertility, and pinecones, immortality. For most Westerners, symbols are secondary to overall decor, but in the same way we make connections with color—"feeling blue," "green with envy," "yellow-bellied," "red hot," in a "black depression"—we make pattern connections. Some patterns are seen as cheap, others expensive; some uplifting, others depressing.

The history and symbolism of pattern: Evolution of themes and elements

Some of the earliest patterns were recreations of nature. To this day, humans appear to prefer natural materials, sources, and renditions. These designs were representations—such as the sun expressed in circle form, sunbursts, stars, serpentine, bird, animal, and wheat design motifs. These are stylized at times, and at other times are drawn as beautifully accurate or remarkably spare recreations in lines or tones. Later, these themes are juxtaposed with triangles, diamonds, squares, stripes, and intricate geometrics. Earliest objects d'art—and function—have been ceremonial cups, jewelry, weaponry, vessels, textiles, and architecture. Throughout history, we have accumulated a rich treasury of patterned images.

African tribal design mimics natural forms closely, in repetitions of simple elements and shapes that create highly intricate designs. Wheat designs, repetitions of hand-drawn vertical or horizontal lines, carved diamonds, and swirls that mimic the swirls of skin on fingertips, become a highly stylized and sophisticated look rendered initially in black/brown and white on barkcloth. Face painting and body piercing carry intricate pattern and symbolism.

From the Americas, Indian art shows intricate bead and feather work, earthworks that replicate serpents, birds and symbolic religious representations in mandalalike sand paintings—all augmented with geometric shapes and forms. Symbolic animals were the eagle, bear, wolf, buffalo, and spider. Totem poles feature elaborate patterns and carvings to invoke spirits. Aztec designs of the 1300s B.C. explore intricate geometric designs, as do Incan designs of the 1400's B.C. Mayan design themes are augmented by highly organic curved lines and depictions of the gods and godesses, serpents, birds, faces, bananas, monkeys, and elaborate astronomical correlations. The Mayan culture used pictorial depictions of the months.

During Egyptian times, beginning in 2,700 B.C., we see stylized representations of lotus blossoms, papyrus, reeds, birds, cone shapes, stars and moon, and symbolic chalice or column designs. Not only were these themes evident on artifacts—such as headware, jewelry, garments—but also in the application of decorative coatings of plaster and paint, which reached new heights of religious, symbolic, and nationalistic meaning. Most of the ancient cultures enjoyed trade with one another, and the decorative arts flourished through the ancient worlds.

In 500 B.C. Greece, pattern assumed a more dynamic form than the stylized Egyptian depictions of royal life. There are pictorial/athletic celebrations, knotted-rope motifs, fretwork, and elaborate leaf designs on drinking and serving vessels And a variety of pattern ornamentation is employed through different architectural periods—as on column capitals and temple structures. Though highly geometric, these designs are interspersed with horse, dolphin, leaf, wave, and stylized circular flower patterns. Oak leaves and laurel wreaths are associated with Zeus. The dolphin is thought to represent love, salvation, and also Poseidon.

Architectural Border Pattern Development

Sanitas for Village

Greco-Roman inspiration

Raymond Waites for Village

Acanthus leaf

Raymond Waites for Village

Interlocking rope border

History of art and architecture classes have drilled into us the differences between Doric, Ionic, and Corinthian capitals. Our purpose here is not to dwell on history of the built environment, but to highlight the evolution of some pattern elements through time, and show cycles at work. Roman designs to 476 A.D. are thought to be heavily influenced by Greek designs and show extensive use of leaf, floral, rosette, scroll, vase, and shell motifs.

Whereas Egyptian designs were intended as a religious accompaniment into the afterlife, wall murals in Pompeii were employed as a

Schumacher African Sun Border

Mosaic-inspired interpretation

purely aesthetic element. Status-conscious and hedonistic citizens decorated their summer homes, brothels, and other sites with graphic and artistic depictions of nature and mythology. There are fruit, scroll, and wave designs, acanthus leaf and grape patterns that give these interiors a naturalistic and lighthearted feel.

In 500 A.D. Byzantine patterns, we find a Far Eastern influence with an extensive organic quality. Interlocked circles, elaborate geometric forms, roped, knotted, beaded, and swirling leaves and small pictographic elements take on an orderly repetition used in mosaic, stone, and other architectural components. "From both Persia and Byzantium came the tendency to subordinate form to rich and sensuous color. Architecture is generally considered the most important of the Saracenic arts; the development of both painting and sculpture was inhibited by religious prejudice against representation of the human form. Most of the products of the arts were embellished with complicated patterns of interlacing geometric designs, plants and fruits and flowers, Arabic script and fantastic animal figures."[3]

As the Byzantine era evolved into the Middle Ages, pattern designs assumed a more allegorical quality with extensive use of stylized motifs—forerunners of the fleur-de-lis, shamrock, trefoil, and cinquefoil, all rendered in rich jewel tones. Other patterns developed more fully during the later Middle Ages include gargoyles, trailing vines, chalices, demons, and pictographic themes. Stained-glass and manuscript ornament evolved into highly developed artforms. Crest and shield motifs emerged during this time to represent courts, fiefdoms, and kingdoms.

Sometime between 400 A.D. and 1,000 A.D., Celtic design developed its own pattern language with interlacing ribbons, ropes, and intertwining knots. Cruciform objects also are ornamented with pictographic renditions of snakes, birds, animals, lizards. The Scandinavian and later Celtic versions added twining foliage, trees, and buds to the earlier Runic knot and ribbon designs. In Chinese ornament and pattern design, the geometric form is developed to a high degree coupled with stylized florals, fretwork, and filigree, leaf and vine themes.

Oriental botanical wall-covering with birds

Raymond Waites for Gramercy

Later Chinese designs included songbirds, scenes, and more elaborate floral motifs. These themes were initially rendered on decorative paper about 200 b.c. The early papers were made to simulate what had been handpainted on silk or other exotic textiles. By the 1600s, a strong import trade had opened with Europe, which introduced not only painted porcelain and silk but paper and other goods. The French took to the scenic murals and decorated entire salons with them, later developing an appreciation for mural scenes of classical ruins, historic scenes, or people in lively settings.

Indian designs show a high development of intricate motifs such as lacy fretwork, paisleys, swirling flowers, and ornamental shapes in rich hues. The bull symbolizes the god of the sky; other important symbols are the lotus, the elephant, and the rat.

In Japan, pattern development evolved to a high degree, and a sophisticated trading network developed between Dutch and Portugese importers and Japanese suppliers. Japanese designs show a highly developed use of small patterns, used for the dress of the Samurai classes, for papers and other household objects. The small-print designs were inspired by hail, rain, and other natural elements. Intricate and tiny geometrics also show more abstract character in designs that are strikingly contemporary. Textiles included early brocades, tiny calico-type prints, lattices, and Sarasa fabrics with insect, fish, grass, leaf themes or tendrils. Other later, larger-scale designs have a painterly watercolor or abstract quality not seen in other cultures. Stripe designs were introduced to Japan from India in the 1300s, and by the 1700s this form of pattern had become highly popular.

The later Middle Ages in Euope saw some of the most ambitious Gothic creations emerge with pointed forms and extensive, rich ornamentation. The triqueta, or three interlocked triangles, circles or stylized representations emerged, as did heraldic themes such as the lion—often used for coats of arms. By the mid-1400s to 1530s Europe saw a lighter and more expansive new design quality emerge. Trade and travel were picking up; new ideas and designs were circulating.

During Renaissance times, vine, leaf, and flower motifs are accompanied by rosettes, ribbons, wings, vases, and urns; fruit; and mythic figures of birds, beasts, and humans or cherubs. Classical forms such as the egg-and-dart motif and beaded themes in many moldings show a phenomenal architectural pattern vocabulary. But excess has been stripped away, and a purer appreciation for the built structure emerges.

Elizabethan English design saw scrollwork and metalwork with interlacing bands ornamented with nail heads or ball-and-diamond designs. Florals appear more stylized and constrained, and we see an emergence of acorn motifs during the 1600s. The acorn is the symbol of potential and immortality. Scottish design develops its own variation on pattern in the famous clan tartan motifs—still popular to this day.

Italian and Southern European pattern and ornament, which generally evolved out of classical traditions, became more highly decorative with the addition of horses, rabbits, small devils and mythic faces, birds, arrows, swag, garland, wreath, torchère, and vase designs. In Spain, printed leatherwork, tile, wood, and metal featured intricate, faintly Moorish designs with gold and embossing.

During the baroque era in the 1590s to 1640s, pattern design reached a new level of excessive ornamentation when a great deal of detail was added to the surfaces the buildings. The passion for splendor and magnificence extended to the enrichment of interiors with gilded surfaces, mirrors, colored marbles, silver and gold, and opulent fabrics and patterns. Rococo design was baroque design to excess, with roses, cherubs, leaves, birds, harps, trumpets, vines, fruit, vases, gilding, and tapestry scenics by the early 1700s. This was followed by a rebellion of sorts in the Federal style of the mid to late 1700s, which brought back greater architectural simplicity and classic forms. The Federal period was followed by Georgian style, with more ornate furniture, greater ornamentation, and patterns depicting crests, shields, mythic beasts, and themes of royalty.

France at this time moved to embrace damasks and reproductions of intricate tapestries and Gobelins in the form of manufactured wallpapers. From hunting, landscape, and biblical scenes, the mass production shifted to more easily replicated, stylized design motifs reproduced with carved wood blocks. By 1840, machine print techniques became common and the production of mass-market wallpaper

Traditional crest/shield design motif

had begun in earnest, including toile designs, flock, and damasks. The Georgian style in England had degenerated into fussy Victorian ornament for its own sake. William Morris of the Arts and Crafts school in England objected to the commonplace designs and poor quality, and advocated a return to certain principles and aesthetic discipline during the 1850s.

Following and overlapping this era, pattern design saw the emergence of the sensuous, curvilinear Art Nouveau patterns with vines and leaves, large blooming florals, and idealized women. Impressionism emerged in France. In the new world, Americans encountered designs of the native peoples in beadwork, feathers, geometric blankets, and the serape. Colonial design evolved out of American primitives into a highly developed craft of its own in Shaker design, which stressed purity of form and craftsmanship.

Mission design in the West later developed as a response to American Victorian, and was a simpler statement in true Arts and Crafts tradition. By the 1920s the jazz age began to usher in new forms and patterns. Art Deco motifs combining geometrics with curvilinear forms offered a new quality to pattern and style.

Humans throughout history have sought to embellish form and function from the earliest artisans—including metalsmiths, stonesmiths, lace makers, Ukrainian egg painters, Romanian embroiderers, Chinese porcelain painters, tribal bead makers, and Norwegian rosemalers—and this embellishment usually includes pattern.

For the most part, and for most people, a natural material in its raw form *was* the flooring and the wall surface: scarcity and subsistence were the norm. Thatched huts, sod houses, tents, and caves were "home." Only the heads of the strongest tribes, and the wealthiest, most powerful rulers, kings, and their courts had access to and command of the artisans. Over time, as the lot of the common peasant improved to "citizen" status, decorative design began to emerge with a more prosperous class of consumer. Ironically, as we enter a new century, there are still nearly stone-age tribal cultures, peasant classes, kings and kingdoms, and cultures dominated by a single religion influencing design outcomes—and all alongside the Western world. And nearly all are exposed to Western television and interior design. We have never before had so much pattern information available to us from so many multicultural sources in so many vehicles: museum archives of artifacts and textiles, architecture, and monuments. Pattern design is both a record of our past and a mirror of our present. It is a unique moment in our collective history, and will be telling in what we take forward.

The connection between exterior, interior, owners, and selections

With the evolution of technique and culture, pattern design has taken many forms, but with common elements and motifs. Many architects and designers through time have attempted to develop guidelines, rules, and practices with regard to pattern design and ornamentation. In Owen Jones, "The Grammar of Ornament" (first published in 1856),37 propositions are set forth as "General Principles in the Arrangement of Form and Colour in Architecture and Decorative Arts."[4] Jones documents in comprehensive fashion Egyptian, Assyrian, Persian, Greek, Roman, Byzantine, Arabian, Turkish, Indian, Chinese, Celtic, medieval, and Renaissance decorative motifs featured on walls, borders, panels, corners, columns, capitals, floors, textiles, and illuminated manuscripts. These propositions form a thorough set of guidelines to the use of pattern design according to 1850s sensibilities around the time of the Arts and Crafts movement. Some of these guidelines are true today, and we have seen confirmation of this in consumer surveys and interviews more than 100 years later.

In his first proposition, that "the Decorative Arts arise from, and should properly be attendant upon, Architecture,"[5] Jones shows cognizance of the integral relationship between exterior and interior environment. We wondered if this held true in an American context of ranch homes, split-levels, Cape Cods, and saltbox-style homes, among other looks. What was the consistency between exterior styles and interior looks? Was a sense of coherence merely an architectural fantasy? What really happens in the marketplace of the late 1990s?

Research from study six: exterior styles and the link with interior looks

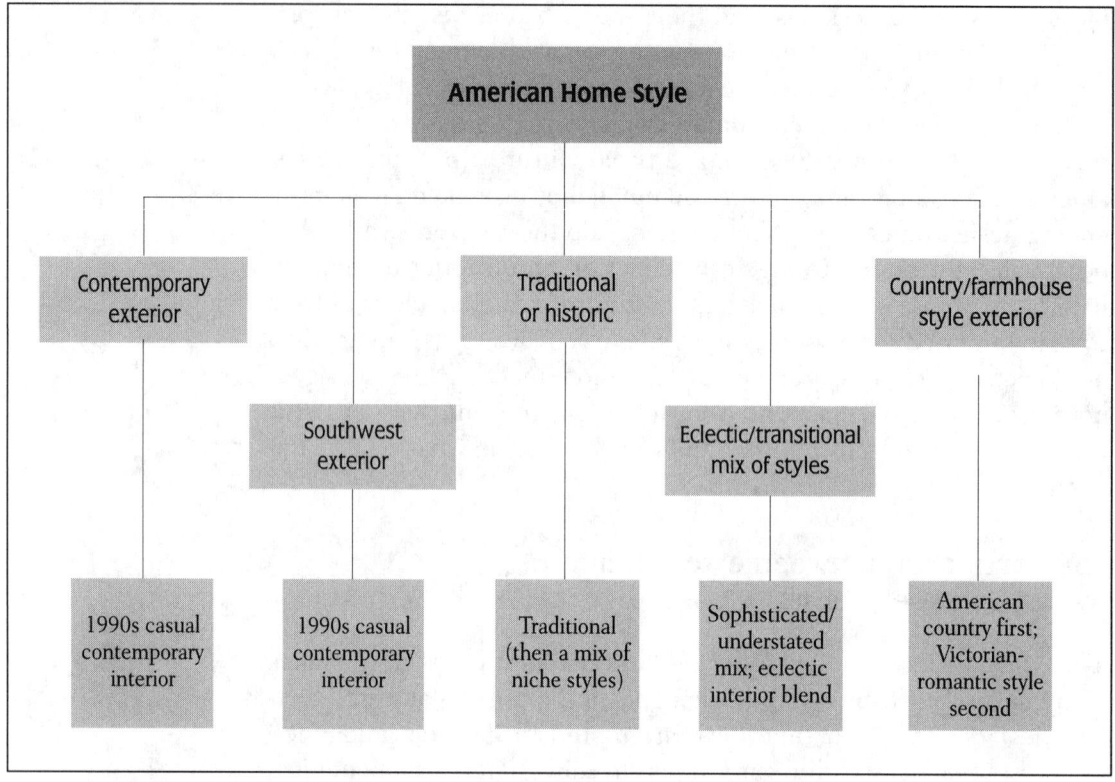

N=3,500. Referenced to specific % and counts. Rodemann, Patricia. © 1996. Study Six.

There is a clear link between the exterior and interior selections in the home. Though for most consumers styles are mixed, we have found consumers typically will select a primary style and three or four closely related styles in designing their interior. This is outlined further in the chapter eight. The exterior/interior link to pattern selections becomes striking at a statistical level. But this goes far beyond demographics, because it begins to define the population, the culture, and the selections.

There is not only a high correlation between the perceived exterior style of the home and the way the interior is decorated—but a link to specific profiles of homeowners. These are general tendencies seen across the entire population of the United States. Of course, there are exceptions. What we have shown is what we are more likely to see. Another general finding is that typical single family homes are more apt to be decorated in traditional or country style; condominiums in sophis-

Study Seven: Who are these home owners more likely to be?
The link between home style and home owner—general tendencies

One-floor ranch—undefinable style mix:

- Primarily Western, then Southern
- Smaller markets <100,000 population
- Middle income
- Service/blue-collar/administrative occupations
- Ages 56–65; less apt to have 4-year college degree

Traditional/colonial—2-story:

- Northeastern, then Midwestern
- Larger markets >100,000
- Upper-middle income
- Professional/technical/management postions
- Age range <45; 4-year college degree

Split-level—undefinable style mix:

- West Coast; then Midwestern
- Larger markets
- Middle income
- Service/blue-collar/administative
- Age <36; 4-year college degree

Contemporary/modern:

- Southern
- Larger markets >100,000 population
- Upper income
- Age <36
- tend to have 4 year college degree

Country/farmhouse—2-story:

- Midwestern
- Smaller markets
- Lower income
- Homemakers/retirees/part-time/blue-collar
- Age 46–55
- Less apt to have college degree

Postmodern/eclectic blend:

- Southern
- More male owners represented
- Upper-middle income
- Professional/tech/mgmt positions
- Age 36–45
- 4-year college degree

Victorian/Gothic/historic—2-story:

- Northeastern
- Smaller markets
- Upper–upper-middle income
- Professional/technical/management
- Age 46–55, then 36–45
  4-year college degree

Southwestern/adobe:

- West Coast; Prairie—Midwestern
- Upper income
- Larger markets >100,000 population
- Age 46–55
- Tend to have 4-year college degree

N= 1000. Rodemann, Patricia. ©1997. Study Seven. Nationally representative database.

ticated mix or 1990s casual style, and duplexes in Victorian romantic, and 1970s naturals/basics style. At any given time, a fairly significant percentage are ready for some type of interior change that involves decorating or remodeling/renovation.

More current times and the impact of the age

Jones Proposition Two, "Architecture is the material expression of the wants, the faculties, and the sentiments of the age in which it is created,"[8] shows an understanding of the interrelationship between culture, psychology, and history. We examined this variable in the age of the home and what it represented in terms of fixed elements and style. We took it a step further in examining styles and color palettes of the 1940s through the 1990s. This is a fascinating look at pattern-design cycles. The Cooper Hewitt design and decorative arts museum featured a retrospective on pattern design that clearly showed the influence of more recent times on our interiors since the Art Nouveau, Arts and Crafts, Mission, and Art Deco movements into the 1930s.

The Art Deco era featured black and white, pink, neutrals, and brighter hues in graceful curvilinear forms and geometrics. War-era designs of the 1940s featured an abundance of florals, plaids, and patriotic themes, and oversize furniture.

The color palette featured cadet blue, taupe, cherry and gold, khaki, brown, pale lavendar, mint green, and dark green. There was a restrictive design quality with the war years upon us. Fifties designs tended to show tiny starbursts, elliptiform shapes, squiggles, and lots of pointy things to go with Danish modern furniture. The palette was aqua, red, turquoise, chrome, pink, and black, along with pastel tints of green, lavender, gray and blue. The feeling was expansionist and modern. As we moved into the 1960s, patterns became larger in scale and brighter in color, to include big daisies, big geometrics, pop art and vibrant, acidic color (orange, magenta, yellow, turquoise, purple), and metallics. The feeling was rebellious—an exploration of freedom. The 1970s saw a natural emphasis with tan, avocado, harvest gold, navy, copper, and brown color palettes, and woven textures, natural plant effects, stylized geometrics, and cultural influences (like batik and sari prints). The feeling was environmental, responsible—a new earthiness coupled with ethnic and high-tech color. A country movement took hold during this time with wheat and weed motifs, ducks and geese. Americans fought plastic with homespun checks and plaids. Denim and layering were "in."

By the 1980s, design themes had gone glamorous, minimal, and uptown with a palette of white, mauve, taupe, charcoal, burgundy, teal, as well as reflectives. Pattern designs featured granites, marbles, smoother textures, stylized geometrics, and stylized contemporary flowers. The 1990s saw a California influence in more casual, textural looks and colors of celadon, pale aqua, apricot, golds, terra-cotta, and cobalt blue. Textile designs featured washed damasks, faded tapestry, old denim, rough muslin, nubby chenilles, sandwashed silks, and leathers.

A historical link between architecture/design and pattern examples of patterns styles from recent times:

Cooper Hewitt, National Design and Decorative Arts Museum, Smithsonian Institution Art Resource, NY

Archives of Columbus
Coated Fabrics, Div. Borden, Inc.

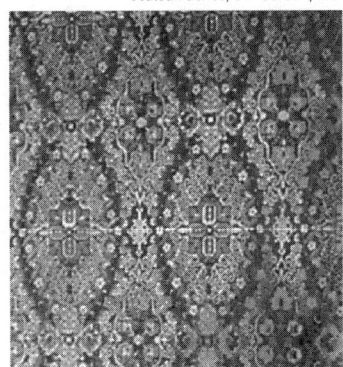

1940s florals in browns and greens, larger scale

Elliptiform shapes, space age whimsy

1960s metallic vinyl, bright hues, "pop art" prints

Furnishing Fabric, 1940; Designer, Stanley H. Coventry; Producer, Stroheim & Romann; Screen printed cotton; Gift of Stroheim & Romann, 1940-115-1

Furnishing Fabric, 1951; Designer, Lucienne Day; Producer, Heal's; Screenprinted; Gift of Eddie Squires, 1992-3-4 1950s

Formica Corporation Archives

Archives of Columbus Coated Fabrics, Div. Borden, Inc.

1970s gold and avocado kitchen, "natural texture" laminate

1980s mauve, gray, and stone looks, cool sophistication

1990s faux effects, organic feel

Pattern designs revisited stuccos, faux looks, stenciling, botanicals, block prints, and whimsy. The feeling was to value and rethink the most authentic and best of historic, cultural, and natural designs in a contemporary context—a glorification of what matters: light, texture, color, nature, and a mixed heritage. Within these style directions and looks are many other trends and themes. However, as macro examples of Jones's propositions, their importance cannot be overlooked.

When we examined the connection between the age of home and interior style, there were some striking findings in studies six and seven that confirm we are a product of our times and our interior design selections are directly related to the architecture of our housing stock from a particular era. This was confirmed in interviews. Throughout all of my research efforts during the past 14 years, and since study one, I have found: *Consumers are extremely conscious of what is "dated." Styles with a more distinct and recognizable imprint in terms of pattern and/or color tended to cause the greatest expression of distaste and disgust by consumers over the age of 40, though nearly one-fifth of the population had at least some elements of the style of a given era 20 years later. It is a maxim that elements of this look will resurrect in some form—in either pattern or color—and be perceived as new again by a new generation of young adults. Our psychological associations form the drama of design that keeps the market dynamic. The fact of the matter is: Pattern sells. Color sells. "New" sells. A constant in nature is change. We expect change in design.*

Perhaps through evolution over time, this is our instinctual way of cleaning out the den, of leaving one nest for another. It is certainly true in nature with the changing of the seasons.

We have examined the link between the style of the exterior and the look of the interior. Knowing the age of the home also leads us to who the home owners are most likely to be. There are several confirmed ways to approach and arrive at pattern selections across the entire population in this contextual way. This demographic/academic view gives us a window on the style selections that lead to pattern (and color) selections.

The link between historic era and owner, style, and pattern
Study seven: A look at home owner types, lifestage, and design tendencies

Homes Built Before 1900:

- Northeastern, then Midwestern residents
- Smaller markets, <100,000 population
- Lower incomes
- Retirees/other occupations; then blue-collar/service
- Age primarily 46–55
- Less likely to have four-year college degree

The owners of the homes built before 1900 are most apt to be middle-aged couples without children, followed by singles, and then middle-aged parents. This group of home owners is most likely to select from the following styles: Victorian-romantic, Federal, Shaker, and then American country. See chapter 8 for patterns that pair with these styles.

N=1000. Rodemann, Patricia. ©1996, 1998. Study Seven. Nationally representative database.

Homes Built Between 1900–49:

- Northeastern, then Midwestern residents
- Smaller markets, <100,000 population
- Lower incomes
- Service/blue-collar/administrative occupations
- Age 36–45
- Less likely to have four-year college degree

Owners of the home built between 1900 and 1940 are more likely to be single, and then middle-aged couples. This group is more apt to feel they they need to make changes and is likely to spend a significant amount to update the home to 1990s living. The styles they are most likely to select from are: Mission, formal French, Victorian-romantic, lodge-lake, Mediterranean, and sophisticated mix

Rodemann, Patricia. © 1997. Study Seven. Nationally representative database.

Homes Built Between 1950–59:

- Northeastern, then West Coast residents
- Larger markets (suburban/urban)
- Middle incomes
- Homemakers, part-timers, or retirees
- Age 56–65
- Less likely to have four-year college degrees

These home owners are most apt to be young couples or retired/older couples without children present. The older home owners are more apt to be what we would describe as "comfortable traditionalists"; younger home owners are more apt to be fashion forward. The styles they are likely to select from are: traditional, Florida, 1980s looks, Mediterranean, or casual contemporary—but these choices are highly region dependent. The same is true for their pattern selections.

Rodemann, Patricia. © 1997. Study Seven. Nationally representative database.

Homes Built Between 1960–69:

- West Coast, then Southern residents
- Larger markets >100,000 population (suburban/urban)
- Upper-middle incomes
- Professional/technical/management jobs
- Age 56–65
- Tend to have four-year college degree and graduate/professional training

These home owners are more likely to be older/retired couples and then young couples without children. They are more likely to take a practical or a traditionalist approach, and value comfort highly. The styles they are likely to select from are: sophisticated mix, formal French, Mediterranean, American country, Shaker and Southwest—but this again is age and region sensitive. Pattern selections must also be evaluated in multiple contexts.

Rodemann, Patricia. © 1997. Study Seven. Nationally representative database.

Homes Built Between 1970–79:

- West Coast, then Southern residents
- Larger markets >100,000 population
- Lower-middle to upper-middle incomes
- White- and blue-collar professions are equally represented
- Age 46–55
- Less likely to have four-year college degree

This group of home owners includes older parents, singles, and then young couples without children. They are influenced by media and planning to do a lot of decorating/remodeling.The styles they are likely to select from are: American country, traditional, casual contemporary, 1980s looks, and Mediterranean. Again, these styles and attendant patterns are age and region dependent.

Rodemann, Patricia. © 1997. Study Seven. Nationally representative database.

Homes Built Between 1980–89:

- Southern, then West Coast residents
- Smaller markets <100,000 population (and suburban)
- Upper-middle incomes
- More likely to have four-year college degree and graduate/professional training

These home owners are most apt to be parents; younger, then older, with middle-aged parents/ school children third. They represent two approaches: fashion impact view and then a practical view. They are more heavily media influenced. The styles they are likely to select from are: Southwest, Florida, casual contemporary, and Mission. There is a smaller but distinct cluster for Federal and traditional styles. For this group, region and lifestyle are important factors that also influence the pattern selection.

Rodemann, Patricia. © 1997. Study Seven. Nationally representative database.

Homes Built Between 1990 to Present:

- Southern states
- Smaller markets <100,000 population (suburban)
- Professionals/technical/management jobs
- Higher income levels/upper incomes
- Age <36
- More likely to have four-year college degree

This group of home owners is most apt to include young parents and then young couples. They are also more likely to be dual income. A smaller cluster of older/retired empty-nest couples follows. The 1990s group tends to be fashion forward and is significantly media influenced. The styles they are likely to select from are: Southwest, lodge-lake, Florida, country French, and sophisticated mix—all escapist design blends. Their taste in patterns is relatively sophisticated, in terms of texture, color palette, and range of looks.

Rodemann, Patricia. © 1997. Study Seven. Nationally representative database.

We have seen how intimate the connection is between exterior, interior, era, consumer demographic, and style/pattern referred to by Jones. Jones expresses a belief "that there is scarcely a people in however early a stage of civilisation, with whom the desire for ornament is not a strong instinct. The desire is absent in none, and it grows and increases with all in the ratio of their progress in civilisation. Man appears everywhere impressed with the beauties of Nature which surround him, and seeks to imitate . . . man's earliest ambition is to create."[10]

A visit to archeological sites and museums full of the artifacts of earlier civilizations show countless examples of the use of pattern. We too are establishing our history, our generational styles in sequential progression, and our imprint on the future. Color, pattern, art, and cultural artifacts augment architecture and remain our legacy. If we were to examine our culture, palettes, styles, and patterns, what would they say about our times? Are we at a similar point to those from the 1850s forward, who faced the twentieth century with a resurgence of Arts and Crafts in the William Morris tradition? Is millennial anxiety an attempt to reevaluate the best and most important elements to take with us?

Each era has its own *cultural* personality expressed via design. Within different historic eras are varied levels of design interpretation and acceptance, often highly dependent on the psychology and cultural influences of the moment.

Design Styles, Colors & Patterns

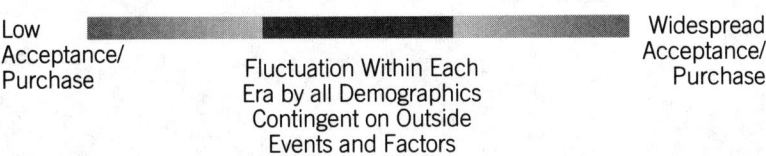

Low Acceptance/ Purchase

Fluctuation Within Each Era by all Demographics Contingent on Outside Events and Factors

Widespread Acceptance/ Purchase

Though each era expresses its own 'personality' through color palette, styles, and mixes, there is something more important at work. Our predecessors symbolized and replicatedelments from their natural surroundings. Through the history of humankind we have been closely influenced by the *exterior* environment. We are keenly attuned to light, climate, wind, precipitation and the natural elements. I have shown a link between the home's exterior style and interior style. We have examined the bonds between era, styles, and homeowners. In chapter ten we explore personality connections. Yet a troubling question remains: *how much of the natural environment do we need to incorporate in the interior environment?* One school of thought held that technology could solve everything. Futurist space voyagers thrive indefinitely in synthetic environments devoid of natural light, plants and authentic materials. I have determined preferences for patterns which replicate or symbolize the natural environment. How successful are we at emulating and incorporating the psychic and environmental cues we need to survive on a bio-evolutionary level? If we have seen differences in how the brain processes pattern and colors, might we assume there are optimum and preferred levels of visual stimulation for physical and mental health which go far beyond consumer preferences and market trends?

We have also shown links between pattern and physiological factors. How successful are we in developing new recommendations for pattern use? Most of the guidelines to date have focused on production technique and suggestions related to replication. Design professionals create and break 'rules of coordination' for the patterns designated for each possible use. With this and other research, we move significantly forward from the edict: 'wide horizontal stripes will make you look fat', and, 'plaids and stripes don't mix'. Recommendations, style direction, the lifestage, and the primary media influence on the decision are only part of the picture when it comes to pattern. The variables are many, and the research design can be complex. It is a closer look at who we are and what we select as we go forward. Will we come full circle to recognize the importance of our ecological link?

Natural elements influence design
creation and selection.

The built environment circa 1999. Designed to protect us from the elements

The electronic environment, designed to connect us with what's
most important, 95% of our day.

References

1. Elsen, Albert. 1962. Children thrive when challenged early. *The Columbus Dispatch,* 11 May.

2. Ibid.

3. McNall Burns, Edward. 1973. *Western civilizations: Their history and their culture.* 8th ed. Volumes 1 and 2. New York: W. W. Norton & Co.

4. Jones, Owen. 1986. *The grammar of ornament.* New York: Portland House. London: Omega Books Ltd.

5. Ibid.

6. Ibid.

7. Ibid.

8. Ibid.

CHAPTER 7

Pattern Rules, Principles, and Techniques

Through time, rules or design principles were developed that governed pattern design characteristics. These were to ensure that design techniques and methods would result in a qualitatively superior product. The appearance of the pattern was supposed to exhibit specific qualities that eliminated contrast and closure illusions, and other phenomena such as tracking, strong diagonal "movement," and other problems. The pattern was to be designed on a pleasing scale and in harmonious color balance. Of course, the principles were to extend beyond *who* was judging the patterns to incorporate the whole design universe through time. This included not only pattern, color, shape, and form but an entire structure.

There are many arguments on the psychology of pattern design. Are we advancing, or is our sensitivity blunted by mass production and the media? Are we in fact ever inventing anything new or just different stylistic derivations? The popular nineteenth-century belief is that a principle of unity encompasses architecture and *all* the arts as representative of their age. But another train of thought is at work. "We have become too much used to identifying the history of art with a sequence of closed stylistic systems, allowing the idea to slip in that every style originates something entirely new. A moment's reflection suffices, how-

151

ever, to realize that in the various styles prevalent in a country there remains still one element in common to them all."[1] The author, E. H. Gombrich, claims that whether the style is *Italian* baroque or *Italian* Renaissance, the common essence is the *Italian artist*—a person in a culture. An example is the Delft porcelain plate with a charming windmill scene, reminiscent of my heritage. However, the plate was produced in the Orient and was painted with a distinctly Asian hand.

Another dilemma that faced the organizers of design principles was, how should a flower, for example, be rendered? "Victorian theory insisted on the need for a clear separation between the forms of applied art and those of high art. The decorator should stylize, the painter should not. A flower on a wallpaper should be flat, a flower in a picture three dimensional."[2] Is a hard-edged interpretation better than a soft-edged, more painterly rendition? Is it acceptable to break the rules? Do any rules of previous vintage still apply? What makes "good" patterns, and what principles should apply? Or does it even matter anymore?

Before elements of a design take shape—line, form, texture, space, pattern, and color—the context and usage should be defined. From the standpoint of the architecture or design professional, *use of pattern design is not in isolation. It is always relational. The flooring is always connected with the walls connected with the furniture, upholstery, textiles, lighting, and function of a space.* This is at the core of a problem, namely, producing art for art's sake. To assume something will always have an application somewhere is arrogant and environmentally incorrect thinking, especially if the decision is made at the expense of thousands of trees or other natural resources and then scrapped and landfilled when it fails to sell. The one-piece artisan approach does not work in mass production. Taking a single open or closed motif, the pattern designer will often put it into one or more common networks or "repeats." Using a square network, a design repeats within the grid, at or along the intersection points in regimental fashion. A half-drop repeat takes every other vertical "column" and drops it by half the distance to create an orderly pattern with more visual interest. A brick motif repeat shifts every other row by half the distance to create an orderly pattern with a sense of stability. Other common repeats are along diagonals, hexagonals, scales, triangles, and ogee or honeycomb shapes.

The repeat of a pattern design is important, because it has a great deal of bearing on the consumer's preference, perception, and cognitive hierarchy. Extremely simple repeats are easy to understand but can become boring or distracting if the pattern motif is also highly simple and closely spaced. So much is also dependent on the form itself. If we are dealing with pure lines, there is a significant difference between the wavy-lined tonal check on white and a sharply regimented check in a strong hue. In most instances, the lighter-hearted, softer version is preferred. The same is true with diagonal designs. If instead of lines we render the pattern repeat in leaves or meandering ribbons, the response is also apt to be somewhat more favorable. With a blooming floral arrangement in the center, the pattern takes on a completely different character than in its earliest repeat format. However, what remains is still directional, still in repeat, and still regimental.

Examples of Pattern Repeats:

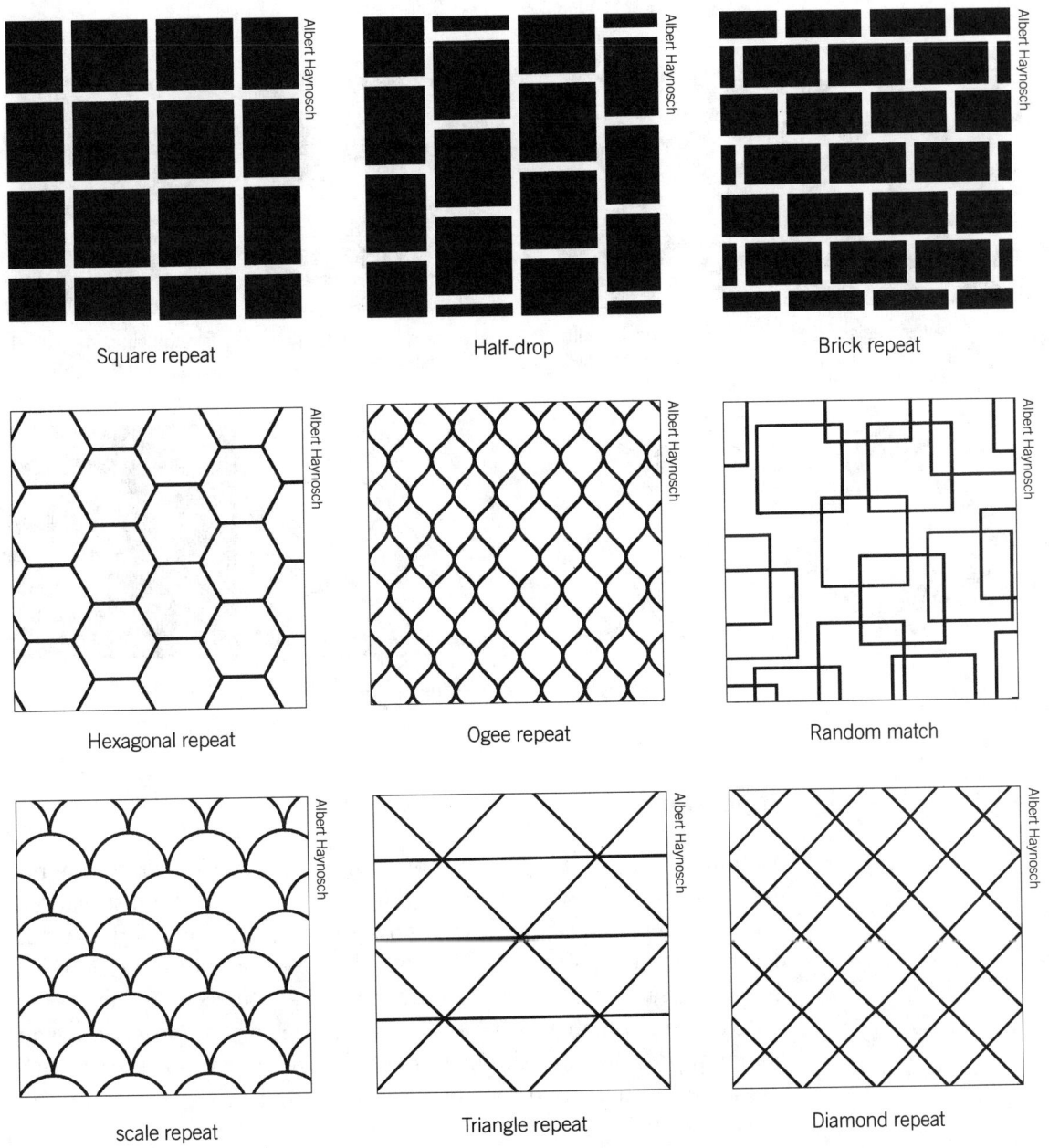

Square repeat

Half-drop

Brick repeat

Hexagonal repeat

Ogee repeat

Random match

scale repeat

Triangle repeat

Diamond repeat

Albert Haynosch

Examples of How a Rendition Changes the Design Character

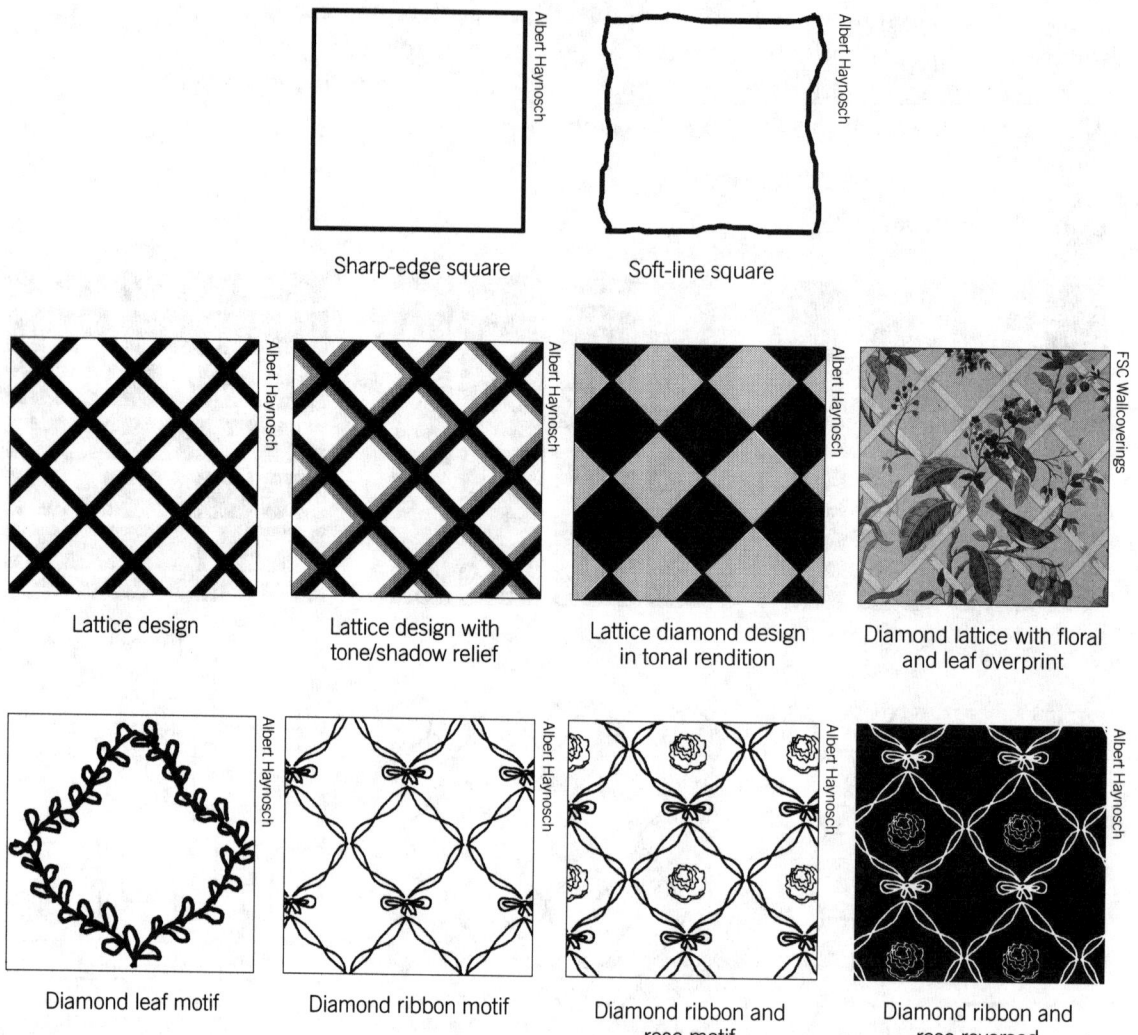

Sharp-edge square

Soft-line square

Lattice design

Lattice design with
tone/shadow relief

Lattice diamond design
in tonal rendition

Diamond lattice with floral
and leaf overprint

Diamond leaf motif

Diamond ribbon motif

Diamond ribbon and
rose motif

Diamond ribbon and
rose reversed

Repetition

Manufacturing techniques introduce specific "repeat" measurements to a pattern design that determine its appearance in the installation. When a selection is made from a sales sample for color and finish, the designer is taking a leap of faith that the inventory or production will match the sample color and that there are no unforeseen effects.

Most manufacturers have testing facilities where optical flaws or potential problems are eliminated before production; however, having conducted sufficient postoccupancy walk-throughs, we know there are still plenty of surprises. Repetition should be a "natural" design phenomenon. It should be expected, serve a purpose, and remain automatic or subliminal. When it becomes redundant, obvious, or overwhelming, the effect is artificial and annoying. Exceptionally high-contrast or smaller-scale designs used too liberally in large spaces can lead to this effect. A closely spaced repeat of a pictorial scenic could be perceived as more distracting than a novelty, stylized floral, or geometric design because we have different expectations of it. A natural degree of randomness, playfulness, or change of texture, pattern, or surface is indicated for repetition to be at its best in pattern-design schemes. A small, highly stylized diagonal check satin-weave fabric in jewel tones is probably fine for an accent chair, but may come across as an overpowering amount of repetition on a large-scale boxy sofa.

Order and Harmony

A painting over the desk features a white farmhouse in what appears to be late summer. Background trees are still green, the fields golden. But the nearby trees are bare; are they dead? The farmhouse windows appear to be open, but smoke is curling up from the chimney. Maybe the lady of the house was baking and her smoke detector went off. Is it the turn of the century? It's art—but this is not harmony! We use this charming but discontinuous scene to illustrate a point. In pattern design, harmony is achieved when motif, repeat, scale, and the color palette follow a distinct and believable order.

Sometimes, to maximize investment in plates, rollers, cylinders, or screens, the design team will be forced to apply color or texture creatively. If a design is intended to print in a typical six-color sequence, the sequence is altered. For geometric, abstract, stylized, and small-print designs, this is not usually an issue. For florals, scenics, novelties, and botanicals, there can be surprises. The harmony of a design, however stylized, is going to be compromised if a typically red fruit appears blue or brown, or the flower an unusual shade of turquoise. In an attempt to gain more sales by introducing another color choice, the primacy of the first design can be diluted. Design harmony is enhanced if the consumer does not have to think about the pattern. Much of our neural-visual processing takes place well below the conscious level at a very high speed. If the subconscious cognitive processing is reinforced, this is usually the case. A pattern of pink horses would disrupt this processing sequence. The example does not have to be so obvious. More subtle effects can also lead to the consumer coming to the conclusion: "That pattern has got to go!" or "I wish I'd never let the designer talk me into that!" or "I'm not sure I can live with that, let's go somewhere else."

Sequence and Continuity

Much as in the alphabet, we expect our letters and numbers to follow a logical sequence, and when they do not we become annoyed. Design writers of the 1800s call a sense of balance in sequence and continuity "repose." This is when all elements are balanced and the eye is pleased. Nothing disrupts the order or is visibly discontinuous. An example of breaking the law would be to remove a key pattern motif out of the sequence. The eye will be expecting the repeat to place the motif at point X. The biggest disruption of sequence usually is improper installation or bad matching.

Example of Figure-Ground Design Relationships

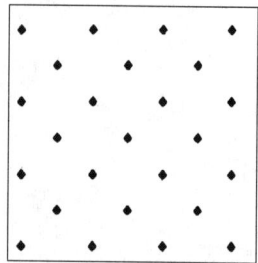 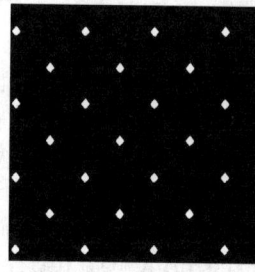  

Diamond on white ground (Studies One and Two)   Diamond reversed   Floral on white ground (Studies One and Two)   Floral reversed

Figure-ground

Figure-ground relationships are very important to pattern design. We have found many cases in which a dark figure on a light ground rates higher with lower-income households, and the same lighter figure on a darker ground rates higher with higher income households. This is regardless of color. A similar phenomenon was noted by the late Carleton Wagner of the Color Research Institute* regarding color value. Light values of a color scored higher with lower household income groups; dark values of the same color scored higher with higher household income groups.

Balance

Balance of the design motifs within a pattern is extremely important. If a stylistic element stands out, once the design is put in repeat the element becomes dominant. A beautifully rendered, vaguely Indian floral/tendril design motif in shades of heavenly blue, pale greens, soft rose with gold accents also featured a large-scale paisley-type leaf. The design was to be used for textile and wallcovering. The sample collection piece was about 12" × 15" high and well laid out with complementary designs. The product arrived on-site for installation and went up like a charm. When the designer arrived and discovered—with shock—just how overwhelming the paisley leaf was and how dominant the repeat turned out, a hasty change to the floor plan placed a large armoire directly in the center of the feature wall to lessen the effect. Artwork, plants, and bolder plain fabrics were quickly put into the room before the client arrived. The pattern was perceived in a very different way from the sample. A similar effect occurred with a young couple who selected a rosy-hued Renaissance marble tile floor. The marble had a faint gray-blue cloud effect, which when installed became far more noticeable across all the tiles, and completely changed the character. Though still pleased with their selection, the couple was shocked to see this element appear so pronounced. It further necessitated a change in wall and border treatments, and decorative artwork.

Issues of Balance:

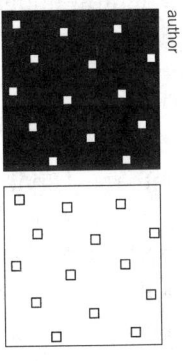

Design sample A

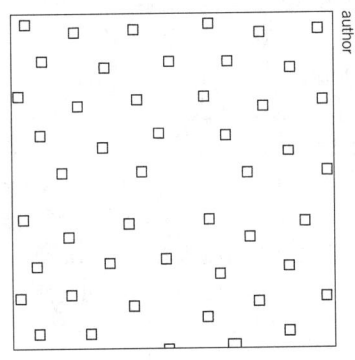

Design A in repeat

Design A installed, perspective

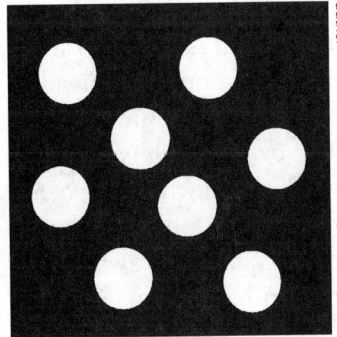

Design sample B

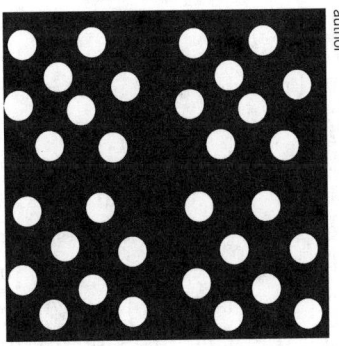

Design B in repeat

Design B installed, perspective

Archives of Columbus Coated Fabrics, Div. Borden, Inc.

FSC, Village, Jacobean design

FSC, Waverly Design

Example of small-scale floral
miniprint design

Example of medium-scale
floral design

Example of large-scale
floral design

Scale

Scale governs the size of the individual motif and the size of the repeat. Large-scale designs tend to be rated more highly by professionals, higher educated and higher income households. Small-scale designs tend to rate better in regions with older housing stock (Northeast), among middle-aged to older consumers, and with women in general. Though highly dependent on the motif itself, small-scale designs tend to rate higher with service, administrative, and blue-collar employees. A calico, snowflake, or foulard design motif appeals to a different consumer than what is referred to as a ditsy dot miniprint, for example. Because the small-scale/miniprint design is easy to incorporate into most style mixes, it is highly rated relative to other design types. Medium-scale designs create more of a statement and begin to narrow the base of consumer appeal. But a great deal is also related to the rendition and palette.

Shape

The shape of pattern motifs also appears to affect the consumer's perception. This seems to be especially true with organic and natural types of designs, botanicals, and florals. If the pattern motif is pointy, prickly, and hairy and the repeat is crawling, the design will not be received as highly. Although we might laugh at this description, some types of design fare better with sharp lines and edges. Novelty designs in which crisp rendition is a virtue, such as a star or a stylized chevron shape, are obvious exceptions. A geometric shape, such as a plaid, has a radically different effect if woven rather than printed. The shapes are softened, and the effect is easier on the eye. If the design has a gradation into another color, the plaid takes on an entirely different character. When the gradation is not overly contrasty, the design tends to rate more

Archives of Columbus Coated Fabrics, Div. Borden, Inc.

FSC, Village wallcoverings

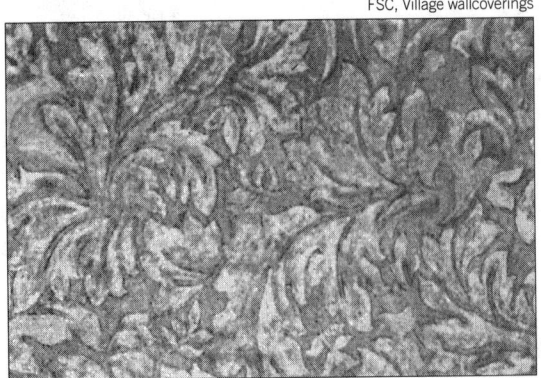

Defined damask

Tonal damask

favorably. In flooring design—such as tiles—the effect from tile to tile is magnified in repeat. In fabric designs, such as damasks, shape implies context. The more defined the shape and the larger the scale, the more apt the design will have greater application for commercial applications—such as hospitality.

Florals tend to rate more highly when rendered with an organic quality, a "sensitive hand." This may be explained by the fact that in nature one does not see outlines as in pattern design. Though stylists of patterns use outlines extensively, in recent years consumers have tended to favor softer, more painterly and abstract renditions of these designs in medium to larger scale.

Flow or Rhythm

Pattern flow is exceptionally important in ogee and border effects. In Pop Art designs of the 1960s, large-scale hourglass patterns in wet look had plenty of "flow" to them. Flow is generally a directional quality of a pattern that is a function of the repeat. Botanicals or florals with an apparent diagonal tracking are negative examples. Flow is a positive effect in small-to-medium-scale designs such as scroll borders on carpeting, sunrise, stripe, or check motifs to enclose other design patterns —as on textile products and art/accessories. Flow is a highly developed concept in Oriental landscape paintings, where the eye is guided up a curved path and into the dimension of the scene. In abstract/watercolor designs, flow may be highly ambiguous but still perceptible. The flow/directionality of a design should not be the first thing one perceives, and it should not be a dominant, overreaching effect. In nature, we look to water, waving fields of wheat or barley, rustling grasses, geese flying, clouds drifting—in short, nothing jarring or discontinuous that signals caution.

Complexity

In the Wagner study,* complex colors (a mix of three or more hues) scored higher with more sophisticated audiences. We have found a similar occurrence with pattern complexity as well. Higher-income households will rate more complex and diverse patterns higher in general; lower-income households will rate them lower. Highly complex patterns are defined as those with many stylistic elements and color pairings such as historic-architectural, stylized designs such as fretwork and filigree, and many ethnic-cultural design types. However, higher-income households are also more apt to rate highly sophisticated, simple tone-on-tone renditions higher. A great deal of the pattern rating is value (as in degree of light/dark) dependent. Finish, texture, and motif rendition will also affect the consumer's perception and the pattern rating in terms of complexity. If an otherwise simple design has a special finish or textural emboss it is classified as "complex."

The more complex a pattern design, the greater the skill of the specifier/user in designing with or around it. Hybrid designs are what we might call complex patterns. These are 50 percent of one pattern element and 50 percent of another, or 33 percent of three different elements. Examples include: a fruit and flower stripe, a damask stripe with

High-end/Narrower Audience Appeal

	Dark value	Complex design	
Income variable			Education variable
	Light value	Simple design	

Lower-end/Broader Audience Appeal

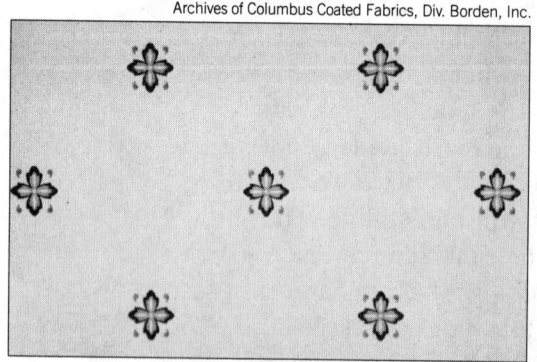

Archives of Columbus Coated Fabrics, Div. Borden, Inc.

Simple small-print motif

York Wallcoverings, Carey Lind Houndstooth

Rich multihued paisley design

a flame-stitch overlay, an abstract motif within a geometric shape with a raw silk texture. If there is little logic and the pairing is contrived or the rendition weak, the design does not appeal to any group or class of consumer. I have also found that pairing a strong design element with a weaker motif will raise the overall perception. In the case of a printed varietal stripe alternating with botanical leaves, the addition of a damask texture or satin finish could raise considerably the overall appeal—as in the case of an upholstery fabric or wall-covering. Again, much is dependent on the design and color palette in question; these are overall observations.

Detail

Detail in pattern design is an important consideration. The more detail, the more is demanded of us in processing the pattern visually. However, at a certain point we shut off cognizance of the pattern image/impression. Different people are attuned to pattern differently. It is perhaps a matter of training and exposure. In my research, designs overwrought with detail were found to be too fussy and unpleasant unless they were scenic, at which point the rendition and quality of the artistic reproduction became exceptionally significant. Consumers are also highly aware of overall design quality. A detailed Indian paisley in rich hues appeals to a much smaller subset of the population, but it is generally the most highly educated, widely exposed, professional, and highest income group. Therefore, detail needs to be considered on a by-pattern category basis. In a small print—typically preferred by the broadest audience—exceptional detail is unnecessary and might actually lower the design rating. A thesis subject claimed such a design took on the appearance of an insect. Texture impacts detail significantly. A two-dimensional print takes on radically different character in woven form.

Density

Density is a direct function of spacing of design motifs or the warp/weft of a textile. It is a function of both repeat and spacing. Having a sense of breathing room in a design is very important to consumers. This first emerged in evaluating textile looks in study two. Textile designs perceived as dense can take on an almost claustrophobic quality on walls, unless richly hued and treated with great design skill in a sensuous visual mix of elements. Designs perceived with adequate spacing were found to be visually pleasing unless—in the case of an abstract motif—the little elements had a tendency to float away from one another. It is a classic case of tension and balance. In floor-covering, design density does not pose the same degree of negative response

Examples of Dense vs. Spaced Designs

Dense ethnic/cultural/historic design. Rich character indicates context.

Spaced French-inspired floral design, with a light-hearted feel.

because of the function inherent in the product itself. However, we have seen that dark, fussy, and dense designs do not score as highly as more open motifs, palettes, and repeats for kitchen and bathroom flooring, health-care settings, and in vinyl or tile products. This is probably because of the "clean" environment cognitive associations.

Vividness or Intensity

Vividness or intensity has to do with hue, but also tonal value. Greater contrast between design elements and figure-ground demands a faster response on our part and a greater sense of attention. For this reason, we become more easily aroused in the presence of high contrast and "vividness" of figure-ground disparity. Consumers describe higher-contrast designs as lively, active, fun, festive, and showy. In the right setting, with skilled design professionals balancing the bold with the elegant and the supporting elements, intense designs are rated positively. On their own, they tend to evoke a love-hate response with about 1 in 5 favoring the design. A certain degree of contrast is important so the design does not appear "fuzzed out" or boring. The criterion is whether a given design will play a statement or background role in the

The following pattern principle appears to be at work:

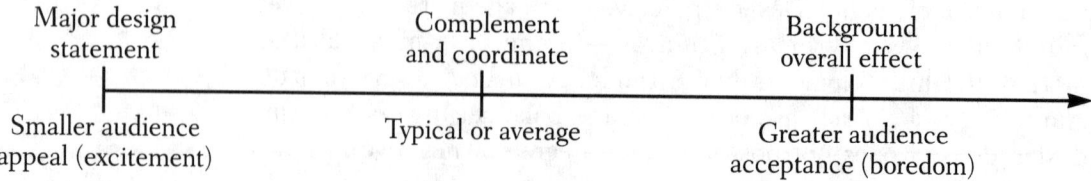

Vivid Design/Background   *Low Intensity Design/Background*

Bolder background diamond motif   Oriental landscape design—tonal

entire interior context. It is well known in color theory that bright colors advance and dark colors recede. Heavily patterned designs advance, whereas less patterning or contrast between figure-ground motifs recede. A great deal depends on the other design elements which will be introduced into the interior: patterns, textiles, flooring, lighting, furniture, walls, and artwork. The outcome is highly dependent on the individual's own arousal curve.

Clarity, Shade, and Shadow

In paintings, shade and shadow are important. They give us the impression of a light source, the presence of illumination and atmosphere. In applied design, more often than not we are dealing with a two-dimensional, "flat" phenomenon. Even so, shadows and shading define the design, adding quality, depth, "believability," and an architectural sensibility. Contour may be achieved on individual elements such as a branch, leaf, or shape with the use of shade and shadow. In woven textiles, this can also be accomplished with a gradation effect. Sophisticated consumers are remarkably sensitive to how a shadow is rendered or misrendered, and the presence or absence of additional tones and shaping to a design. In surface printing, where tones are not as easily replicated as in gravure printing, a design carries specific inherent limitations. In this instance, the designs appear opaque rather than naturally soft. The same is true of highlights. We expect to see an indication of "clarification" to our designs by our natural conditioning.

Gramercy Design

Oriental-inspired design. Note the depth and definition of the tree branch, which has a three-dimensional quality.

Mystery (Depth)

Mystery is defined as uncertainty, that which is undefined, tentative, or ambiguous. A perception of depth in a Renaissance painting, or a misty path in an Oriental landscape painting, lends an aura of mystery or deep interest to the subject and invites more complex cerebral processing than a more limbic (gut-level) response—as would be found in a pattern design of black and red squares. This is supported by neurological research. The more literal and photographic the pattern rendition, the more we are apt to want to compare it with the real thing and find it comes up short. The more artistic in a painterly sort of way, the more we are apt to value it above flatter, cruder versions except for the playful or deliberate. Consumers pass value judgments along similar lines when reviewing patterns. These judgments are always reaching to define a context and usage. The sense of mystery goes beyond what those French people are up to in the toile fabric, or what the crocks in the country-border design contain. In many cases, the sense of mystery is an intangible, inherent to the design motif itself. Celtic fretwork and knots show a sense of mystery in their infinity. They intertwine forever with no beginning and no end. When natural designs are placed in repeat, they can lose their sense of natural mystery—as in marble, granite, alabaster, and many woods. The more evident the repeat or the more repetitious, the less believable and less precious. A new home buyer found to her great annoyance that the side panels to her oak kitchen cabinets were actually wood-grain laminate. The evident repeat became a source of great irritation to her in contrast with the real wood trim and drawer fronts. Another home owner discovered a "loss of mystery" in installing a faux-marble wall-covering that could not be returned. The repetitious character of the marble design elements on a large wall took away the natural random quality of the design. The end effect is not always apparent from sample selections. A lot of trial-and-error learning goes on in the design arena.

Texture and Finish

Adding a third dimension visually or via finish or embossing adds a great design element to a pattern. Consumers respond favorably in many cases. The entire character of a design can be greatly altered—enhanced or cheapened—by the type of finish chosen. A dark, dense floral design that otherwise would fare poorly can be enhanced if it is rendered in an in-register or light reflective embossing. Using texture and finish with a design can elevate it to the consumer's perceived next higher level of socioeconomic status. Perceptions of stripe, floral, fabric looks, abstract/watercolor designs, and marble/stone designs can be improved by these treatments. A satin flamestitch over a dark upholstery print often raises the price point.

In some cases, a design may be cheapened by taking on too much iridescence or a shower-curtain quality. In contract design, solid-color embossings in wall-coverings have been the norm for many years. Woven designs with a burlap quality are perceived as dated, and rate lower than vertical silk embossings. There has been an overall movement toward greater complexity with layered metallics: burnished, brushed, irides-

Gencorp; Essex Dynamic Finishes, Mosque Tile

Retail lighting captures subtle embossing.

Formica Corporation

Depth and drama to faux marble

Gencorp; Genon Apex, Berkshire & Fissure Designs

Dramatic embossing enhanced by lighting.

cent, and translucent pigments; and surface treatments. This is a sophisticated and well-received use of surface that has tremendous design potential. Because of the surface change, the multidimensional use of color, finish, texture, and the organic qualities of "pattern" design, the specifier is more closely able to approximate what humans are most attuned to in the natural environment: variety and interest. Luminous design elements can be particularly effective under specific lighting conditions—such as canister, up or down lighting—as in corridors and public spaces of theatres, hotels, lounges, restaurants, and corporate suites. It is an effect that can be most effective in transitional areas. Embossings also pick up light and add subtle surface interest.

Translucence/Transparency/Glimmer

A design feature that has received much attention in recent years is a quality of translucence or transparency. Sheer fabrics, sheer window treatments, sheer layers of shimmer, even in the tiniest flecks, or pearlescence in paint, laminates, and flooring have captured market fancy. Similarly, flickers of brass, gold, brushed metals, nickel, copper, and silver have added a new appeal to upholstery, wall-coverings, and woven textile products. Pattern designs take on a heightened sense of quality if these effects are not overdone and/or have the patina of age (verdigris) or high tech (fashion fabrics).

Overlapping leaf design

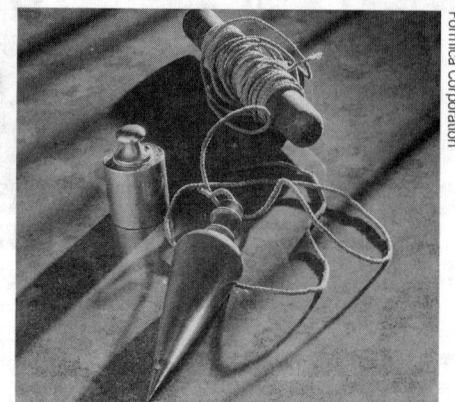
Depth/patina—laminate surface

Formica Corporation

Formica Corporation

Overlap/Overlay

When design elements overlap we expect it to feel natural and follow a certain order. In printed textiles and wall-coverings, this effect is more pronounced than in carpet or woven textile designs. An angel overlaid on a floral-and-leaf motif may leave us wondering what the designer was thinking; a paisley on a vine or a stripe of leopard spots mixed with foulard paisley may be jarring to some. This simply is pushing creative freedom. Clusters of ivy atop a lattice rather than underneath it do not cause us a problem. It is a question of balance and aesthetics. The designers and authors of principles and rules would no doubt object to the freedom that followed in the twentieth century, — "If it can be done it will be." The new maxim is, "If it will sell, it will be made." Does the shell belong on top of Greek fretwork? We may well ask who cares, but the consumer votes "no" in the marketplace.

Typically, a question of overlap concerns botanical and leaf designs, but can also extend to granite and stone patterns, and architectural designs. Granite designs when placed in layers for production can sometimes create disparate color blobs or pairings that create an unpleasant cluster motif not noticeable at first. In abstract and water-color designs, translucent overlays of successive color are usually well received. Many times — as in the above cases — questions of overlap are questions of color sequence. In other cases, it is a question of pigment: whether the design consists of successive transparent or tonal overlays or is opaque and distinct. Sometimes it's a question of colors that must combine to make another color within a pattern or not combine (trapping) to maintain design integrity. Technique is critical. The day the cyan, magenta, yellow, black (CMYK) dot sequence of the Sunday comics didn't line up is a blatant example of bad overlay or out of register. In home decor products, consumers are aware of more subtle overlay/overlap issues, sometimes subliminally at first. When they finally distinguish poorer versions, they become annoyed as if a bad hoax just dawned on them. The more subtle and naturalistic the effect, the stronger the design.

Qualitative Differences in Design Perception

How do consumers rate different types of designs exhibiting different traits, and who prefers each design type? Are there differences?

Archives of Columbus Coated Fabrics, Div. Borden, Inc.   Raymond Waites for Village   Gramercy Designs

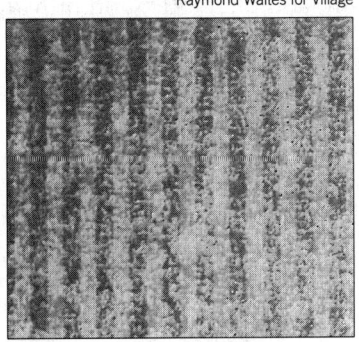
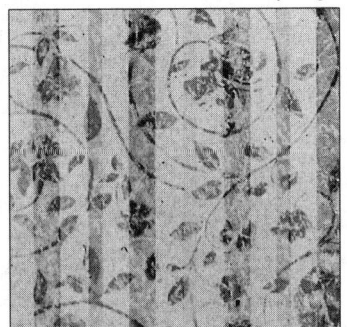

Simple stripe   Marble tonal stripe   Broken, brushed, multihued stripe

Study six: design traits[*]

Design			Improved Design		Trait Difference
Stylized design—flat	6%	vs.	Stylized design—embossed	27%	Texture
Abstract color overlapping	18%	vs.	Abstract translucent colors	23%	White space
Multihued marble	23%	vs.	Multihued marble in repeat	8%	Repeat
Pointy leaf floral	18%	vs.	Soft, rounded leaf floral	20%	Rendition
Dense floral	11%	vs.	Spaced floral	24%	Spacing
Tiny sharp-edged shell	7%	vs.	Small soft-edged shell	22%	Scale,
Stylized/square repeat	–		Painterly/square repeat		Rendition

*Designs rated on a scale of 0 to 10 with 0 completely unlikely to consider and 10 definitely consider this type of design for home. 7 to 10 high likelihood scores shown here.

N=3,500. © 1996, Patricia Rodemann.

We examined research data to see what, if any, the differences might be. Are pattern-design traits and rendition measurable and meaningful qualitites in the consumer marketplace? Is this a function of use or demographics? Is it a matter of simplicity or complexity? Is the difference between patterns projectable or measurably noticeable?

The difference is visible in consumer preference and *perceived design value*, all other factors being equal. Much can be said about the design rendition and the need for principles governing pattern usage. It is my belief that much of the usage centers around context and that more pretesting and consumer research needs to be done. Though a great deal has been written about design theory, little consumer testing has confirmed the theory. The rules and ratings are different too, whether we are talking about wall-covering, floor-covering, printed textiles, or upholstery. "You can get away with more as you move toward the floor," one designer commented on density, scale, and rendition.

Good design is thorough design from conception to production to specification and installation. There are no excuses for poor pattern design and poor quality. Outstanding pattern design can change a space dramatically, add character, and provide a unifying quality. Do we want anything less?

References

1. Gombrich, E. H. 1984. *Sense of order: A study in the psychology of decorative art.* London: Phaidon Press.

2. Ibid.

3. Wagner, Carleton. Color Communications, Inc. (formerly Color Research Institute), 4000 West Filmore Street, Chicago, Illinois 60624.

4. Ibid.

CHAPTER 8

Color Combinations, Styles, and Pattern

Rarely do we see and perceive color in nature in a flat form. We are dealing with light, dimension, constant change, texture. This is one issue with the idea of flat color indoors. It is a falsehood. And though light affects the individual perception of interior color throughout the day and night, we are dealing with a different phenomenon from the natural environment. What color is grass? We cannot say "green," because it is a lie. Grass is alive. It is at times yellow, ochre, tan, wheat, brown, new-growth light green, and deep greens with multiple textural signals under varying lighting conditions. The same is true of tree bark. It's not just brown, and we know what it feels like from looking at its texture. From our first waking moment of the day, we open our eyes to light. Every moment of the day we see color, light, pattern, and texture. We are processing rapidly at a subconscious, automatic level and at a highly aware, focused level. Between the environment, the eye, and the brain, sight and what it communicates to us is a miracle.

Throughout the day, we are bombarded with color, pattern, texture, and dimensional stimuli to which we attach meaning. When we look at the sunrise, it changes from one milli-second to the next, infusing the sky with ever-changing light and color. Sunlight and moonlight cast their influence over everything in patterns of light and shadow. The

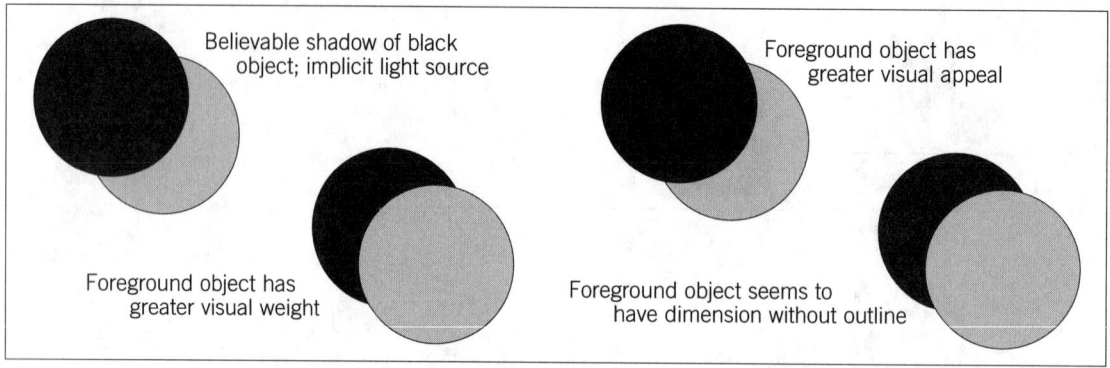

Believable shadow of black object; implicit light source

Foreground object has greater visual appeal

Foreground object has greater visual weight

Foreground object seems to have dimension without outline

Effect of light and outline on shape and color

perceptions of color are altered by dappled sunlight filtered through leaves, shade, and shadow. Synthetic interior lighting augments, illuminates, and changes our temporal understanding of texture, color, and pattern in a marvelous symphony of perception.

Through learning by exposure and education, we discriminate all the nuances, cues, and cultural associations that go with color, light, and pattern. We build expectations of the way things are supposed to be. Our zebras don't have red stripes, our giraffes aren't patterned in lavender, we expect our leopard spots to be black, brown, and white—and our household tabby isn't green. The late Carleton Wagner claimed that 60 percent of all product decisions involved color.[1] Color was the most important single factor. But we seldom see our colors in pure isolation. Research shows that we also expect our style looks such as country, traditional, contemporary, or lodge-lake to feature a specific palette, much as we associate harvest gold, avocado, brown, tan, navy, and rust with the 1970s.

Similarly, we expect patterns to be rendered in specific styles and colors, and seek those colors and pattern designs in the marketplace. Because only about 10% of design purchases are based on impulse, the consumer is making a premeditated search—nearly half said they identified highly with this shopping approach.[2] When the palette/pattern rules are broken, as when there are too many incongruous colors, the design fails to appeal to a broad base of consumers. Many of the pattern-design observations (rules) also apply when pattern is coupled with color. Balance is critical. Repeat, spacing, and flow may be enhanced or disrupted by high-contrast or vivid accents or combinations. My purpose was to research common motifs in common categories.

I began my thesis research in a neutral range, and expanded to thousands of colors and combinations of colors—of the same and different designs. I examined palettes derived from common color schemes in fabrics, flooring, and wall-covering; and I examined individual color usage by room. If a pattern is rendered in one or more colors from the most used, most popular palettes, it will rate significantly higher than patterns with disparate or less popular color elements. The objection of designers was that in this one perpetrates a static, never-changing look, and that the new colors and looks must somehow be introduced continuously. I believe three marketing principles are at work: 1) As one or more new *colors* ascend in popularity, they are incorporated into popular pattern-design statements through printed textiles, accessories, area rugs, and household items; and later, borders, wall-coverings, furniture, upholstery, and floor-coverings, appliances, and tile. 2) As one or more new *pattern motifs* ascend in popularity, they usually incorporate *one or two colors* from one or more previous palettes as a bridge to the new look or style. 3) Completely new colors and color combinations are successful in pattern only in so far as they appeal to those forming new households or can be easily integrated by their use, function, or incorporation of other stylistic elements.

There will always be a dynamic tension between the new and the old. Few consumers have the luxury of starting completely from scratch every time a new palette is introduced. If a color scheme has been built and added to over many years, updating is the more likely scenario. Color is highly connected with a specific era, much as are pattern motifs and architectural styles. Our purpose is to show the link with color and pattern and the different styles consumers *expect* to be rendered in specific palettes. Consumers may *dislike* a style or a pattern design, but *like* a palette or colors within that palette. Though they may make compromises, more often than not, if they cannot find the perfect pairing they will opt for the safest solution. An error in pattern design occurs when the design team gives them too many colors so that they are sure to find the right combination or single colors within the palette. One incongruous color, and the whole pattern design is ruled out. Often the extraneous color doesn't pair well with other pattern designs already established within the home or contract setting.

Another problem at the retail level is rapid change to satisfy the hottest trends the buyer sees, without regard to the reality of the situation in the home. The close-out market and off-price catalogs thrive on these gaffes. It was our intent to also determine which individual colors were most dominant today and track their change over time.

One consumer complained about being unable to find matching patio furniture a mere two years after investing in a distinct color palette. This is why we have seen a trend toward classic and timeless design statements, especially with regard to pattern color on products with a longer life cycle: flooring, furniture. The longer the life cycle, the more critical this issue becomes. In this case, small adjustments in tints and shades of existing color families to complement broad shifts in the market are the best the design team can hope for, much as they would like to provide wild and crazy accents in the latest hues. The newest households entering the market are most apt to adapt to and embrace the latest; however, one-fourth are also designing around what we have termed "heritage mix": hand-me-downs, antiques, heirlooms, or "finds."

As much as we like to believe in creative freedom, setting the trends, reaching for the stars, and artistic license, the consumer market has distinct programmed associations and preferences, which we have attempted to define via research. Fortunately, consumers are also highly attuned to change, but not in a slavish or fad-oriented sense. Research study shows that ~5 percent identify highly with the decorating approach: "I like to keep up with latest trends and colors, and decorate to fit the latest styles." Fewer than 15 percent identify "somewhat" with this approach.[3] These are what could be termed "early adapters" in the first group, and perhaps "strivers" in the second group. *Flexibility and the ability to change a color palette are exceptionally critical elements in pattern design.* The patterns of flooring, wall-covering, and textiles allow the designer to completely change the look of a space by introducing new colors, serving as a bridge between eras. The ability of a pattern design to completely change a room's appearance with all its openness, scale, rendition, repeat, and color palette is an integral story throughout human history. In this context, we review color by individual palette and then by pattern category. The eras and palettes we have shown are commonly recognized. Consumers viewing the 1970s palette will say, "Oh yeah, I remember that. My kitchen had those colors." Consumers viewing the 1980s palette will say, "Our house was built in the '80s, and we have all this mauve and dark gray. We need to update the look."

Interestingly, the "Asian" palette showed much higher statistical acceptance among Asian Americans; the Southwestern palette, among residents of the Southwest; and the African palette, among African-Americans. Palettes were not tagged with names. The newer palettes and the less recognizable country French-impressionist palette scored highly with the same audiences who rated the style higher. These results taken together indicate a good degree of internal validity. Color palettes, as with patterns, are highly linked to room usage and other lifestage variables. Consumers typically do not adapt all the hues in a given palette—as the designer will recognize. With the thousands of textile and related color-pattern designs available, our purpose is to simply illustrate how linked color is with pattern and era. Of course, several palettes are available at any point in history, as my initial study of 18 palettes shows.

Study six was an attempt to understand what was happening in the marketplace and to whom different palettes were meaningful. What were the correlations with pattern, style, and era? Is color preference predictive? What does preference mean to us? How can we better understand each of the consumer types?

During the course of one study, I found unusual individual color combinations that led me to notes in the margin explaining how the consumer had fallen in love with a particular fabric pattern. More often than not, looking at the built environment for a decade, one finds palette stories in place across nearly 20 percent of the homes built during that era. *Typically, two to three hues within the palette will be more meaningful than others, which may only be accent colors or not used at all,* as explained in the survey. Multiple palettes may be used. Shades and tints are also components within each palette shown here. These colors have been selected based on extensive sample search, historic research, the dominant media presence, frequency during the time period, and consumer familiarity and memory association with the indicated era.

Beyond palette preference, there are also physiological, sociocultural, and psychological preferences at work. We are born with our response to individual colors, color pairings, and illumination levels. "Contrary to popular belief, people's first response is not to the aesthetic 'look' of a color. They respond at various, often subconscious, levels, and in some cases, the aesthetics of a color never significantly influence the response. It is the subconscious response to color, not just the aesthetics, that must be taken into account."[4] We arrive at evaluating *pattern* color combinations with all our uniquely human predispositions. Looking back, we see the color stories of other times and cultures; now, we write our own.

PATTERN PALETTES:[5]

Sophisticated palette (warm neutrals) (See color insert)

It appears consumers find the warm neutral palette safe and soothing, and highly sophisticated. There is a distinct correlation of this palette to specific rooms, with consumers more likely to select elements of this palette for home office, study/den, family room, and living rooms.

Which Individual Colors Rated Higher

1. Ivory, and/or cream
2. Tan
3. Clay/copper
4. Black
5. Brown

Studies Six, Nine, Ten.. © 1996, 1998 Patricia Rodemann.

It is apparent that all the hues remain in the palette going forward. All derivations of warm neutrals remain in highest use, and this is by far the dominant palette of choice among new and recent movers based on study ten data. Many styles are being reinterpreted in this palette to give them broader appeal and a newer look. Tints and shades of these neutrals—and tan—should be closely studied, because the shift between yellow-based, blue-based, or red-based tints can be dramatic. A tan that appeared neutral under synthetic lighting conditions took on a green cast under natural light and made an unpleasant statement in an otherwise coordinated interior. The same is true for yellow-based almonds, which now appear to be shifting to a slightly warmer, toasted quality. The warm neutral palette is seen at the higher end of the market in more complex hues and combinations; and at the lower end, if one of the medium to darker hues is dominant. The palette is seen in all product categories: textiles, flooring, furniture, and wall-coverings. Anecdotally, from a personality standpoint, the individual who selects the palette typically has an active life in other areas. The palette rates highly among new and recent movers.

Major Styles Most Likely to Be Paired with the Warm Neutral Palette

- 1970s basic, natural, earthy, simple
- American country
- Casual contemporary
- Sophisticated upscale mix

Study six: N=3,500. © 1996 Patricia Rodemann

Most Likely Pattern Categories

- Marble/stone/granite looks
- Graphic/novelty prints
- Natural-texture prints
- Architectural/historic motifs
- Stripes

Study six: N=3,500. © 1996 Patricia Rodemann

Cool Neutral Palette (See color insert)

Cool neutrals appeal to a smaller subset—about half—of the population than warm neutrals. This palette correlates highly to specific rooms and to specific styles. Consumers are more likely to select this palette for the family room, foyer, a high-tech kitchen, home office, or a modernist living room. Typically, color accents such as red, burgundy (closer to the '80s palette) or warm-hued woods and accessories/art add life to the interior palette.

Which Individual Colors Rated Higher

1. White
2. Light gray
3. Taupe
4. Black
5. Medium gray
6. Charcoal

© 1996, 1998 Patricia Rodemann

All hues remain important in this palette, and are often paired with textures from the smooth: brushed metals, laminates, stones, leather, and concrete; to the rough: deeper pile or flokati rugs, wovens, aged tonal damasks, chenilles, bleached-aged woods, berber, corduroy, velvet, and plaster/faux effects. As with warm neutrals, tints and shades of these neutrals should also be closely studied because the shifts between green-based or blue-based tints can be dramatic. A gray that appears neutral under one light can appear greenish under another. Gray can also take on a purple cast, similar to certain tans that can take on a green cast in the warmer palette. Greater complexity in both warm and cool neutrals seems to be evolving into widespread consideration for home decor. The cool-neutral consumer is more typically younger in an urban setting. From a personality standpoint, control and practicality seem to be more important.

Major Styles Most Likely to Be Paired with the Cool Neutrals

- Modern
- Casual contemporary
- 1980s postmodern
- Sophisticated upscale mix

Study six: N=3,500. © 1996 Patricia Rodemann

Most Likely Pattern Categories

- Marble/stone/granite looks
- Geometric patterns
- Abstract designs
- Natural textures and prints
- Graphic/novelty prints

Study six: N=3,500. © 1996 Patricia Rodemann

1980's Color Palette (See color insert)

It appears consumers find the 1980s palette very familiar and, with the exception of teal, easy to adapt to. There is a distinct correlation of this palette to specific rooms, with consumers more likely to select elements of this palette for bedrooms, master suites, powder rooms, family room, den/study, and home office. The palette appeared in laminates and flooring products, bedding and furniture; in new builds and in renovations. Anecdotally, there appear to be specific personality traits that pair with this palette, such as a greater sense of responsibility. The palette rates higher with upper-middle-income and professional home owners.

Which Individual Colors Rated Higher

1. White
2. Rose
3. Burgundy
4. Mauve/pink
5. Light gray
6. Teal
7. Taupe
8. Charcoal

© 1996, 1998 Patricia Rodemann

It is apparent that the all the hues remain in the palette going forward, but with less emphasis on teal. A new version of this palette substitutes brown and green to balance the "cool" feeling and add a touch of Victorian nostalgia, while maintaining the rose/mauve/pink hues. Thirty-two percent are highly likely to consider use of some variation of a pink/rose hue. All derivations of rose/pink/burgundy remain in highest use. Tints and shades of this hue—and gray—should be closely studied because their appearance and direction can change dramatically in the presence of other colors. An introduction of other hue pairings enables consumers to update.

Major Styles Most Likely to Be Paired with the 1980s Palette

- Homes of the 1980s
- Victorian-romantic
- Casual contemporary
- Sophisticated upscale mix

Study six: N=3,500. ©1996 Patricia Rodemann

Most Likely Pattern Categories

- Marble/stone/granite
- Small/miniprints
- Sports/kids/characters

Study six: N=3,500. ©1996 Patricia Rodemann

Federal/Formal Palette   (See color insert)

Colors that were popular in Federal and formal French palettes focus on pinks, soft rose hues, pale salmon, light green, pale heavenly blues, and soft golds. Many consumers find these hues very attractive, and interpret traditional and casual contemporary styles in this palette. This palette has a softer quality than the heavier traditional palette of navy/wine/burgundy with gold and plum accents, and often updates the original look via introduction of new patterns and accessories. The palette is versatile, accommodating many styles.

Which Individual Colors Rated Higher

1. Rose
2. Angelic blue
3. Blush pink
4. Golden light
5. Mint candy
6. Salmon mousse

©1996, 1998 Patricia Rodemann

COLOR COMBINATIONS

The color combinations shown here represent some typical color families seen in common decorating schemes and sofa/chair fabric, curtain, or wallpaper patterns. Usually, two or three main colors are used with one or more accent colors.

Warm neutral-sophisticated, understated palette

| Ivory | Tan | Clay/copper | Brown | Black | Antique brass |

Cool neutral palette

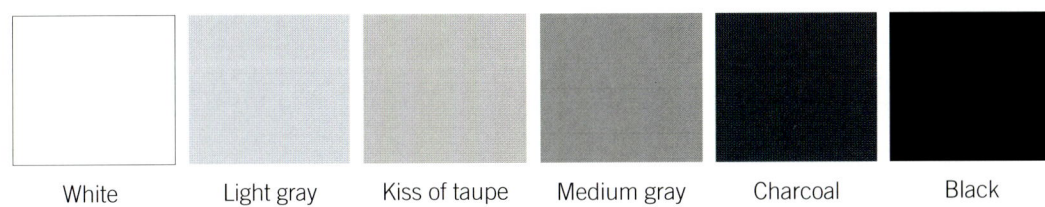

| White | Light gray | Kiss of taupe | Medium gray | Charcoal | Black |

'80s mauve, gray, and teal palette

| Mauve | Gray | Pink | Warm taupe | Burgundy | Charcoal | Teal |

Federal/formal palette

| Rose | Angelic blue | Blush pink | Golden light | Mint candy | Salmon mousse |

Victorian–romantic palette

| Pink | Taupe | Rose blush | Burgundy | Leaf green | Brown |

California sunbaked pastels palette

| Stone | Light yellow | Celeriac to tumbleweed | Aqua tint | Peaches | Clay/terra-cotta |

Lodge-lake north woods palette

| Navy | Northern blue | Forest green | Berry | Stone | Clay/copper earth | Brown |

Florida/tropical palette

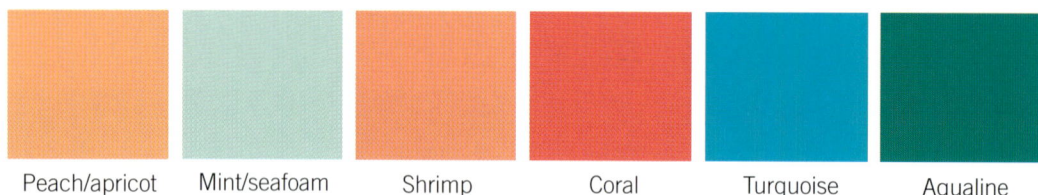

| Peach/apricot | Mint/seafoam | Shrimp | Coral | Turquoise | Aqualine |

Arts and Crafts revisited palette

| Sage green | Ochre | Cypress green | Cobalt | Wineberry | Spanish stucco |

1970s naturals palette

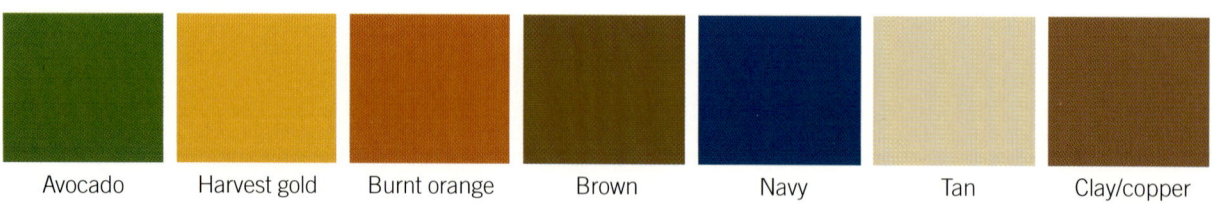

| Avocado | Harvest gold | Burnt orange | Brown | Navy | Tan | Clay/copper |

American country palette

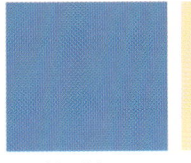    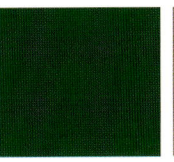 

| Sky blue | Wheat tan | Barn red | Sunny yellow | Cornfield green | Copper kettle |

Traditional/country club palette

| Navy | Hunter green | Bordeaux | Brass | Royal plum | Gold |

Shaker palette

| Honest green | New moss | Golden | Pennsylvania blue | Garnet | Mulberry | Velvet brown |

1950s retro palette

| Pink | Aqua | Turquoise | Red | Black | Silver/chrome |

Country French palette

     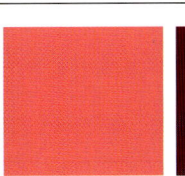 

| French blue | Daffodil | Poppy | Salmon | Waterlily green | Rhododendron | Iris |

Oriental/Asian palette

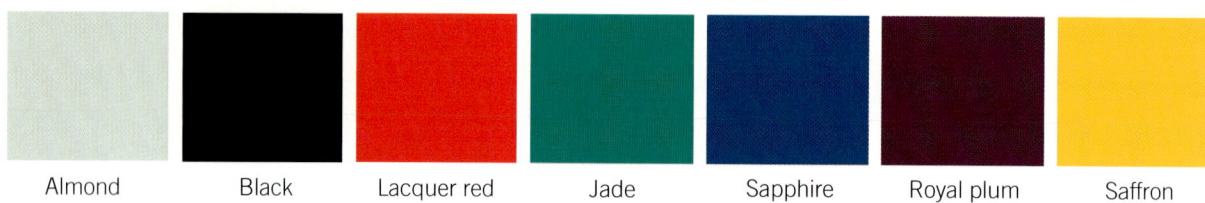

| Almond | Black | Lacquer red | Jade | Sapphire | Royal plum | Saffron |

Southwestern/western palette

| Pueblo tan | Turquoise | Indian clay | Teal | Magenta | Fire poppy |

African tribal/ethnic palette

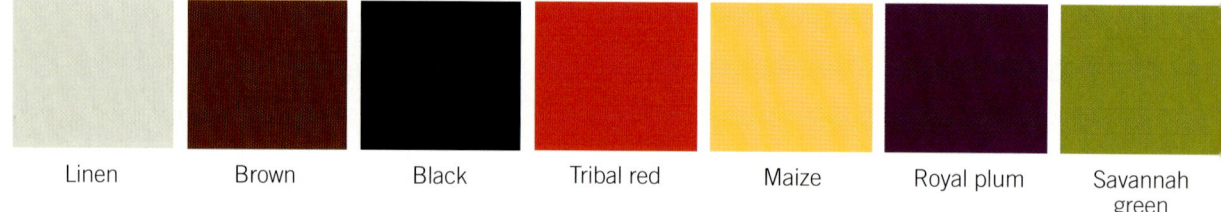

| Linen | Brown | Black | Tribal red | Maize | Royal plum | Savannah green |

Modern/minimalist palette

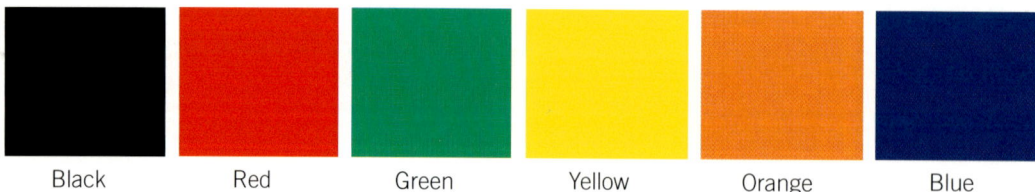

| Black | Red | Green | Yellow | Orange | Blue |

1960s brights palette

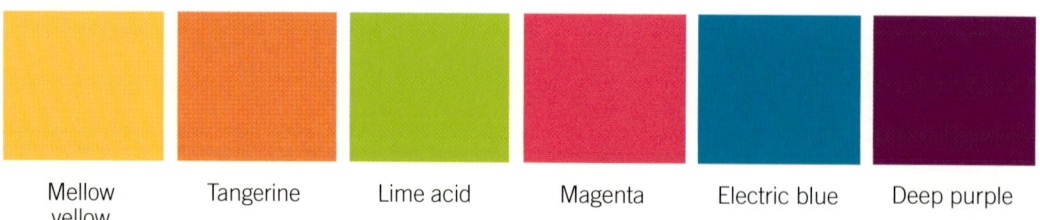

| Mellow yellow | Tangerine | Lime acid | Magenta | Electric blue | Deep purple |

Consumers typically combine rose and lighter-medium blue, at times with accents of the popular hunter green as an anchor hue or medium blue paired with rose and light blue-gray. These hues combine well in certain pattern pairings and act as an anchor to the candied almond quality of the palette. Recent introductions of chartreuse and yellow-greens in textile patterns coincide with the resurgence of these hues in the marketplace in general. However, these newer yellower greens are still not ranked very high overall on a broad scale. The palette typically appeals to a consumer in a suburban setting with a middle/upper-middle-income level. From a personality standpoint, sociability and home and family life define the individual.

Major Styles Most Likely to Be Paired with the Federal/Formal Palette

- Federal/colonial/Adam
- Formal French
- Traditional
- Casual contemporary

Study six: N=3,500. © 1996 Patricia Rodemann

Most Likely Pattern Categories

- Botanicals
- Textile effects/prints
- Floral designs
- Mini/small prints
- Stripes

Study six: N=3,500. © 1996 Patricia Rodemann

Victorian-romantic palette   (See color insert)

It appears consumers find this palette charming, romantic, and familiar. There is a distinct correlation of this palette to specific rooms, with consumers more likely to select this palette for dining room, home office, study/den, family room, master suite, and living rooms. This palette personality seems to pair with a sense of nostalgia and a desire for stability.

Which Individual Colors Rated Higher

1. Dark green
2. Rose
3. Burgundy
4. Pink
5. Sage/leaf green
6. Taupe
7. Brown

© 1996, 1998 Patricia Rodemann

It is apparent that the all the hues remain in the palette going forward, but with less emphasis on rose and dark green, and more emphasis on the lighter greens and brown. All derivations of pink/rose and dark green remain in highest use, but these will need to be coupled with transition hues to new patterns that blend. Tints and shades of creamy neutrals have an antique or tea-stained quality. The palette is an update of the 1980s colors. Suburbanites and professionals prefer this palette.

Major Styles Most Likely to Be Paired with the Victorian-romantic Palette

- Victorian-romantic
- American country
- Casual contemporary
- Sophisticated upscale mix

Study six: N=3,500. © 1996 Patricia Rodemann

Most Likely Pattern Categories

- Botanical designs
- Medium- to large-scale florals
- Natural-texture prints
- Small/miniprints
- Sports/kids/characters

Study six: N=3,500. © 1996 Patricia Rodemann

1990s California sunbaked pastels   (See color insert)

It appears consumers find the 90's sunbaked palette casual, relaxed, new, and uplifting. There is a distinct correlation of this palette to specific rooms, with consumers more likely to select this palette for master suite, bath/powder room, study/den, dining, guest room, and great room. The palette personality type seems to have a more easygoing response to life in general. Residents of both coasts rate this palette higher.

Which Individual Colors Rated Higher

1. Pale blue/aqua tint
2. Light yellow
3. Celery green
4. Peach/apricot
5. Clay/terra-cotta

© 1996, 1998 Patricia Rodemann

It is apparent that all the hues remain in the palette going forward, but with less emphasis on the heaviness of the clay/terra-cotta hue. Tints and shades of these neutrals—and tan—should be closely studied, because the shift is to a linen and natural raw material feel. "Sheer" is a quality associated with hues of this palette. Other hues such as lavender, Aegean, and cerulean blue accent this palette.

Major Styles Most Likely to Be Paired with the Sunbaked Pastel Palette

• 1970s basic, natural, earthy, simple
• Casual contemporary
• Traditional classics

Study six: N=3,500. ©1996 Patricia Rodemann

Most Likely Pattern Categories

• Botanical designs
• Natural textures, textiles
• All other patterns rated lower; this is a nonpattern style and palette with color and texture the main statements

Study six: N=3,500. ©1996 Patricia Rodemann

Lodge-lake north woods palette (See color insert)

It appears consumers find the lodge-lake palette upscale with a certain sense of freedom. This palette is familiar to residents of the Pacific Northwest, northern Minnesota, or Georgia. Without the cool notes, it becomes a Western palette with warmer, brighter red, more vivid blues and green, and a hint of gold. Nearly half of all households—Study Ten—are highly likely to consider the green color family. The same is true for the blue color family. This palette is most often seen in L. L. Bean clothing, or designer products such as Bob Timberlake textiles and furniture. There is a distinct correlation of this palette to specific rooms, with consumers more likely to select this palette for family room, den/study, master suite, child's room, and living room. This personality type seems to link to analytical qualities and desire for upward mobility. Higher-income professional households are more likely to rate this palette highly.

Which Individual Colors Rated Higher

1. Stone, ivory, and/or oyster
2. Forest/dark green
3. Berry
4. Light northern sky blue
5. Navy
6. Clay/copper
7. Brown

©1996, 1998 Patricia Rodemann

It is apparent that the most of the hues remain in the palette going forward, but with less emphasis on green and light blue, and more emphasis on berry, navy, and brown. This is because consumers typically will seek coordinates to match what they've already invested heavily in—dark green and light blue. Filler, accent, and analogous hues will be more important. Yellow/golds may infiltrate in new accent pattern combinations, and/or eggplant and deeper purple hues. The palette has a heavily Northern outdoors feel, which will maintain popular appeal.

Major Styles Most Likely to Be Paired with the Lodge-Lake Palette

- Traditional
- Victorian-romantic
- American country
- Casual contemporary

Study six: N=3,500. ©1996 Patricia Rodemann

Most Likely Pattern Categories

- Geometric prints/plaids
- Stripes
- Architectural/historic motifs
- Botanicals and Florals

Study six: N=3,500. ©1996 Patricia Rodemann

Florida/Tropical Palette   (See color insert)

It appears consumers find the Florida palette regional and tropically bright in its purest form. One would expect that what goes in Miami's South Beach would not necessarily fly in Brooklyn or Boise. There is a distinct correlation of this palette to specific rooms, with consumers more likely to select this palette for bedroom, master bath, powder room, and child's or guest rooms. Used as accent hues or in tints coupled with neutrals, the palette shows up in family-room/great-room areas—but this has a regional predisposition. The personality that pairs with this palette appears to desire escape. This palette is most often seen in bedding, bath textiles, and tabletop accessories. Southern and West Coast residents favor the palette.

Which Individual Colors Rated Higher

1. White, ivory, and/or cream
2. Mint/seafoam
3. Peach/apricot
4. Teal green
5. Coral/shrimp
6. Turquoise
7. Aqua

©1996, 1998 Patricia Rodemann

It is apparent that the mint/seafoam hues remain stronger in the palette going forward, but with some oppotunities to explore accents of less saturated coral, aqua, and turquoise hues. Fewer than 10 percent rate the peach and coral families as highly likely to use. All tint derivations of neutrals remain in highest use. New pattern combinations may introduce accents of lavender and a pale, sunny hue taking a stand to update palette combinations.

Major Styles Most Likely to Be Paired with the Florida/Tropical Palette

- Florida/tropical regional styles
- Casual contemporary
- Traditional
- Victorian-romantic

Study six: N=3,500. © 1996 Patricia Rodemann

Most Likely Pattern Categories

- Medium- to large-scale florals
- Small/miniprints
- Ethnic/cultural prints
- Botanical designs
- Graphic/novelty/modern motifs
- Abstract/watercolor looks

Study six: N=3,500. © 1996 Patricia Rodemann

Arts and Crafts revisited palette   (See color insert)

It appears consumers find the revisited Arts and Crafts palette solid and timeless, and highly sophisticated. The palette has had a "new wave" revival of sorts with the popularity of Mission furniture and style. It rates higher among professional occupations. There is a distinct correlation of this palette to specific rooms, with consumers more likely to use it for home office, study/den, family room, and living room. The yellow/golds have increased in popularity in recent years.

Which Individual Colors Rated Higher

1. Spanish stucco
2. Cypress green
3. Wineberry
4. Medium blue/cobalt
5. Sage/leaf green
6. Gold/ochre

© 1996, 1998 Patricia Rodemann

All the hues remain in the palette going forward, but with more emphasis on medium to lighter tint values of these hues. All derivations of stucco/tan neutrals remain in highest use. Whereas some consumers take a purist approach, many are opting for different and lighter-color palette mixes with this style of furniture and architecture. The palette is most seen in textiles and paint treatments designed to coordinate with the style. Cabinetry, furniture, and construction focus on woods, metal, mica, and organic materials. The personality type associated with the palette seems to be progressive.

Major Styles Most Likely to Be Paired with the Arts and Crafts Palette

- Mission, Arts and Crafts
- Victorian-romantic
- Sophisticated upscale mix
- Traditional

Study six: N=3,500. ©1996 Patricia Rodemann

Most Likely Pattern Categories

- Architectural/historic motifs
- Geometric prints
- Medium- to large-scale florals
- Stripes

Study six: N=3,500. ©1996 Patricia Rodemann

1970s naturals palette   (See color insert)

It appears consumers find the 1970s palette familiar and dated, yet it is coming back in selected use. The palette remains most visible in appliances, flooring, wall-covering, and patterned textiles—less so in upholstery. The current use is in flat-color paint, accessories, and slipcovers. There is a distinct correlation of this palette to specific rooms, with consumers more likely to select it for home office, study/den, family room, and living room. The personality type associated with this palette seems to be pragmatic and "laid back." Midwesterners and Westerners rated this palette higher.

Which Individual Colors Rated Higher

1. Tan
2. Navy
3. Brown
4. Clay/copper
5. Harvest gold
6. Khaki/avocado

©1996, 1998 Patricia Rodemann

It is apparent that navy and tan were the hues that remained in the palette going forward, with less emphasis on brown, khaki, copper, and harvest gold. As these colors have been reintroduced in different palettes and products—generally in solids rather than patterned—they have taken on a new character. All derivations of neutrals remain in highest use. The neutral tints, tan, and brown from this era had a yellow base. Initially, the result that 20 percent of the consumers still had major elements of this style 25 years later came as a surprise in the early '90s. But in true cyclical fashion, as new home owners and young adults emerge on the scene, the colors appear fresh in new uses and combinations. It is worth mentioning that the 1990s palette is a natural transition and a younger, cleaner version of the 1970s palette—a natural graduation. About 20 percent are considering some variation of clay/brown for their home decor.

Major Styles Most Likely to Be Paired with the 1970s Naturals Palette

- 1970s naturals, basic, earthy, simple
- American country
- Traditional
- Casual contemporary

Study six: N=3,500. © 1996 Patricia Rodemann

Most Likely Pattern Categories

- Graphic/novelty and modern motifs
- Small/miniprints
- Natural-texture prints
- Botanicals

Study six: N=3,500. © 1996 Patricia Rodemann

American country (See color insert)

It appears consumers find the American country palette specific to a look, region, and heritage. These are the colors of "down home" and farm country. This palette is found in tabletop accessories, kitchen textiles, print and woven fabric, and craft finishes. It is more likely to be found in deeper, more sophisticated hues for furniture finishes—closer to the Shaker palette. These hues are found in gingham curtains, check tablecloths, red-and-green geranium prints, and spatterware. About one-fourth plan to consider some variation of red for home decor. There is a distinct correlation of this palette to specific rooms, with consumers more likely to select this palette for kitchen, bath, child's room, master bedroom, and great room/dining area. This palette is preferred by Southern and Midwestern residents.

Which Individual Colors Rated Higher

1. Dark green
2. Tan
3. Sky blue
4. Copper
5. Barn red
6. Cornfield green
7. Sunny yellow

© 1996, 1998 Patricia Rodemann

It is apparent that the light blue and tan neutrals remained popular and continuous in the palette. Red, green, and yellow remain popular accents. The newest higher-end versions of the palette continue to feature light blue and white/cream coupled with newer sage/leaf greens, pale yellows, and reds that either visit the warmth of the Native

American hue or raspberry patch. The palette is rated higher by Caucasian Americans.

Major Styles Most Likely to Be Paired with the American Country Palette

- American country
- Traditional
- Victorian-romantic
- Casual contemporary

Study six: N=3,500. ©1996 Patricia Rodemann

Most Likely Pattern Categories

- Graphic/novelty prints
- Geometric/plaids/checks
- Stripes
- Botanical designs

Study six: N=3,500. ©Patricia Rodemann

Traditional/country club   (See color insert)

It appears consumers find the traditional palette rich and country-club-by. Elements of the palette were most often seen in designer use by names such as Ralph Lauren. One consumer lamented that her entire home was done in hues of blue, hunter, and bordeaux and that the latest color introductions were beautiful spring greens. She felt it would be easier to sell the house than to change color palettes. This is how an era or style becomes "entrenched." There is a distinct correlation of this palette to specific rooms, with consumers more likely to select this palette for family room, living room, den/study, dining room, child's room, and master suite. Upper-middle-income households rate this palette highest, as do Southerners.

Which Individual Colors Rated Higher

1. Hunter green
2. Bordeaux
3. Navy
4. Brass/gold
5. Royal plum

©1996, 1998 Patricia Rodemann

The dark green hue is clearly dominant, with navy and wine next as accent hues. Consumers seeking to update and add accent colors have introduced brass and gold, rose, and lighter values of green to soften the effect. In pattern designs, tapestries and historic crest/shield motifs come to mind. Upholstery textiles, bedding and wallcovering, carpeting, and accent pillows are more apt to feature these colors than hard-surface flooring, though deep-hued marbles gained in popularity. The consumer personality can be described as striving and feeling that they have "arrived."

Major Styles Most Likely to Be Paired with the Traditional Palette

- Traditional styles (Federal)
- Sophisticate upscale mix
- Victorian-romantic

Study six: N=3,500. © 1996 Patricia Rodemann

Most Likely Pattern Categories

- Geometric/plaids
- Graphic/novelty prints (horseshoes, etc.)
- Stripes
- Sports/kids/characters (golf borders, etc.)
- Medium- to large-scale florals
- Architectual/historic prints

Study six: N=3,500. © Patricia Rodemann

Shaker   (See color insert)

It appears consumers find the Shaker palette familiar and a "traditional classic" with its richer hues. However, there is a reluctance to use the palette in large, unrelieved doses, and it is more likely to show up in furniture finishes, upholstery, and accessories than in printed textiles and wall-covering. There is a distinct correlation of this palette to specific rooms, with consumers more likely to select this palette for home office, study/den, family room, living room, and dining room. One is less apt to see the palette with more than three of its colors. The palette was more likely to appeal to upper-middle-income households, professionals, and males.

Which Individual Colors Rated Higher

1. Honest green
2. Garnet
3. Pennsylvania blue
4. Velvet brown
5. Golden
6. Mulberry

© 1996, 1998 Patricia Rodemann

It is apparent that green and blue are the most popular hues in the palette, but garnet, mulberry, yellow green, golden, and velvet brown allow consumers to update and transition to other looks. These hues are a brighter, clearer palette than those in the traditional palette, often used in a simpler fashion and with a quality of greater transparency, as in stains. This consumer is less likely to use a lot of pattern in the home. This is a higher-income audience than that of American country. This group of consumers may be described as having a solidly traditional outlook that favors craftsmanship; and includes collectors.

Major Styles Most Likely to Be Paired with the Shaker Palette

- Sophisticated upscale mix
- Victorian-romantic
- Traditional
- Shaker
- American country

Study six: N=3,500. © 1996 Patricia Rodemann

Most Likely Pattern Categories

- Ethnic/cultural prints—paisleys, foulards
- Medium- to large-scale florals
- Architectural/historic motifs
- Printed/textured fabric looks-solids

Study six: N=3,500. © Patricia Rodemann

1950s Retro (See color insert)

The 1950s palette is highly contextual, and many consumers recognize it as such. In small group situations, there are usually stories about the colors in this palette in connection with products from the era. There is a distinct correlation of this palette to specific rooms, with consumers more likely to select it for child's rooms, powder rooms, themed rec rooms. There are regional overtones, because many of the hues cross over into the Southwest palette.

Which Individual Colors Rated Higher

1. Pink
2. Silver/chrome
3. Black
4. Red
5. Turquoise
6. Aqua

© 1996, 1998 Patricia Rodemann

Black, red, or silver give the consumer the opportunity to shift style stories most readily. Pink, turquoise, and aqua can transition into a Florida palette with the addition of other hues. This palette is often seen in retro products, updated and reintroduced from furniture to printed textiles, laminates, and accessories. It is less likely to show up in upholstery or wall-coverings. The palette is connected with memories of diners, automobiles, jukeboxes, café chairs, and poodle skirts. This consumer personality type is decisive and likes a degree of recognition. Northeasterners were more comfortable with this palette, as were non-Caucasian consumers.

Major Styles Most Likely to Be Paired with the 1950s Retro Palette

- 1950s retro
- Florida
- Asian
- Modern/minimalist
- Southwest/West

Most Likely Pattern Categories

- Graphic/novelty prints
- Sports/kids/characters
- Ethnic/cultural prints
- Abstract/watercolor/free-form stripes

Country French   (See color insert)

Consumers are less likely to embrace the country French palette than two or three colors or tints based on the palette, and those will most likely be derived from pattern selections. Neutrals are also important in balancing the palette, which is often used primarily for printed fabric for chairs, tabletop accessories, window treatments, wall-covering, tile, and bedding. An example of this type of palette/pattern might be found in the Pierre Deux collection and in many specialty catalogs. Females preferred the palette; urban residents and college-educated.

Which Individual Colors Rated Higher

1. Daffodil
2. French blue
3. Waterlily green
4. Salmon
5. Poppy
6. Iris

The spring hues of daffodil, waterlily, and French blue are used most often. French blue is also a familiar component in kitchens when paired with daffodil. The palette is also found in bedrooms, dining rooms, powder rooms, and master suites. This is a consumer who knows what she or he wants and seeks romance in life.

Major Styles Most Likely to Be Paired with the French Palette

- Casual contemporary
- Traditional
- Victorian-romantic
- Country French

Most Likely Pattern Categories

- Ethnic/cultural prints—tiny foulard, paisley, Indian
- Graphic/novelty prints
- Geometric prints
- Medium- to large-scale florals
- Miniprints
- Textured fabric looks/effects

Oriental/Asian   (See color insert)

The Asian/Oriental color palette is highly sophisticated; its use derives from furniture, home products, and textiles. It is most likely found in the market in printed and woven textiles — particularly satins, silks — in the garment trade. Because of the color saturation, this palette is usually seen in smaller doses and is less often seen in wall-covering or floor-covering except in single- or two-color renditions. It demands finesse and a less cluttered environment. The palette is most seen in kitchen, living, den/study, dining area, and bedroom. West Coast residents rated the palette higher as did Asian-Americans by 2:1. This was more likely to appeal to a highly educated, professional consumer.

Which Individual Colors Rated Higher

1. Ivory and/or almond
2. Sapphire
3. Jade
4. Black
5. Lacquer red
6. Saffron
7. Royal plum

© 1996, 1998 Patricia Rodemann

Though the percentages of those selecting these colors remains lower, ivory, black, red, and sapphire are important colors with this look. Other hues are usually accents — saffron and jade. This palette has strong Feng Shui connotations. The personality type of those rating this palette more highly is traditionalist with pride and honor as strong traits.

Major Styles Most Likely to Be Paired with the Asian Palette

- Casual contemporary
- Oriental/Asian
- Modern/minimalist
- Sophisticated upscale mix

Study six: N=3,500. © 1996 Patricia Rodemann

Most Likely Pattern Categories

- Ethnic/cultural prints
- Architectural/historic motifs
- Abstract watercolor and free-flowing stripes
- Geometric motifs/fretwork/stylized
- Sports/kids/characters

Study six: N=3,500. © Patricia Rodemann

Southwest/Western   (See color insert)

The Southwestern/Western palette has strong regional connotations in both saturated and lighter tints. The palette is most often seen in printed and woven textiles, contemporary wall-coverings, and art/accessories. There is a strong correlation with Southwestern-style architecture such as adobe, ranch, and pueblo style homes. This palette is most often found in great rooms, rec rooms, master bedrooms, bath, and child's rooms. Midwestern, Western, and Southern consumers rated the palette higher, as did males.

Which Individual Colors Rated Higher

1. Pueblo tan
2. Clay/copper
3. Teal
4. Black
5. Magenta
6. Turquoise
7. Fire poppy

© 1996, 1998 Patricia Rodemann

Rarely are all hues used in total combination or saturation in a large space, but often in prints and textiles, blankets, pillows, and art/accessories. The palette has a strong outdoor/desert feel to it. Tan, off-white (57 percent), and clay/copper are the core architectural colors in many related tints, with the balance of the palette providing accents to woods, leather, metals, and natural materials that are core to this style. Consumer personality types are more likely to be highly relational, affable, and enjoy their leisure time. In recent years, apricot, sage, denim, and cactus have brought a softer feel to the palette, which thrives on the hues of the regional environment.

Major Styles Most Likely to Be Paired with the Southwest Palette

- Casual contemporary
- Victorian-romantic
- Southwest/Western styles
- Florida/tropical

Study six: N=3,500. © 1996 Patricia Rodemann

Most Likely Pattern Categories

- Graphic/novelty prints
- Sports/kids/character
- Ethnic/cultural/native
- Architectural/historic motifs

Study six: N=3,500. © Patricia Rodemann

African Tribal/Ethnic (See color insert)

The African palette is derived from textiles, accessories, and tribal garments. The most prevalent use of the palette is with three or four dominant colors derived from patterns. Recent printed textile introductions of zebra, leopard, tiger, leaf, giraffe, and related prints have captured the fancy of the market in bedding, window treatments, wall-coverings, and art/accessories. Batiks provide similar color pairings. African-Americans rated this palette higher by 2:1. Urban residents and service/blue-collar occupations also rated this higher.

Which Individual Colors Rated Higher

1. White, ivory, linen, flax
2. Safari tan
3. Maize
4. Savannah green
5. Black
6. Tribal red
7. Brown
8. Royal plum

The palette is dramatic, sophisticated, and sometimes quite upscale. Tan and the neutrals coupled with brown and black are the "safari" staples of the palette, with other hues such as red providing the color accents. The personality type associated with this palette has strength and independence. The palette is most often seen in living room, family room, study/den, and master bed/bath.

Major Styles Most Likely to Be Paired with the African Palette

- 1970s basic, natural, earthy, simple
- Mission, Arts and Crafts
- Casual contemporary
- Sophisticated upscale mix

Study six: N=3,500. © 1996 Patricia Rodemann

Most Likely Pattern Categories

- Natural texture/natural prints
- Stripes
- Printed/textured-fabric looks
- Marble/stone/granite looks
- Novelty designs

Study six: N=3,500. © Patricia Rodemann

Modern/primaries/minimalist (See color insert)

The minimalist palette was originally one of natural materials; later one of primaries. It is the palette of iconoclasts and purists—and is usually found in a context of white walls/cabinets and with accent or solid-colors as in duck cloth, canvas, parachute cloth, leather, or in patterned Asian textile brights. The palette is most often seen in kitchen, living room, or

Which Individual Colors Rated Higher

1. White
2. Blue
3. Black
4. Red
5. Green
6. Yellow

Note: pure hues, primaries

child's room. Brighter hues of cobalt, raspberry, coral, apple-green, violet, pumpkin, and marigold have begun to redefine this palette for today without losing the "punch."

White and blue are popular individual hues in the palette that can take on a nautical character or even a delft or British Willow-ware feel. Red and white has a similar effect. The primary hues offer the colors from many flags, allowing a theme or rec-room application. In pattern, stripes often echo this look. This consumer personality tends to celebrate precision and order. Males rate the palette highly, as do Midwesterners. It is predominantly rendered with white or black as dominant hues.

Major Styles Most Likely to Be Paired with the Modern Palette

- Modern/minimalist
- Oriental/Asian styles
- Casual contemporary

Study six: N=3,500. © 1996 Patricia Rodemann

Most Likely Pattern Categories

- Architectural/historic motifs
- Abstract or watercolor prints — Mondrian, Klee
- Marble/stone/granite
- Ethnic/cultural prints (India/Asia)
- Sports/kids/character

Study six: N=3,500. © Patricia Rodemann

1960s brights (See color insert)

Consumers fall into two groups regarding this palette.: those who lived with it in the 1960s and those now setting up households, for whom this is new and fresh. Many older consumers are willing to move into new color stories from this revisited era, but not in a large way, and are concerned about how they will integrate these hues with their current home decor.

What is true in apparel does not always translate into enduring home furnishings, but often begins "infiltration" via accessories, higher-priced furnishings, and printed textiles. New color palettes often begin via solid-color introductions. In this sense, new looks are more sophisticated than their forbears. In pattern, new color pairings and more contemporary renditions of previous pattern stories begin to appear in

Which Individual Colors Rated Higher

1. Electric blue/cobalt
2. Mellow yellow
3. Lime green/apple green
4. Magenta/melon
5. Deep purple
6. Tangerine/orange

© 1996, 1998 Patricia Rodemann

beddings, tabletop accessories, wall borders, accent rugs, and occasional furniture. Rooms for this patterned palette are most often bedroom, child's bedroom, bath/powder room, and kitchen. Single colors extend to other rooms.

It is difficult to say what the staying power of any individual color or the entire palette will be based on one or two studies at any point in time. It should also be recognized that a color palette will usually seldom be picked up again in its original form and that there is approximately a 2–3 year lead time before a pattern, color story, or style really takes hold. Certainly if 5 to 7 percent decorate to keep up with the latest trends, we will see continued and ongoing adaptation to the newest palette or elements of the palette. Bright lime-green accent chairs, electric-blue sofas, watermelon-hued accent pillows offer a fresh modern take on this palette in solid hues without the clichés of pattern overkill or old shapes and prints. The consumer personality that embraces this palette tends to be adventurous and sometimes ahead of the pack.

Major Styles Most Likely to Be Paired with the 1960s Brights Palette

- 1960s retro and emerging re-dos
- American country revisited
- 1990s casual contemporary
- Modern/minimalist

Study six: N=3,500. © 1996 Patricia Rodemann

Most Likely Pattern Categories

- Ethnic/cultural looks (Indian/Southeast Asian)
- Graphic/novelty looks
- Botanical designs
- Medium- to large-scale florals

Study six: N=3,500. © Patricia Rodemann

There are many ways to look at color: individually; in single-color families; two-color pairings, which may be complementary or contrasting; or larger palettes, which may or may not be tied to an era. No single approach is right for all situations. Color, especially linked with pattern, is always contextual, temporal, and referential.

Color perception and color palettes are a blessing and a gift to each era. They are derived from us and synthesized by us in tandem with the sociocultural forces that inform us. It is important that we understand the coherence of color and pattern in a wider architectural context: continuously evolving, forever reflecting energies, happenings, moods, and emotions of our times. Media—tv, movies, magazines, sitcoms; the economy—global, Wall Street, and personal; war/peace-time; labor market; family/household formation, add up to affect our collective design psyche and dreams for the future.

CHAPTER 9

The Style Language of Pattern in Home and Workplace

Downtown at Broad and High there is a bank on every corner. One bank's logo and interior/graphics scheme is blue, white and gray. Another bank is "green," yet another "red," and the fourth "black with shots of purple and teal." Who is going into each bank? Are the demographics different beyond the basic interest rate and service offer? You bet! If you stand there long enough to discover the art director isn't going into the blue, white, and gray bank you already know the CPA is! Although this is an exaggeration, corporate images depend a great deal on appealing to their clientele, meshing with their generation, or "our kind of people" as if an exclusive secret club initiates those belonging to it through color, pattern, symbol, and hidden meaning. Advertising messages reinforce the bond.

Pattern design has its own classification system, much as color does. Certainly pattern is not an isolated element of the interior and connects powerfully with the overall style message — the image. We will look at overall styles and their perceptions, as well the individual component elements that add up to overall "meanings" in this chapter. Early studies began to point to the link between styles and the resultant palettes and patterns. Walking endless miles of trade shows one begins to wonder what, if any, measurements of style have been done and to what degree. Consumers describe their style as country, contemporary, or traditional — but what does that mean? Did they really understand? And how would this translate to palette and pattern? Charged with the responsibility to know and predict the next great thing, who knew what would appeal to consumers and what would wind up on closeout? Of all the thousands of style, color, and pattern statements, which combinations would be meaningful to consumers for their next home purchases? How popular were the ever-present niche styles that ascend and decline periodically?

Initially, I began to research several styles for the thesis studies, and to examine each style as representative of the consumer's look today versus intended look tomorrow. In this manner, I began to benchmark the overall preference for and acceptance of each style and to derive a certain degree of directionality or intent in national surveys. In a further dialogue with consumer audiences, I reviewed photographs of representative looks within each style category and from that arrived at rated photographs of styles as a supplement to style descriptions.

There are, of course, plenty of interpretations of these styles and looks, which necessitates ongoing research and fine-tuning. Consumer responses are a snapshot in time of a specific collection of images (not shown here) gathered across America from thousands of individuals collectively representing each demographic. It's important to take a new snapshot regularly to stay abreast of change.

Variations of the research methodologies continue to evolve, allowing us to determine more fully which consumer type is most likely to embrace each style and which portions and percentages of the market each style represents. Though consumers will decorate with a mix of styles, it is within an overall context with a primary overall style direction. Although the primary three styles — country, traditional classics, and casual contemporary — remain fairly constant, it is the secondary and niche styles that fluctuate in appeal and bear watching.

Sometimes core rooms like the living and dining rooms will feature the primary style and other rooms will feature secondary or niche styles: for example, a traditional living room with a lodge-lake–style rec room or a Victorian-romantic bedroom. However one views style and style mix, it is intextricably linked with pattern and personal preference. It is these audiences we will explore.

Broadly speaking, the styles may be grouped into *traditional, formal and historically derived looks,* including Federal/colonial, Oriental/Asian, traditional mix, Victorian-romantic, formal French, and neoclassic. More *humble heritage looks* are American country, Southwest/Western, lodge-lake, Mediterranean, Mission, Shaker, and country French. More contemporary *lifestyle looks* are: casual contemporary, African, Florida/tropical, Art Deco, 1980's chic/postmodern, Modernist, and the upscale sophisticated eclectic blend. *Niche looks* — or "still hanging on" — styles would be 1950s retro, 1960s revisited, 1970s naturals, and shabby chic (better known as "hand-me-down heaven"), and those styles capturing a very small percentage of the overall market. Let's review how pattern, style, and people intersect.

STYLES BY PEOPLE TYPES, PATTERNS BY STYLE

Traditionally and historically derived styles

"Traditional Mix"

Traditional classic mix living room

York Wallcoverings, Ronald Redding Designs, Masculine

Traditional pattern

Traditional classic mix dining room

Traditional mix is a highly-rated style in the traditional/historic group and overall. This style today is more of a country-club feel, though it derives from English and colonial design traditions featuring Queen Anne, Windsor, Hitchcock, Hepplewhite, Georgian and seventeenth- and eighteenth-century styles. Many of the designs that are embraced now have taken inspiration from these time periods in fine reproductions and/or there may actually be authentic antique pieces in the traditional mix. This style has a classic timelessness and mixes well.

Regionally, the consumers are more likely to be Southerners or Northeasterners—extending to the South Atlantic states.

Pattern selections are consistent with the style, with florals, small prints, textile effects, stripes, faux-marble looks, and plaids most associated with traditional mix. Pattern-style correlations are independ of the palette-pattern relationships in chapter eight.

"Victorian-Romantic"

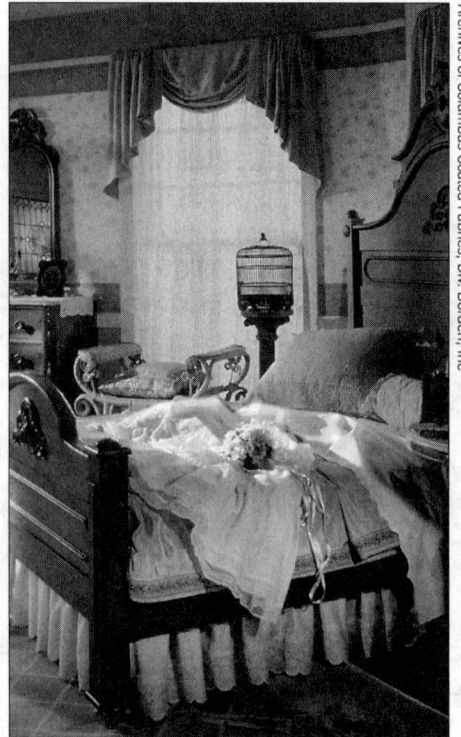

Victorian-inspired bedroom   Victorian-inspired bedroom with antiques   Victorian "feel" pattern

Victorian-romantic style is very appealing to American consumers. Though the style has its origins in Victorian England in a time of opulent ornament, it has a quality of romanticism that consumers seem to be drawn to. This design style was actually a mix of Gothic, Georgian, and other styles done to ornamental excess—typically in dark woods with deep hues and much attention to fabric: lace, brocade, moiré, velvet, damask, and tapestry. The American version was a frontier-town opera house and Southern mansions with swagged and tasseled, heavily draped windows, patterned carpets, and sentimental themes. Today's version is typically lighter, with selected elements mixed with other styles. Those who like the style tend to live in smaller towns or country settings. Females are much more likely to embrace the look, and they tend to be younger (under age 36). Young couples and first-time parents are most likely to feel "romantic."

Pattern selections associated with Victorian-romantic style are floral trail designs, nosegays, medium- to large-scale florals, small prints, faux marbles, botanicals, fabric looks, and stripes. Most importantly, the look must capture a sense of nostalgia.

Federal/Colonial

Formal Federal style sitting area

York Wallcoverings, J. Chesterfield Studios, York Traditions

Botanical document pattern

Queen Anne dining room

Federal design style differs from traditional mix in that it tends to focus on Queen Anne, Chippendale, Sheraton, Revival, or Adam styles and has a much more formal quality. There are many separate styles over time and regional interpretations to this overall moniker. The color palette tends to feature hues of rose, lighter Wedgewood blues, mint/lighter greens, ivory, summer corn, and pale pumpkin rather than the deeper hues of traditional mix. It is perhaps, a purist version of traditional mix.

Original antique pieces feature a more delicate, finely detailed quality and there are many excellent reproductions available. Woods are cherry, walnut, and mahogany. Consumers for this look are most likely to live in Southern and South Atlantic states, with Northeastern consumers having above-average interest in the style. Upper-middle income households favored Federal style. This style is preferred most by an older age group. *Formal fabric effects—damask, watered silk, velvet, moiré—stylized designs, and florals tend to be associated with Federal/colonial style.*

Formal French

York Wallcoverings, Carey Lind New Orleans, volume 2

Formal French mix

Archives of Columbus Coated Fabrics, Div. Borden, Inc

French library nook; bergere chair and aubusson rug

York Wallcoverings, Antonina Vella

Damask stripe pattern

Formal French style appeals highly to a smaller subset of the population. This overall nomenclature typically features furniture from the separate looks from the Louis XIVth and XVth eras, which are more clearly baroque and rococo in style. After the Louis XVIth era, the style evolves to the Napoleanic classicism of Regency and Directoire. Draping and tassels are a big style element. Furniture may be fruitwood, pecan, or even gilded, as is popular today. A whitewashed finish was also popular for a time—as well as hand-painted pieces. The color palette features "candied almonds" in shades of peony pink, mint, and seafoam green, palest blue, pale violet, and light golden. The style adds a touch of elegance and is usually mixed with other looks. Formal French pieces—*bergère* chairs, accent tables, or bombé chests—are versatile enough to go with sophisticated mix, casual contemporary, African, Asian, or the more predictable, traditional Victorian-romantic and Federal styles. The consumer who rates formal French highest tends to live in the Northeast or on the West Coast. Females favor the style, and it rates highest among those with higher household incomes. Formal French patterns are typically small prints such as fleur-de-lis, the royal bee, small floral stripes, damasks, moiré, watered silks, tapestry, and stylized overall motifs. Frequently the style is paired with Oriental hand-painted silk wall-coverings. It is an opulent look.

Oriental/Asian

Oriental tea room

York Wallcoverings, Ronald Redding Designs—Masculine

Archives of Columbus Coated Fabrics, Div. Borden, Inc

Sitting area

York Wallcoverings, Carey Lind Designs, Teahouse Rose

Oriental/Asian-inspired pattern

Oriental style seems to be an ever-present market niche that has periods of popularity when Western imagination is captured. New discoveries, museum tours, and trade missions introduce us to new aspects of the look. In the public view, this style is most associated with dark woods, black-lacquer furnishings, bright reds, jade greens, rich cobalt blues, saffron yellow, and gold-hued silks of China. The Japanese garden, the shoji screen, rice paper, printed batik cloth, futons, and bonsai trees have enhanced Western appreciation of the beauty of simplicity. The style is most apt to mix with other looks such as modern, sophisticated mix, traditional, formal French, and neoclassic. Oriental pattern-design motifs are most typically botanical/floral and geometric—fretwork, filigree, and scenics—though stylized themes of lotus blossom, sunburst, and natural textures are also featured. As with formal French, this buyer is most likely to be Northeastern or Western with high household incomes.

Neoclassic in the 1990s

Archives of Columbus Coated Fabrics, Div. Borden, Inc.

Neoclassic, '90s take

York Wallcoverings, Antonina Vella La Rosa

Apartment sitting room

Raymond Waites for Gramercy

Acanthus leaf border

Neoclassic style bloomed again in the 1980s, two hundred years after it had swept Europe. Neoclassicism is best known for its recreation of styles of art and architecture from Greece and Rome. Patterns mimic architectural looks. This look includes deep-hued woods, black and gold finishes and accents, and ornamented furniture with gilded leaves, wreaths, rosettes, lion or griffin heads, swans, and spare lines and curves to the silhouette. In Britain, Regency style of the late 1700s to early 1800s appears lighter and more delicate than its stuffier predecessor styles. The color palette features gold hues, light blues, rich reds, salmon and watermelon hues, medium greens, and neutrals paired with black. One is most apt to see this style mixed with sophisticated, casual contemporary, modern, formal French, or Federal as accent pieces. Southern consumers were most apt to rate the style highest, followed by both coasts. The neoclassic consumer is most represented in the higher household income group, and the style also appeals to a younger consumer.

Humble heritage looks

American Country

American country dining area

American country kitchen

Archives of Columbus Coated Fabrics, Div. Borden, Inc.

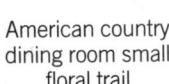

American country
dining room small
floral trail

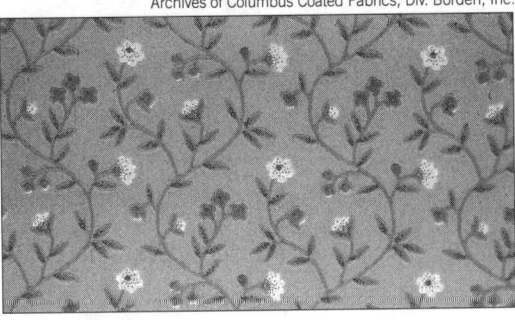

American country has long been a favorite style of many consumers, but the style has evolved and changed focus significantly during the past two decades. The style has its roots in farmhouse and prairie settler design born of pioneer heritage and honest practicality. Waves of immigrants added their imprint to colonial styles in simpler, less expensive, more functional versions of furniture. Textiles tended to be *homespun weaves and checks, and quilt-motif designs,* now supplemented with denim, flannel, canvas, and woolens. Finishes include painted and sponged effects, in addition to ornamented motifs of Pennsylvania Dutch, Amish, and American Primitive themes. *Whimsical and natural*

treatments of patterns include farm animals and farmhouses, apples, sunflowers, wheat, daisies, watermelon, and berries. American country is today an eclectic mix of collectibles with a lighter, cleaner assembly and palette than in its 1970s discovery and heyday. It is a nostalgic style. The palette is drawn from nature with barn red, cornfield green, yellow grain, and sky blue tempered by whitewash and weathering. Finishes typically are oak, painted woods, pine, and natural maple.

The style preferred by Southern consumers, followed by Midwesterners and then New Englanders, and typically from a smaller-size town or rural area. This is more likely to be a lower-middle-income consumer.

Shaker

Archives of Columbus Coated Fabrics, Div. Borden, Inc.

Thomasville Furniture, Inc.

Shaker inspired home office nook

Shaker-inspired bedroom

York Wallcoverings, J. Chesterfield Studios, Great Outdoors

Simple leaf pattern, Shaker in "feel"

Shaker style developed in the 1700s as the contribution of a religious order that placed a premium on pure form, honesty of design, and simplicity in all things. It is a spare version of colonial, which avoids unnecessary ornamentation and has a minimalist quality. Its attention to exceptional craftsmanship stresses natural materials and finishes, though color is used for furniture and architecture. Color is often referred to as a grayed primary palette and includes slate blue, apple red, late-summer green and amber. Black wrought-iron metal is in contrast with the more expensive brass associated with colonial decor. *Patterns seem limited to simple checks, braid, and weaves of chair, textile, and basket design. But often, American Primitive designs and miniprints seem to find their way into coordinating furnishings and textiles,* and in other reproduction pieces. It is most typically a "go-with" style. I have seen growth in acceptance of this style. The Shaker consumer is most likely to be Midwestern and then a Northeastern resident in smaller-population markets from an upper-middle-income household.

Country French

Country French inspired kitchen patterns, chair

York Wallcoverings, Carey Lind, Weatherby Woods

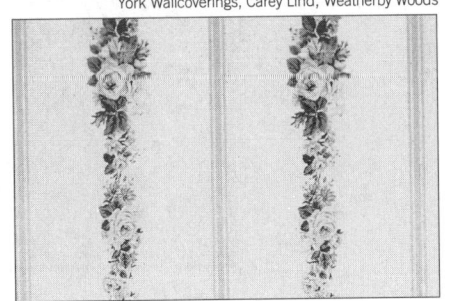

Country French floral stripe

Country French dining area, New Orleans interpretation

Archives of Columbus Coated Fabrics, Div. Borden, Inc.

Archives of Columbus Coated Fabrics, Div. Borden, Inc.

Country French style is derived from the village and farmhouse life of France and has evolved into its own style statement: a simpler, rustic version of formal French. Country French design typically features furnishings with the same gentle curves but with more natural and lighter-finish woods, rush seating, and small-print fabrics. In recent years, Americans have fallen in love with the style form and sought to create their own country-chateau style. Tile, terra-cotta, stone, plaster, and other natural materials are integral to the look. *Pattern designs are often brilliant calico-type prints; whimsical roosters, hens and rabbits; botanicals; and stylized overall patterns.* Country French mixes well with other rustic and humble heritage design styles. The style is preferred by females 2:1.

Lodge-Lake

Archives of Columbus Coated Fabrics, Div. Borden, Inc.

Eisenhart Wallcoverings

Lodge-lake look with beamed ceiling, rustic feel

Cabin at the lake kitchen

York Wallcoverings, Carey Lind Houndstooth

A fishing border plus fly fishing wallpaper design

Lodge-lake style may originally have had its roots in the grand vacation homes of yesteryear. Americans today most identify the style with log cabins, ski chalets, lake homes, and rustic mountain retreats. The style has grown in popularity (along with four-wheel-drive vehicles and SUV's). There is a sense of both the familiar and the sentimental in this style, which can be termed "escapist." *Pattern themes are represented in textiles by natural weaves, plaid and buffalo checks, along with botanical and novelty themes such as scenics, moose, bears, birds, wolves, waterfowl, pinecones, eagles, and fish.* This consumer is more likely to be Midwest-ern or live in the plains or mountain states in small towns.

Mission

Courtesy of Sunworthy, Santa Fe Collection

Raymond Waites for Village Arts and Crafts design

York Wallcoverings, Ronald Redding Designs—Monogram

Example of mission style mix   Arts and Crafts design   Arts and Crafts design in style of William Morris

Mission has emerged again in the late 1990s as a popular American style, with a fair number of American consumers highly likely to consider the look or have elements of this style in their home. Mission design evolved out of the Arts and Crafts movement in the United States and heralded a simplicity of form in finely crafted Stickley furniture, which was linear and sturdy in quality. Tile, mica, geometric metalwork lamps, and hardware coupled with a warm palette gave the style a distinctive look. *Pattern elements are geometric, floral, botanical, and organic in feel.* Twenty-eight percent said they were highly likely to consider this style and/or already had these style elements in their home today. The Mission consumer tends to be middle income, working in professional/technical and management occupations. Like lodge-lake, Mission is a young style, with devotees under age 45.

Southwest/West

Southwestern inspired patterns

Archives of Columbus Coated Fabrics, Div. Borden, Inc.

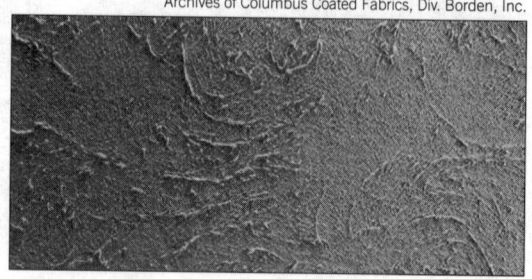

Naturals and stucco patterns, in addition to ikats, SW geometrics

Southwest/Western inspired dining area

The Southwest look originated in Arizona, New Mexico, and Texas with touches of Native American, cowboy, and Hispanic cultures. There is a reliance on natural materials of stone, adobe, weathered woods, and the brilliant palettes of natural rock formations and high desert. The look is highly regional in appeal, though many will recapture the style in family rooms or as a strong secondary look to another style—usually casual contemporary in other parts of the country. *Patterns are typically derived from Navajo and native cultures in geometric blanket, ikat, and ornamental design, though abstract watercolor themes and novelty patterns also capture the feeling.* This consumer tends to be a West Coast resident by a high percentage, with the reach extending to Western south-central states and mountain regions. The look appeals to two age ranges: the under-36 group and a "fun in the sun" 56–65 group.

Mediterranean

Archives of Columbus Coated Fabrics, Div. Borden, Inc.

Mediterranean inspired surfaces

The Mediterranean style used to represent dark, heavy, lower-end, and chunky styles two or three decades ago. The style has been rediscovered and reinterpreted with a Tuscan spin. The Mediterranean region can be said to include Italy, Greece, Spain, southern France, and Portugal. It is a natural transplant to other parts of the world, with its rustic and natural ambience. The new Mediterranean style includes weathered plaster and stone, terra-cotta, tile, and distressed woods. *Pattern designs tend to include many of the stone looks, architectural and historic designs, stylized ethnic and cultural motifs, casual wide stripes, and natural textures.* This consumer is more likely to be from the West Coast, with secondary interest on the East Coast. It is a younger and urban style and somewhat more likely to be favored by males and higher-income groups.

Lifestyle Looks

Casual Contemporary

Casual contemporary rec room area, geometric pattern

Sophisticated eclectic-blend casual dining

Casual contemporary computer work area with soft floral

Archives of Columbus Coated Fabrics, Div. Borden, Inc.

Casual contemporary is a 1990s take on "transitional." It is also known as a California look. This style has evolved from Danish-modern lighter woods to 1970s pit groups and a more transitional look in the 1980s to a more natural and grown-up 1990s sensibility with style. The light, sunny outdoors feeling so currently popular is easy to design with and around, but the primary attribute of the style is comfort and unpretentiousness. It is what we call an easy-lifestyle look that works well for families with older kids, suburban homes, and busy two-income households. This style joins traditional and country to round out the top three styles. There is a relaxed, playful character to this style. *Pattern designs that are identified with this look are faux stones, stripes, natural textures, woven and casual fabric effects, abstract watercolor effects, modern motifs, and small prints such as stars, half-moons, and diamonds.* Casual contemporary is most preferred by Southern/South Atlantic and West Coast/Western residents. This consumer usually lives in an urban market and is what we would classify as having an upper-middle-income level. This is a younger consumer group. The look does especially well in a multicultural environment and for those whom Northern European country heritage looks have little appeal.

Sophisticated Eclectic Blend

Eisenhart Wallcoverings, Ashford House

Sophisticated eclectic-blend casual dining

Archives of Columbus Coated Fabrics, Div. Borden, Inc.

Sophisticated foyer

York Wallcoverings, Carey Lind Quiet Contemporary

Complex multilayered background pattern

Sophisticated blend is an upscale version of casual contemporary and offers the consumer a more elegant deliberate interpretation, which can include neoclassic pieces mixed in with frankly modern elements. It is a style that requires taste and skill to assemble effectively. It is international and confident in character. Interviews with consumers made light of the differences between casual style and sophisticated style. As one colleague said, "My son would have his feet up on the coffee table and be eating cheese curls in front of the television with casual contemporary. With sophisticated style you simply don't eat cheese curls, and you're probably never home to sit on the sofa!" *Likely patterns in this style are natural and handcrafted textures, multilayered abstract effects, fabric textures and looks, stone and wood blends, and architectural/historic designs.* Finish and authenticity are important to the look. The style is both understated and eclectic. Northeastern, Atlantic, and Southern residents from urban areas are most likely to rate sophisticated mix highly. This group tends to have a high household income level.

Florida-Tropical

Archives of Columbus Coated Fabrics, Div. Borden, Inc.

Florida novelty patterns add touch of humor

Archives of Columbus Coated Fabrics, Div. Borden, Inc.

Florida casual with abstract contemporary patterns

Archives of Columbus Coated Fabrics, Div. Borden, Inc.

Florida space

The Florida/tropical look has a distinctive casual quality with vibrant color, multicultural and Caribbean influences, and a sense of fun. The Florida style mixes natural materials such as wicker and outdoor furnishings with plants and lots of white and sun-drenched pastels. The style is popularly recognized as typical to shore homes, condominiums, and vacation escapes. *Pattern elements include graphic novelty designs such as fish, shells, starfish, seahorses, natural textures and abstract/ watercolor prints, along with familiar plaids and stripes in freer line form and brighter hues.* The style is readily picked up for a secondary theme room, such as a family room, bath, or exercise/sunroom area. This middle-income consumer is most likely to reside in Southern/South Atlantic and Gulf states, but also in the Northeastern/ North Atlantic region.

1980s Chic/Postmodern

Example of '80s charcoal grey sofa, mauve and grey
patterned *wallcovering design*

1980s kitchen

1980s patterns: cool-neutral palette—mauve/gray/teal

Eighties postmodern style is most recognizable by its palette—white/mauves/grays and teal—and materials   stone, steel, and "cool" glamour. It is a postmodern style without superfluous ornament, layers of fabric, or tradition-bound decor. It is a less casual version of contemporary, but a less deliberate version of modern. Most homes and offices built or renovated in the 1980s feature elements of this style. The 1980s renovation might be a SoHo loft or an adaptive reuse of a warehouse. *Patterns identified with this style are stone, metallic, and faux textures; botanic leaf and abstract floral designs; geometrics, small prints, smooth-finish textile effects, and pinstripes.* This is more likely to be an urban or suburban resident, and tends to be a middle-income consumer. A big priority will be updating the 1980s fixtures, furnishings, and palettes to incorporate newer looks in the next several years.

Art Deco

Art Deco inspired bath with geometric mini-print

Art Deco was a popular style in the 1920s and 1930s. The style mixes well with modern, sophisticated, casual contemporary, Asian and African looks, and has staged somewhat of a comeback. This is most typically a 'go with' style today. It is recognizable for its palette, ziggurat geometrics, curvilinear forms, and distinctive cubist motifs. The palette features rose-pink, gray, black, Nile green, gold, brown, and taupe. This is associated with the jazz era. Torchère lamps, reclining couches, distinctive mirrors, and round-armed overstuffed chairs are all elements of the style. *Pattern motifs are geometric, novelty graphics, stylized overall designs, and some swirling abstract elements.* The Art Deco consumer is more likely to be Northeastern, then from Southern states. This is most likely to be an urban consumer.

African Inspiration

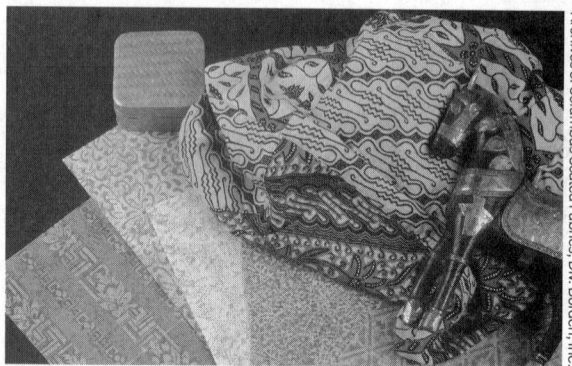

African inspired patterns; batiks, ethnic, and cultural stylized prints

Border pattern—African animals

Traditional "clubby" take—African-colonial

African style has become popular in the marketplace as a distinctive individual look in recent years. From batiks and patterns of Morocco to the animal-print designs reminiscent of a Kenyan safari, consumers have begun to recognize the appeal and beautiful decorative character this large continent has to offer. Though some of the appeal may derive from a spate of movies beginning with *Out of Africa,* a larger percentage may be because African-Americans are a distinct growing and important demographic with interest and pride in their heritage. However, this look is by no means restricted to one population subset, as Western nations recognize the precious environmental heritage and uniqueness of the African continent. *Pattern designs are likely to include all natural-inspired designs and botanical elements, novelties—such as animal-skin motifs—birds, geometrics, organic small prints, stripes, and overall abstract and faux designs.* This is more likely to be a younger, middle-age consumer in urban markets. Males preferred the look over females and African-Americans by a significant percentage.

Modernist

Courtesy of Frigidare Corporation

High tech stainless and laminate surfaces

Archives of Columbus Coated Fabrics, Div. Borden, Inc.

Textural background pattern with light

Thomasville Furniture, Inc.

Modern and "fun" living room

Modernism derived from a school of architecture that stressed a purist approach to structure and function. This meant avoidance of superfluous ornament and decoration and a focus on purity of form and architectural geometry, with natural material often in raw form providing its own beauty: steel, concrete, leather, wood, glass. The spare quality of modernism extends to furniture and artwork. Though Le Corbusier and architects of the Bauhaus usually eschewed pattern and superflous color, today's popular interpretations use architectural materials in tandem with color, light, and artwork to create a lively 1990s take on the look. *Pattern elements might appear in rugs, Mondrian, Klee, Cubist, Pop Art or other modernist artwork in bold primary hues, geometrics, whimsical motifs, stripes, and other abstract designs.* The black leather Mies Van Der Rohe Barcelona chair might sit on a bold primary–hued abstract rug on a concrete floor. There may be elements of Memphis style or a Breuer Wassily chair against a Finnish wall hanging. This consumer is likely to be young and urban. Males embraced the look by 3:1.

Niche Looks

1970s Naturals

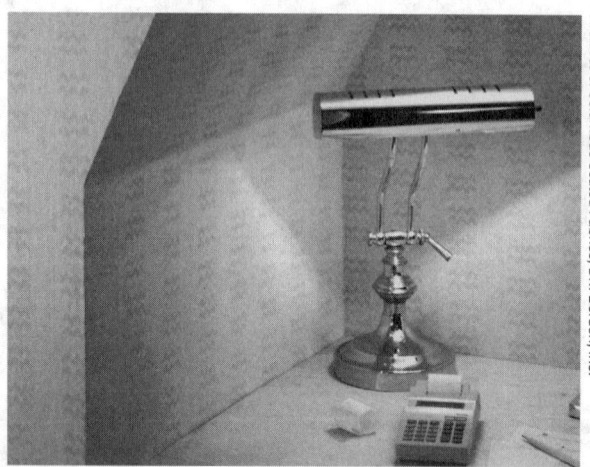

Natural chevron weave

A look at the '70s office waiting area; tan rope effect vinyl wallcovering; burnt orange chairs

Seventies style went through many phases emerging from the 1960s Pop Art effects to a love affair with ethnic prints and a more drab back-to-basics naturals movement that included mixed transitional furniture, pit seating groups, glass-top and chrome tables, and rock-group denim and grunge looks. *Patterns and textures include Haitian cotton, grass cloth, burlap, multicolor weaves, and bold geometric and tree/leaf motifs.* These patterns accented the avocado/harvest gold/brown/tan/navy and dark orange palette. Fewer than twenty percent of the consumers live in 1970s-era homes—where renovation is past due, under way, or recently completed. Many elements of the 1970s naturals are being rediscovered, such as authentic materials, and botanical and natural textures and weaves by a younger audience eager to preserve the better design ethic of the era.

The 1970s naturals (basic and earthy) consumer is typically in the 56–65 age range and is more likely to live in Southern or Midwestern regions. We are likely to see demographics continue to change as the style is embraced in a retro-revisit—as with looks of the previous decades.

Shabby Chic

Bright color, retro wall pattern liven up minimal furnishings

Retro mix and hand-me downs against abstract wall print

Chic midtone floral adds drama for the 20's era bath

In recognition of the Gen-X and baby-boomer echo or millennial generation, shabby chic as a separate style category appreciates recycling, adaptive reuse, flea-market finds, and hand-me-down mix. This style also celebrates creativity, antimaterialism for its own sake, and funky, new wave interpretations and artsy approaches. Shabby chic can take on a sassy sophistication all its own with Fiesta ware, painted antique chairs, unusual color and pattern mixes, and rule-breaking eclecticism. *Patterns are revisited from earlier eras and often reintroduced in new pairings or with new finishes to mix with other acquisitions.* Color, finish, and material are also important traits of the style. HGTV has introduced *Awesome Interiors,* a show that elevates this style to a place of its own, and there are several books on the market dedicated to the look. This young consumer is more likely to be Northeastern and then a West coast resident in a larger urban market. Females were slightly more likely to rate the style highly, and this group tended to have lower household incomes.

1950s Retro

1950s retro diner style eating space

This classic diner pairs '50s chrome swivel chair with beautiful, natural wood finish surface.

The 1950s style has become associated with suburbia, "American made," the exuberant postwar love affair with the automobile, and the advent of television. Synthetic materials (laminates, melamine, plastic), new colors such as turquoise and aqua, and whimsical jet-age patterns captured our fancy. Chrome kitchen tables with a Formica tops and diner-style chairs on black-and-white check linoleum flooring say "fifties" as much as the Danish-modern chair with the plaid upholstered cushion and the kidney-shaped coffee table. Fifties style is seldom seen in complete original form, but has been revisited as typically American and worthy of preserving. *Patterns are space-age whimsical as well as geometric.* Typically, fifties retro appears in a family room with jukebox and records or in a kitchen with chairs, chrome wall clock, and other memorabilia. This consumer is more likely to be younger and from urban markets. Males are significantly more likely to rate 1950s retro style highly. (We won't ask who collects cars, *Happy Days,* or Elvis memorabilia!)

1960s Revisited

'60s floral   '60s geometric

The sixties made a style imprint all its own with tulip chairs, plastic furniture, Pop Art brights, wet-look wallpaper, bold flower prints, and tie-dye fabrics. *Graphic patterns, geometrics, and swirling abstract designs characterized 1960s designs alongside ethnic-cultural prints and bright in-your-face colors.* This style has reemerged to celebrate pattern blocking, bold prints, colors, and large-scale stylistic florals (daisies) in lemon-lime, orange, purple, pink, and bright yellow; but is coupled with pale blue and dark brown in fashion. This is definitely a niche style. The original consumer is age 56–65, from smaller market areas with lower household incomes. Newer consumers (age 25) just discovering the revisited 1960s will continue to alter the demographic.

STYLE, A RECAP

"Style" is revisited, reinterpreted by each successive consumer age group. The '50s rendition of lodge-lake style is quite different from the '70s or the '90s version, as it was in the grand resort "cottages" of the 1890s. The same is true of "traditional." Traditional design in the '60s had a far more formal and rigidly defined quality than the "traditional classic mix" of today. This is where consumer attitude and behavior affect how we live with style. Our preoccupation with "casual" today extends all styles.

When we look to pattern, *how* the pattern is rendered affects its potential rating significantly under the umbrella of style. If a floral tends to the botanic or casual feel, the perception and saleability may be much higher than if the floral tends to the Jacobean or Oriental because of the relatively higher ratings of those looks today. When color is factored in, the potential success of a given pattern is further determined. Working with the range of today's popular hues, tints, and shades is preferable to a historic throwback or completely unconventional, difficult-to-integrate, new hue palette. The best designers do have an intuitive feel for this rule, which, when coupled with their own research, can serve both the public and the manufacturer well by tracking the winds of change without stepping too far afield to the detriment of sales and the ability of the consumer to work with the new pattern entry.

The research process began by defining elements of each style, including color palettes and patterns. I subsequently established a firm link between the era and the style, the style look, and the consumer types drawn to each and the degree of popularity and trending of each style and mix of styles within the marketplace and the attendant patterns. As much as we attempt to be timeless and classic, change in the marketplace, materials, and the world at large cause us to recognize we will never quite get there.

In my study of the connection between occupation and pattern-design types selected, I found in general that style and pattern associations carry over into the work environment. Looking at each type of installation, here is what the public believes is acceptable in pattern palette and style selection.

Commercial spaces

Increasingly, architects and design professionals stay away from "style" per se, focusing instead on excellent, timeless design. It is the realization that "been there, done that" formulaic design does not work over the long haul and is neither financially nor environmentally sensible. Yet style, pattern and clientele are inextricably linked in the commercial setting. The style-image statement recalls memories, and cues us how to behave. The consumer visiting a dental office with furniture, wall-covering, or a color palette from more than a decade or more ago might question the age of the equipment and the continuing education of the staff. One consumer told of just such a panic-inducing environment in a health-care setting in a small rural town. Admitted to a 1950s vintage hospital after a waterskiing accident, he nearly fainted in fear after seeing the postwar green tile and the "ancient" 1960s-style furniture. The competent young medical residents could do little to allay his fear with thickly accented commands.

A high-level professional dinner held in a well-regarded Mid-western restaurant raised eyebrows for one or two of the team members who noticed the dated—and somewhat faded—stained carpet and late-1970s dusty vintage memorabilia mix. A few of the diners changed to "safer" menu items. A female conference speaker attending a regional conference walked into a well-known hotel lobby in a resort area and immediately recognized the lodge-lake style of the early 1980s with its velveteen pit group, copper hearth, and adjacent dark-paneled disco lounge. Many of the female guests of the conference ordered room service and the hotel dining room remained empty. Bookings increased at the newer hotel across town. We may snicker at these examples, but they are far too prevalent to dismiss. Consumers *do* care and understand the rules of the style-association game.

Mannington Commercial, Saint James School, St. James Maryland

Timeless design: visual interest in diamond ceiling border, school colors and emblem, red bordering.

Public/governmental spaces: Consumers expect to see Federal, traditional mix, or a contemporary-modern look. In historic or buildings by notable architects, Art Deco, Mission, or neoclassic might appear. Older—in need of renovation—spaces might feature 1970s naturals. Obviously, different rules and greater functionality apply; these spaces are not the same as the associated residential styles.

Formica Corporation

Subtle natural patterns get dramatic geometric accents.

Financial institutions: Consumers expect to see Federal, traditional mix, or a contemporary look. With the trend toward retail banking and banking without walls, modernist and high-tech looks have emerged. Investment-banking firms might employ sophisticated electic mix, neo-classic, or elements of regional/cultural styles.

Health-care settings: Consumers expect professional versions of homelike ambience. With the great variation in health-care settings, many of the residential styles apply—differently—and many of the regional styles influence the interior outcome. Casual contemporary is more prevalent in health-care settings; but American country, Southwest, Mission, Victorian-romantic, Florida, Art Deco, Oriental, lodge-lake, and Shaker influences are all felt in the casual contemporary context. For lobby areas, senior centers, and more conservative regions, one is apt to see traditional mix, Federal, Victorian-romantic, and formal French. For a plastic surgeon's office, one might see sophisticated eclectic mix, elements of country French, 1980s postmodern, or Mediterranean. There is a much greater sensitivity to palette, pattern, architecture, and specific clientele in determining the style direction for health-care settings, with the best environment for healing uppermost.

Mannington Commercial, Kingston Hospital Family Maternity Center, Barbara DeStefano, Design for Healthcare

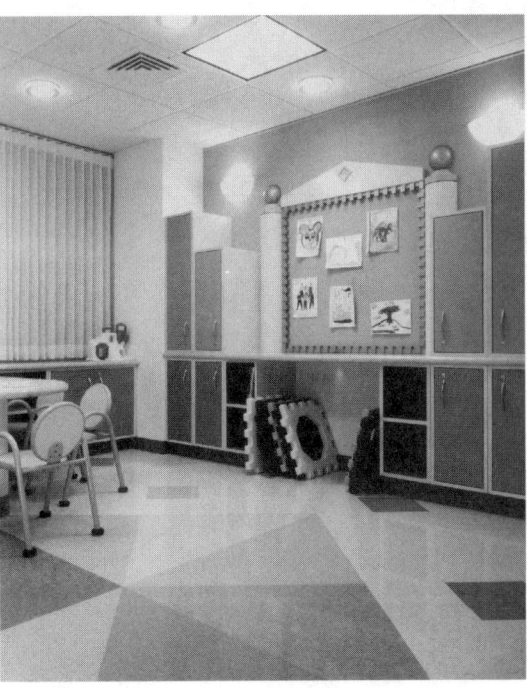

Mannington Commercial, Children's Memorial Hospital, Chicago Illinois, Wendy Borg-Borg Design

Lively use of geometric and stripe design with art mural

Intricate use of colored VCT architectural fixtures creates pattern interest

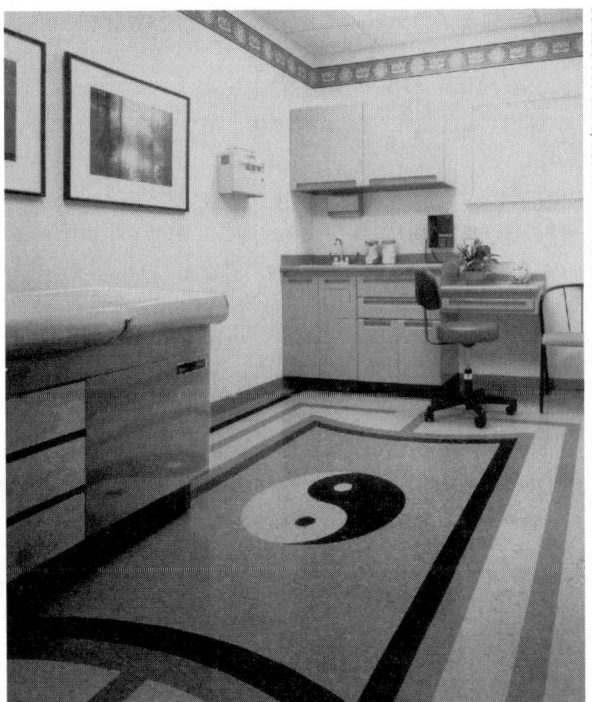

Mannington Commercial, Rainbow Healing Arts Center, Hyde Park New York, Barbara DeStefano, DeStefano & Associates

Use of symbolic pattern yin/yang motif in flooring; cross-symbol border motif

Mannington Commercial, The Neenan Company, Fort Collins, Colorado, Deanna Thompson, designer

Archives of Columbus Coated Fabrics, Div. Borden, Inc.

Hospitality banquet room/reception; swag border, damask, and moiré wall treatments

Excellent visual interest in flooring pattern and cut-out wall; cafeteria

Hospitality settings: Consumers expect and gravitate toward specific styles that match their demographic in hospitality settings. There is an understanding of each brand and franchise, and the appearance of the property associated with it. Convention hotels and banquet facilities are often more closely linked with regional setting and architecture; but many times there are niche looks within a single site. Retail principles of return per square foot will increasingly apply—as much as occupancy rates have—as a measure of success, and style will become an important component of that equation.

Corporate offices: Image and performance are powerfully linked with the visual cues of style. Though the cue is often architectural or regional, much depends on the nature of the business. Consumers are keenly aware of dated looks associated with commercial settings, and offices that serve the public are no exception. Increasingly, safe generic approaches that are vaguely contemporary have been the "out of the box" solution taken by budget-conscious facility managers. Component pieces—seating, case goods, accent art/accessories in limited statements—set a secondary style stamp on the site and allow for greater flexibility in the corporate arena at the end of the twentieth century. The environmental "green" movement has contributed greatly to our understanding that it is no longer desirable to install and rip out repeated cycles of more faddish styles, and a new classic design ethic has emerged, which will extend into other types of commercial environment. The corporate office setting must increasingly be highly adaptable to the changing needs of a flexible workforce.

Courtesy of Formica Corporation

Surface interest created by faux granite stone—longevity!

Coping with demands of electronic equipment, the need for greater worker productivity, and an ever-changing corporate situation demands the utmost from office facilities. It is not enough to portray the company image—which could change tomorrow. Design is now a "movable" investment that supports and enhances the people who compose the entity in providing products and services worldwide.

Home interiors, like commercial spaces, are a changing landscape. There are differences between the styles rooms have been recently decorated in and the styles consumers are planning to decorate with next. Though I have gathered specific annual product, style, and palette data, we focus here on broader design considerations.:

Home interiors

Children's spaces: Children's rooms are heavily theme influenced, and marketing, media, and entertainment have the biggest impact on which designs a child will select. Children's television viewing significantly impacts the direction of the design decision for bedding, which in turn impacts color and other elements of the child's room.

Living rooms: Traditional mix is often a top style, followed by sophisticated eclectic, American country, and then casual contemporary. Victorian-romantic was a strong secondary style to traditional for this room. The living room was less likely to feature a regional or niche look than other rooms. The lowest amount of impulse decisions go into living-room furnishings and decor: This is after all, the presentation of self to the "public."

Family/rec rooms: The primary styles are often 1990s casual or sophisticated eclectic, then traditional mix. Often, the secondary style is a strong regional or historic variation, such as Southwest, Mission, lodge-lake, country French, or Shaker. Themes are popular in this setting, but this is highly dependent on whether the family room is part of the main floor/great room or a segregated basement room.

Bedrooms: There is great variance between the number of rooms in a home. For single- or two-bedroom homes, either 1970s naturals (low-end) or sophisticated ecelctic (urban) emerges as the primary style. For three-bedroom homes, 1990s casual, American country, traditional, sophisticated eclectic, and Victorian-romantic all emerge as important styles with significant regional and demographic variation. Department stores and bedding producers are keenly tuned to this and always offer ensembles for all the core styles.

Bathrooms: Consumers are most apt to recreate niche looks and theme rooms in the bath and powder room; though core styles are similar as for the bedroom.

Kitchens: Early research identified traditional and casual contemporary as the top two overall directions, with country rated highly though perceived as dated. Later research began to identify sharper distinctions with Mission, Shaker, country French, Mediterranean, Victorian-romantic, high-tech, and Old World mix emerging, with specific wood finishes and niche directions within each depending on demographics (age, income) and region.

Having shown some recent style-design research, I would like to add that a *professional's role is to push the envelope, break the rules, produce cutting-edge (and delightfully unexpected, fresh) design. How is that to be accomplished with such a profound, unspoken rule book?* With evolving roles, changing career patterns, and growth in the multicultural workforce, we have the latitude to reinterpret what design means — which patterns will be used, and how. Consumers will tell us how far to go comfortably and economically. There is no substitute for thorough preplanning and evaluation, and the earliest stages of the design process should not be compressed or dismissed. We are caught in between balancing return with the delight and necessity of new discoveries. Design researchers, planners, and postoccupancy evaluations will continue to measure what works and what does not. There is no room for arrogance or absolutes. We must be fluid and adaptable. We still have to be visionary by measuring the moment while grounding ourselves in what we currently know to be true.

CHAPTER 10

Working with Pattern for Specific Effect

Though many architects will start with site, determining the feeling and personality of a space is at the very least the second consideration, but often follows well after structural and functional decisions. What behaviors is the space supposed to stimulate?

Casinos in Las Vegas and other gaming/vacation/resort destinations use bold and unlikely pattern designs in highly stimulating and contrasting colors, unusual materials, and new applications with the express purpose of exciting and driving gambling and consuming behaviors. It works. But there are more subtle examples of how pattern can signal behavior.

The little shots of a black-and-white checkerboard tile motif—an acuity pattern—can quickly attract attention to the restaurant bistro or retail setting. The bordered rug with a different color center signals exit elevators in the health-care clinic. The formal moiré stripe of a banquet area leads to a playful geometric companion design in the adjacent meeting rooms. Professionals know these things intuitively, but there isn't much research on it. Study three demonstrated that business interactions dropped significantly—with no other influencing factors—when a distracting "speed space" acuity pattern was installed on one wall of a quick-print company.

Environmental psychologists have identified several important psychological characteristics with regard to one's living/working space: a sense of control, privacy, expression of identity, sense of security and

Pattern Signals: Personality

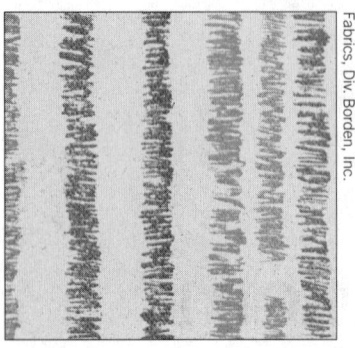
Archives of Columbus Coated Fabrics, Div. Borden, Inc.

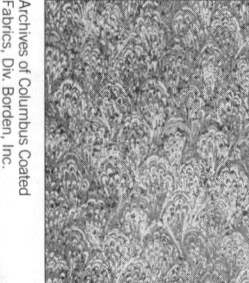
Raymond Waites for Village

York Wallcoverings, Carey Lind Houndstooth

Playful stripe   Studious book paper   Opulent paisley

safety, order and organization, and variety. These include stimulating and relaxing aspects to space, aesthetically beautiful or pleasing qualities, freedom of choice/change, and a background that enhances interaction with others/relationships in one's life.[1]

CONTROL

Having a sense of control over one's space is related to our territorial urges. We define our boundaries with design. We define our rooms and spaces by styles, colors, and patterns. The executive dad who spends much time working at home defines his study/home office space with specific wood finishes, color palette and patterns. Realtors are quick to recognize and point out the appeal of the "male study" patterns: small geometric prints, stripes, faux finishes, and deeper hues. The space is defined as "dad's office" and carries with it an off-limits character and specific status.

Different control issues are expressed via pattern design in different spaces. Clearly, Victorian-romantic floral designs in the master suite might not be the male spouse's first choice, but it is a room in which he willingly submits to nurture and romance. The adolescent child with a black or purple room and heavy-metal posters on the wall is establishing independence and control over his/her own life.

Some rooms of the home have a more egalitarian quality. The balance of a relationship and comfort level between a couple and/or their children may be seen in how the home is designed and who made the decisions. In commercial spaces, large corporations used to have rules of status that determined the office accoutrements. The positioning of the desk, the size of the desk, the wood finish, and the presence of raw-silk wall-coverings, plants, and Oriental carpet all determined the exec-

Dad's office—male cues, male patterns, male themes   Dad's office

utive status. One colleague told of making a dreadful error in ordering a replacement wastebasket of the wrong (higher) "status cue" for a midlevel executive, which became the talk of the break room. It was assumed that because the executive also personalized his space in other ways and "dressed up" that he was power hungry, and many people implied he was a control freak—all because of a wood-grain square wastebasket.

"Control" can be a subtle perception. If a carpeting, flooring material, or wall-covering pattern statement extends outward from an office to adjacent areas, it may be assumed the individual controls that function too. In multilevel health-care facilities, care is taken to define boundaries for cardiology, pediatrics, ophthalmology, obstetrics/gynecology, and gastroenterology by using different palettes, materials, furnishings, finishes, styles, or accessories. In the generic "big box" approach, one could only distinguish the difference by dog-eared magazines and brochures, assuming one did not get lost and wind up in the wrong waiting room. This sense of control extends to design for "*our* demographics," "*our* patients," because perceived comfort levels often translate into profitability via more patients, more word-of-mouth referrals, and other intangibles.

The public feels uncomfortable in being unable to control personal space or other elements of a setting. Control behaviors extend to spreading one's things around and accessing adjacent chairs and tables.

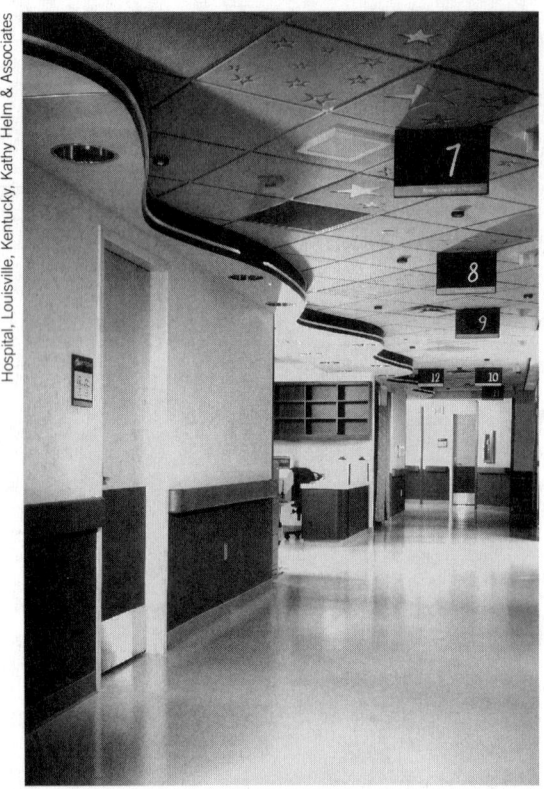

Mannington Commercial, Kosair Children's Hospital, Louisville, Kentucky, Kathy Helm & Associates

Star pattern walls, ceiling, cubicle curtains, and use of shapes add to visual interest and positive energy.

A small New York office interior lobby off the elevator bank was designed in exceptionally minimalist style with two unmovable square modern chairs. The only way the telephone could be accessed was by standing and bending over. The lack of control was accentuated by the gray metallic-look patching-compound effect on the walls, too-low chrome and glass table, black-granite floor, and tiny downlights, with no obvious switches. It did not encourage lingering. Design for shrinkage (high-theft environments), institutional spaces (correctional facilities) are examples of diminished-control environments. These types of space remove a basic human expectation or need for control.

A young woman found herself the design victim of a controlling mother-in-law whose taste in pattern and design did not match hers. The ruffled calico pillows and tie-backs simply did not belong with the Italian leather sofa and torchère lamps. Control takes many forms in design. Pattern is used as a tool of control—or is at the very least the root cause of a difference of opinion.

PRIVACY

The commercial-office environment uses partition systems to both control the space and enhance productivity by promoting a sense of privacy. A sense of privacy can also be enhanced by palette/style and pattern selection. Privacy is both a spatial consideration and also related to the control of information to and about oneself. Privacy is related to solitude and retreat—a sense of escape. In one office, though partition systems provided separate work areas for staff side-to-side, they all faced onto a busy corridor with glass fronts and completely open entrance, with no door or other control over their ability to work privately and unobstructed.

The distraction led to many having to work overtime, away from the office, or changing hours to times when they could be alone, concentrate, and engage creatively in tasks at hand. In this case, the neutral and minimal textile/textural patterning was an asset; but the office systems design was less than optimal. The neutral design scheme was reengineered to include a more vibrantly colored carpeting, patterned and light-reflective wall treatment, and brighter lighting. Increasingly, the staff expressed a sense of distraction and agitation. Both absenteeism and turnover increased without the root cause being addressed: the need for privacy.

Controlling information about oneself can extend to pattern selection. Whereas some people are an open book, others would not dare let people know their taste or design preferences. Like the suddenly desperate guy whose date announced she hated those glib types of operator with tiger bedspreads, people can become fairly selective about their private places. There is a phobia associated with having designers first visit the home. Consumers are afraid they will hear the dreaded and embarrasing refrain, "Oh my God! That *must* go!" as private spaces are invaded. In many commercial offices with an overzealous eye to the bottom line, cosmetic renovation is deferred far too long as an unnecessary expense, until a important buyer/visitor makes a rude comment to the CEO about the colors, patterns, and materials on a visit to the private spaces beyond the confines of the new conference room. How can pattern promote a sense of privacy? It is related to the expression of identity. The woman in the bold plaid suit is effective in high-profile sales. Her pattern choice exudes confidence. So it is with our interior selections—they express what we want to convey.

SELF EXPRESSION

"I don't care what anyone thinks. I love it. It's totally me!" meets "Ugh, I hate that; whatever was he/she thinking. It's so tasteless." The self-expression issue in pattern is at the root of many an argument. Somewhere between, "It's kind of neat," and "Yeah, well, it's not my taste," is a rating scale for each pattern type.

Rating Scale for pattern type (self expression)

Yuck   Not my taste   OK   Kind of neat   Totally me

Finding and matching others and ourselves with styles, palettes, and patterns is at a very basic level an extension of demographics, culture, and individuality. As we change, so too do the Design Expression of who we believe/wish ourselves to be.

Was then   Me, now   Wanna be someday

The Victorian-style home exterior sports a gingerbread front, manicured lawn, small picket fence, and regimental little barberry shrubs.

Once inside, past the restored front door with antique knocker, is a startlingly contemporary interior completely incongruous with the exterior. "It's like having a split personality," laughed the historic/arts district resident-owner. "Other friends of mine have done the Victorian interior to the nines" he said and shook his head, "but that's not me. I love what the area offers, but you'll never catch me going that style route."

Typically, research points to young parents with a new baby in a Victorian-romantic-style and pattern phase. Families with older children tend to embrace casual contemporary or more traditional mix classic looks, depending on other demographic variables. Strong secondary styles are "escape" looks or "alter ego" looks, such as Southwest, country French, Mediterranean. These selections express "wish-fulfillment" fantasies. Styles are supplemented by palettes, finishes, and patterns to express how people feel about themselves, memories of special times or places, and dreams of what they wish to be or how they wish to live. One frustrated designer worked with a client who claimed no particular interests and lived a very basic life with not much socializing after a

If your walls could speak, they should speak your language.
Who are *you?*

day in the auditing department. After designing a pleasant, functional space, the designer heard the client complain that it didn't offer nearly the personality of a colleague's home. As it turned out, the client was obsessive about a particular television show and this offered the only vehicle to unlock identity or "alter" identity in design.

Environmental psychologist Clare Cooper conducted a study of individual and home environment that strongly pointed to the connection between ourselves and our spaces as expressions of us.[2] In further research study[3] comments, hundreds of consumers reaching life-stage changes in their fifties age and/or retirement in their early sixties seek to recreate their smaller (highly correlated) "image" home. The new home sports colors, materials, finishes, patterns, products, and styles they have aspired to and couldn't or wouldn't embrace until now. This self-expression can take the form of sophisticated style, as these empty-nesters give away and sell off traditional, Victorian, country, and other styles of furnishings and patterns from their old lives. Midlife divorces can also trigger extensive renovation and redesign, as individuals express themselves apart from an "other." This independence phase can result in significant pattern statements. A divorcée in her late forties left her Georgian-style home for new quarters and chose sleek, contemporary black and gray office furnishings, a black baby grand piano, teal dining chairs at a glass table, and a contemporary abstract-patterned sofa grouping. Upstairs, in her own suite, was a dainty traditional rose floral–patterned comforter on a brass bed, lace curtains, and soft rose hues. It said, "I need TLC and romance, and I am vulnerable." Touring the home was revealing, and she felt suddenly "exposed" to the outsider. The psychology of design offers fruitful ground for analysis: "If your kitchen (bedroom, office) could speak, what would it say about you?" has become inspiration for a slogan for a wallpaper company. It is an interesting thought.

SENSE OF SECURITY AND SAFETY

In study two, subjects selected a chair that either faced a plain or patterned wall, or the door. One individual commented that the pattern seemed to be crawling on the wall behind him/her and preferred instead to face it. Some designs create a familiar, homey ambience that connects an individual with a nostalgic past: small prints and small-scale designs frequently fall into this category. In flooring design, this feeling relates to wood, brick, and slate. In other cases, the feeling is related to the spacing of design elements; more closely spaced elements imply interdependence rather than independence. Quilt patterns are examples of bedding design, and also wall borders and wall-covering that may relate to a feeling of security. Certain types of plaids also correlate with "blanket" connotations. Specific fabrics—flannels, wovens, woolens, chenille, and deeper piles—have a homespun feeling and invite cognitive association with warmth, comfort, and protection. Denim and corduroy are casual and familiar. Leather and natural materials connect us with the environment through a sense of durability and timelessness. Classic, traditional, and heritage designs also strongly connect us with our past in a world of rapid change. The sense of security translates into cautiousness in design terms. My research shows over half of all consumers identified highly with having a cautious approach to design of their home. They were much more likely to be Southern, Midwestern, and from smaller markets. They were more likely to be on polar ends of the income spectrum and either quite young or nearing retirement. Females were more likely to describe themselves as cautious. Cautious individuals are most apt to take the approach "I don't know about that pattern . . . that tint of gray is too bold . . . I'm not familiar with this look."

ORDER AND ORGANIZATION

We tend to prefer a sense of order to our patterns, and our home and work interiors. The interrelationships between the patterns in our spaces and in defining separate spaces either leads to greater cohesion or disrupts our information-processing flow. Highly complex spaces with a multitude of pattern types require us to put two and two (or four/five/six) together. When patterns are rendered in similar or complementary palettes or contrasting scale relationships, we are more comfortable. The rules are broken when cushions don't match body fabric—for example, the recent slipcover rage and/or when chintz, stripes, plaids, and small prints fight for attention with a floral rug and moiré wallpaper in a less-than-successful adaptation of English country style. There is something quite deliberate about created order, unlike natural order, which is far from precise and has an inherent organic quality to it. Grasses don't come to the forest edge and stop like some sharp dividing line of a suburban lawn. In nature there isn't a stone retaining wall to keep the mulch neatly in the "tree area."

Similarly, in defining rooms within a larger area, we face transition and continuity issues. Our personalities overlap with the created order of an office in sometimes quite dramatic ways. An executive of a New York textile company defined his space with plants. In spite of the rather stark modern decor, the individual office had a startling conservancy quality that calmed and delighted as he "transcended the boundaries." Study six sought to discover how many preferred color continuity throughout the home; how many preferred mixing many patterns, colors, and textures within each given room; how many didn't have a choice in the aquired mix; and who typified each approach.

Study Six: Individual's Decorating Approach*

I tend to coordinate rooms throughout the house with similar colors	43%
I like to mix colors, fabrics and textures in a given room	40%
My home is a mix of hand-me-downs and doesn't look "decorated" at all	26%

*% expressing high agreement defined as "7 to 10" on 0 to 10 point rating scale.
Study six: N=3,500. © 1996 Patricia Rodemann.

A sense of order and cohesion from coordinating colors throughout the home is either a highly sophisticated approach or a fearful response. Typically, high-income households agreed most with this technique, and households with higher educational levels. Southern and West Coast residents felt strongly about using a similar color palette throughout the home. African Americans were more apt to use this tool, and homemakers, retirees, and professional/technical/management employees were also more comfortable using the same palette; the "coordinators" were most likely to be in the 56–65 age range.

Comfort with mixing colors, fabrics (patterns), and textures to achieve a relative degree of design cohesion is most common to higher-income households in the 46–55 age range. Females, homemakers, and Hispanic Americans are more likely to use this technique. The "mixer" group tends to have higher educational levels. This is more apt to be a West Coast/Western customer. Lower-income households are less comfortable with both approaches. In this case, one tends to see greater use of solid colors and "safer" patterns that are room specific. Consumers who have difficulty creating a sense of design continuity with a mix of styles, looks, patterns, and hand-me-downs are more likely to live in smaller towns and country settings, work in blue-collar/administrative and service positions, and be under age 36, and then 36–45. More homemakers and part-timers are represented in this group. One young dad wrote: "We have three children under age four; our taste is sophisticated, but right now our style is a mix of shabby chic (hand-me-downs) and country; but And it's going to stay that way until the kids go to school and my wife goes back to work, or until we can't stand it anymore!"

One challenge in establishing a sense of order is in the mix of advancing and receding pattern elements. The foyer with the black-and-white stripe wall or black-and-white check floor motif demands a bolder treatment in other furnishings, art and accessories, rugs, and pattern-color mix. A wimpy scale, color palette, or poor lighting will create a sense of disharmony and dated quality. Because higher-contrast patterns advance, other patterns and elements need to create a "transition" to that which recedes, to lead to a sense of balance. The sense of flow is highly important within a single room and between rooms. Patterns that promote the transitions are often complements to the themes of connecting rooms. Consumers are well attuned to hallway patterns and will often comment that a stylized design, natural texture, stripe motif, or abstract pattern would make a good stairwell or transitional motif—in both flooring and wall treatments. A sense of organization is more important to males than females. Over half of American consumers identify highly with having an organized approach to the decorating and design of their home. Upper-middle income households felt that sense of order and organization was most important, with younger consumers more likely to feel this way.

VARIETY/SIMPLICITY/COMPLEXITY

Any design professional will recognize quickly how different human beings are in their need for design simplicity or complexity. This can also relate to conventional or unconventional types of interior and individuals, as Weisner and Weibel pointed out in a home-environments study reported in *Environment and Behavior*.4 Complex interiors have a full complement of objects, a variety of things going on, a color/pattern/texture mix, and much decoration. Antiques, books, photos, prints, and pictures on the wall; rugs, pillows, and the like represented the complex interior. People who describe their look or approach as "simple" frequently have white walls, limited pattern mix, and tend to shop mass merchants and have difficulty identifying, accepting, or recognizing trends; their home is orderly, and they tend to prefer American country, casual contemporary, and Shaker styles. A growing percentage of consumers want to embrace "simplicity" in their look and approach.

In recent years, the shift to simple, simpler, and simplification seems to be a backlash to the high-speed, high-tech, and highly complex environment we have fostered in this culture and time. Relaxation and "chill time" is increasingly a priority. *Relationships* are more important than *places* for relationships, or places that get in the way of time together by virtue of the complex care and investment that must be expended in maintaining them. I have noted this from logging thousands of written survey comments. In styles, traditional classic mix style has less complexity than Federal/colonial style, Victorian-romantic, or formal French. Shaker and today's interpretation of Mission offer less complexity than typical American country looks. Casual contemporary is less complex than 1980s postmodern, neoclassic, Oriental/Asian, modernist, and sophisticated mix looks.

The more monochromatic the color palette (i.e., warm and cool neutrals), the higher the correlation with a greater need for simplicity and a sense of relaxation in the home environment. In one sense, the sophisticated individual is the "powerhouse" or the "color" in the calm

From Study Three installation; too complex for most people.
Checkerboard design is intense.

space where he/she must recharge. In other cases, the individual draws strength from interior variety and the complexity of a different style mix and has created a self-contained "island" approach.

Complex environments speak to our need for variety. We have noted this in the style mixes people select and use to express themselves. "Pattern upon pattern" describes a specific type of individual; artistic, innovative, complex, and less conventional then when the mix is deliberate, created, or spontaneously acquired. One dominant pattern is enough for most people; especially those for whom simplicity and relaxation point to more tonal pattern treatments. Beauty may be in the eye of the beholder; but it is also important to distinguish here between what one appreciates in other spaces and what one could live with day to day. "I like this look for this space now, but I could not live with this at home," commented a showhouse visitor.

WHAT MAKES A SPACE AESTHETICALLY PLEASING

There is a great deal of difference between the "done" space and the "evolved" sapce. The reason is time and real-life usage. "I could stay here for a week and never leave this home," commented a landscape designer, "There is something unique and interesting in every room, every angle; it's all so tastefully done, yet not 'done'," He added, "I usually don't feel this way about *interiors*."

Increasingly, consumers prefer natural patterns and textures and stone/wood/plant-derived effects. They value relaxed versions of classic fabric looks and textile-finish patterns, authentic botanical designs, and looks that have a patina and the authentic quality of age. These are perhaps a reactions to our technical, synthetic, and manufactured times. Even modern style is being revisited in playful new colors and shapes with a new sense of comfort.

VIEWS/NATURE AND INTEGRATION

Gardening rates highly as an American pastime. More than three-fourths of Americans have higher-than-average interest in outdoor gardening. The most avid gardeners tend to be over age 46. My research found many consumers also placing a premium on landscaping, and there is an increasing desire to integrate interior and exterior views and vistas. The ability to control light and view via shutters, miniblinds, and verticals is important to consumers; but so is the ability to frame the outside by including decorative rods, draperies, and swag treatments in creative new ways. The interior-exterior integration is also expressing itself in the use of more natural flooring materials: stone, tile, hardwood, and natural-look laminates and vinyls. The *natural* world offers us *ever-changing* light and pattern stimuli, which have a uniqueness we

Author's collection

Natural patterns; light and shade

are seldom able to capture indoors. We derive a sense of mystery from the aliveness of the natural world and are inspired by it: The sounds, colors, and light of the environment are unlike any experience within the built environment. This essence is what we seek to recapture indoors.

For many, the best the interior environment has to offer is comfort. About 80 percent of the consumers in my research gave high levels of agreement to the statement "Comfort is more important than being stylish." Other research firms confirm the increased importance of comfort.

This explains why we have seen a shift away from the highly bold and dramatic pattern statements in the last two or three decades. Visual comfort is derived from the natural environment. We are learning more about the role of light, water, plants, scents, and views in promoting health. Patterns of the natural world are part of that learning experience.

CHANGE AND FREEDOM

Having the freedom to change our environment as we change is exceptionally important in creating interiors that uplift and heal us from the stresses of life. We are used to change in daily light levels, seasonal palettes, and conditions, and are acutely hooked into the biorhythms of life. But each of us approaches interior change differently. There are the clichés about the woman who took the lamps out of the box and never removed the plastic covers for 25 years. One creative woman, highly accustomed to variety and complexity, found herself in a rather uninspiring townhouse living room with mandated white walls, tan carpeting, and modular furniture. Within seven months, she had rearranged the grouping five different ways, changing artwork, plants, throws, pillows, and occasional tables. Colleagues joked about how her husband took it. A friend a few doors down never moved or changed a single object, except to clean it, over a period of five years. It is apparent we have different thresholds for change and stimuli.

Consumers change bedding designs approximately every 4–6 years, and window treatments (draperies) about every 11–12 years. Wall-covering typically is changed within 10 years and floor covering, about every 12–13 years—though all are estimates subject to demographics, regional variation the economy, and product types and price points.

Understanding these cycles of design, puts palette and pattern usage into a different context. Undoubtedly, household economics also has something to do with the timetable. Our desire for change is far greater than product obsolescence.

About a third of Americans agree highly that they are ready for change today. These are younger consumers in urban markets. Fewer than one-fifth agree highly with the statement, "We'll wait until we move to make big-ticket decorating purchases." This group of consumers tends to be young (under age 36) and middle-income professionals. My research has also discovered high agreement with the statement, "Once I get a room the way I like it, I keep it that way for a long time." This group tends to be higher-income professionals in the 46–55 age range. Our need for change and environmental stimuli may be part of learning and maintaining/growth of the brain. Recent discoveries have shown the importance of a rich sensory and educational environment for long-term high-level mental functioning. Conversely, one wonders if the sense of exhaustion that comes from shopping may be an "overload" of our typical sensory alert cue system with advancing, high-stimulus, high-color, high-impact, heavily patterned products, sounds, smells, and motion, and with order and organization turned upside down. We cannot and should not look at our need for change—with respect to design—as a marketing-induced phenomenon alone.

PATTERN INSIGHTS AND OBSERVATIONS

Beyond historic period, design era, style, palette, demographics, and personality, there are other, deeper human needs to which pattern research is beginning to point. Pattern design research is at its initial stage of exploration, similar to the position color perception research held a few decades ago. In my research, I probed design approach and personality type: Is it possible to understand more fully who is more likely to approach the design/pattern decision in a specific way?

DESIGN APPROACH AND PERSONALITY TYPES

Adventurous types are the fearless folks who try a bold new color first; who mirror the ceiling, adopt a new style, or spring for the esoteric pattern. Entrepreneurs are more likely to be adventurous. This personality type is more likely to live on the West Coast, and then in the Northeast, and is more likely to be an urban resident. The adventurous type is in an upper-middle- to upper-income household and is young (age 36–45). This maverick is more likely to be male. In pattern designs, the adventurous individual is more apt to select designs that make a statement and embrace a full complement of finishes, coordinating patterns, and eclectic furnishings and accessories. This type will be more comfortable with new colors, concrete floors, stainless steel counters, and industrial looks in fixtures.

Cautious types are hesitant to try new palettes, colors, or patterns. They lack confidence in their ability to visualize and combine styles and designs, and are careful not to make a mistake. This group was far more likely to be Midwestern and from smaller markets, female, and on opposite ends of the income spectrum. The cautious consumer was also more likely to be a homemaker and younger, or retired. Cautious consumers are more likely to select small-print patterns, plaids, checks, and smaller-scale florals in simpler renditions.

Traditionalist types are more likely to select a style, look, palette, and pattern mix from a familiar recognizable historic era, and place design elements in predictable places. The traditionalist is more likely to be Northeastern, from larger population centers, and earn the highest household income. This consumer is more likely to have a college education and work in professional/technical and management positions. The traditionalist age range is 46–55. Patterns are stripes, plaids (tartans), small prints, medium- to large-scale florals, fabric looks (damask), and botanicals.

Analytical types study the material, the decision, and the source for the products and design advice. This group of consumer will leave no stone unturned and often selects stone and fine-quality natural materials. The analytical consumer is more likely to be Northeastern, live in an urban market, and earn the highest household income. Unlike the traditionalist, the analytical consumer is less predictable in style and

Traditionalist pattern designs

younger (age 36–45). This consumer is also likely to have college and/or postgraduate training and work in professional/technical and management positions. Pattern types are architectural/historic, ethnic/cultural, stone/marble/faux, stripe, and geometric. Males are much more likely to identify with this approach.

Artistic types have the imagination and ability to execute their vision in creative ways. This is the individual who masters special paint techniques or marquetry, creates one-of-a-kind window treatments, or combines furnishings in unusual mixes. The artistic consumer is most likely to be Northeastern or from the West Coast, from smaller markets, and female, by far. This individual is more likely to be upper-middle income or lower income and young (under age 36). The artistic individual is either a homemaker or works in a professional/technical/management position and is likely to have a college degree. This individual is comfortable with many pattern styles, including abstract/contemporary, stone/natural/faux looks, graphic novelties, natural textures, historic/architectural, and ethnic/cultural prints.

Loyalist types stick to schemes, brands, looks, and retailers. This is a faithful consumer who may like other styles, but will commit to a palette, for example, and continue room by room until the house is completed—moving before changing. Midwesterners, Southerners, females, and upper-middle-income households are more likely to be loyalists. Market size makes little difference. This consumer is less likely to have a college degree and tends to be a homemaker in the 56–65 age range, or nearing retirement. Pattern types are similar to those of the traditionalist, with the addition of themes and novelty looks—though there are regional style considerations.

Intuitive types are most likely to say, "I just know it will look great." This type of consumer discovers just the right item—on sale at an unlikely time and place. This consumer can visualize almost as well as the artistic consumer, but tends to make up what they can't on faith. Intuitives are most apt to be West Coast residents, from smaller markets, and upper-middle income. Gender makes little difference. Intuitives are more likely to be homemakers, part-timers, self-employed, and to have a college education. The age range for intuitives is more likely to be 36–45. Intuitive pattern selections tend to be graphic/novelty prints, florals, abstracts, stone/faux looks in deeper hues, printed fabric effects and stripes in larger scale. The intuitive is confident, or at least projects an aura of confidence, and often influences friends and family to try new things.

Other types of consumer also exist; and I continue to refine types and methodologies. It is both instructional and amusing to understand the connection between pattern and product design selection, demographics, shopping behavior, and personality type.

PATTERN DESIGNS FOR SPECIFIC PURPOSES

Over 14 years or more, I have observed specific pattern applications through many installations and research studies. I would like to encourage the reader to add to, edit, and refine this list as pattern use changes and renditions vary over time—as we change individually, as a culture, and through differing world circumstances.

A Research Summary of Pattern-Behavior Traits

To grab attention: High-contrast figure-ground relationship (black/white), checkerboards and geometric designs, stripes, graphic and novelty prints, sports/kids/characters, medium- to large-scale floral designs, and selected ethnic/cultural prints.

To soothe emotionally distraught: Lower-contrast, smaller-scale enveloping overall designs in light-midrange hues (blue, sage, rose, etc.), medium-scale florals, softer geometric prints, abstract/watercolor, small/miniprints, natural textures, finishes and prints, botanical designs, printed/textured fabric effects, and some scenic/graphic novelty.

To promote business: Highly contextual depending on financial, service, retail, and so on. In a general corporate sense: medium- to larger-scale designs in lower to moderate contrast, figure-ground relationship in an appropriate palette (e.g., deeper hues: navy/burgundy/forest green, etc.) for the demographic audience; stripes, marble/stone/granite looks, geometric prints, architectural motif, small medallion/stylized, natural-texture prints and finishes, printed/textured fabric looks/finishes, stylized abstract and graphic novelty.

To promote learning: Low- to moderate-contrast figure/ground, but smaller scale or less descript pattern elements in midrange hues— highly age and context sensitive—abstract/watercolor, geometric prints, marble/stone/granite, architectural/historic motifs, small/miniprints, printed/textured fabric looks and finishes, graphic/novelty.

To enhance a feeling of confidence: Moderate- to higher-contrast figure-ground relationships in moderate- to larger-scale in midrange shades rather than pale tint values except when finishes/textures used. Medium- to larger- scale floral designs, geometric prints, marble/stone/granite looks, architectural motifs, ethnic/cultural prints, natural-texture prints and finishes, printed/textured fabric looks, sports/novelties, stripes.

To promote a sense of healing: Small- to moderate-scale designs with lower-contrast figure-ground relationships—except in the case of visual impairment (seniors)—in midtone to lighter hue palettes with judicious (limited) use of textures/finishes. Small to medium-scale florals, geometric prints paired with specific softer rendition—faux-stone, graphic and small prints, less abstract-quality motifs, architectural motifs, natural-texture prints, botanical designs, printed/textured fabric effects, medium to wider stripes in specific softer rendition and/or hybrid versions.

To uplift and enhance spirituality: Low-contrast between figure-ground and tonal; medium- to larger-scale in pale tints or dusty shades of midtone hues (light blues/blue greens, apricot, rose) in abstract watercolor, marble/stone/granite, architectural/historic, natural-texture prints/finishes, print/textured fabric looks, stripe hybrids.

To encourage fun: Moderate- to high-contrast figure-ground—any scale—in lighter, brighter palettes including medium- to large-scale florals, geometric prints, abstract designs, graphic novelty prints and modern motifs, ethnic/cultural prints, natural-texture prints, botanical designs, sports/kids/characters, and stripes.

Pattern is one powerful piece of the natural and designed environment. Our designed environment is an important contribution to "us," and an extension of self. Because we continue to grow and change over the course of our lives, it is exceptionally important to seek to understand each element and its impact on us. We open our eyes not to flat color or a singular light source, but a multitude of visual stimulation—much in the form of pattern. We are walking through a patterned, textured environment—working within it—all day long, and often processing much of that information on an unconscious level. We are at the threshold of a new and exciting understanding of the brain's ability to process and respond to pattern stimuli. Physiologically, we barely understand response to pattern stimuli and often only in pathological or extreme states and conditions. Cognitively, we appreciate the depth of rich and personal associations to patterns in our lives. Historically, we are left with a treasury of images, eras, and applications. Demographically, we are the sum of what we choose. Pattern should not and cannot be overlooked and relegated to a minor role—an afterthought. Pattern reveals, conceals, and predicts who we are and who we are becoming.

References

1. Miller, Stuart and Judith Schlitt. 1985. *Interior space: Design concepts for personal needs.* New York: Praeger Publishers.
2. Cooper, Claire. "The House as symbol of Self," *Designing for Human Behavior.* ed. J. Lang, Stroudsberg, Pa. Dowden, Hutchinson & Ross, 1974.
3. Rodemann, Patricia. © 1998. Study Nine.
4. Weibel, J.C. and T.S. Weisner. "Home Environments and Family Lifestyles." *Environment and Behavior.* 13 (1981) pp 417–460.

BIBLIOGRAPHY

Amedeo, Douglas, and R. A. York. "Indications of Environmental Schemata from Thoughts about Environments." *Journal of Environmental Psychology* 10, no. 3 (1990).

The American Society of Interior Designers (ASID), 608 Massachusetts Avenue NE, Washington, D.C. 20002-3480.

Bahrick and Boucher. "Retention of Visual and Verbal Codes of the Same Stimuli." *Journal of Experimental Psychology* 78 (1968): 417–422.

Balling, John D., and F. Falk. "Development of Preference for Natural Environments." *Environment and Behavior* 14, no. 1 (1982).

Belk, Russell. "Possessions and the Extended Self." *Journal of Consumer Research* 15, no. 2 (1988).

Birren, Faber. *Creative Color.* New York: Van Nostrand Reinhold, 1961.

Blakeslee, Sandra. "Experts Finding How Brain 'Sees' Things You Think." *The New York Times,* 31 August 1993.

———. "Seeing and Imagining." *The New York Times,* 31 March 1993.

Bloch, Peter. "Involvement Beyond the Purchase Process: Conceptual Issues and Empirical Investigation." *Advances in Consumer Research* 9 (1982).

Brebner, John. *Environmental Psychology in Building Design.* New York: Applied Science Publishers, 1982.

Bruner II, Gordon, and Paul Hensel. *Marketing Scales Handbook: A Compilation of Multi-Item Measures.* Chicago: American Marketing Association, 1994.

Canter, David. *Psychology for Architects.* London: Applied Science Publishers, 1974.

Cherulnik, Paul, and S. Winderman. "Symbols of Status in Urban Neighborhoods." *Environment and Behavior* 18, no. 5 (September 1986).

Colby, Barbara. *Color and Light: Influences and Impact.* Glendale, Calif.: Chroma Productions, 1990.

Corcoran, D. W. J. *Pattern Recognition.* Middlesex, England: Penguin Books, 1971.

Crick, Francis, and Christof Koch. "The Problem of Consciousness." *Scientific American* (September 1992): 153–159.

Danby, Miles. *Grammar of Architectural Design*. London: Oxford University Press, 1963.

Deitz, Samuel. "The Experimental Analysis of Human Behavior: History, Current Status, and Future Directions." *Psychological Record* 37 (1987): 29–33.

Deregowski, J. B. *Illusions, Patterns, and Pictures: A Cross-Cultural Perspective*. London: Academic Press, 1980.

Ellinger, Richard G. *Color, Structure, and Design*. International Textbook Co., 1980.

Elsen, Albert E. *Purposes of Art*. New York: Holt, Rinehart & Winston, 1962.

Emery, Irene. *The Primary Structures of Fabrics*. Washington, D.C.: Watson-Guptill Publications/Whitney Library of Design, The Textile Museum, 1994.

Epilepsy Foundation of America, 4351 Garden City Drive, Landover, Maryland 20785.

M.C. Escher web site: http://lonestar.texas.net/ªEscher/ or Cordon Art BV PlO. Box 101, 3740 AC The Netherlands.

Frankl, Paul. *Principles of Architectural History*. Boston: Massachusetts Institute of Technology Press, 1968.

Fuhrer, Urs. "Bridging the Ecological-Psychological Gap: Behavior Settings as Interfaces," *Environment and Behavior* 22, no. 4 (1990).

Gallagher, Winifred. *The Power of Place. How Our Surroundings Shape our Thoughts, Emotions, and Actions*. New York: Poseidon Press, 1993.

Gibson, Clare. *Signs and Symbols: An Illustrated Guide to Their Meaning and Origin*. New York: Barnes & Noble Books.

Gifford, Robert. *Environmental Psychology: Principles and Practices*. Boston: Allyn & Bacon, 1987.

Gilliatt, Mary. *Period Style*. New York: Little, Brown & Co., 1990.

Gombrich, E. H. *Sense of Order: A Study In the Psychology of Decorative Art*. London: Phaidon Press Limited, 1984.

Gregory, R. L. *Eye and Brain: The Psychology of Seeing*. New York; Toronto: McGraw-Hill, 1966, 1972.

Guyton, Arthur. *Basic Neuroscience: Anatomy and Physiology*. Philadelphia: W. B. Saunders Co.,1991.

Hansen, William, and I. Altman. "Decorating Personal Places: A Descriptive Analysis," *Environment and Behavior* 8 (1976).

Harris, Jennifer, ed. *Textiles: 5,000 Years*. New York: Harry N. Abrams, 1993.

Hasell, Mary and Frieda Peatross. "Exploring Connections Between Women's Changing Roles and House Forms." *Environment and Behavior* 22, no. 1 (1990).

Healy, Jane. *Endangered Minds: Why Our Children Don't Think*. Simon & Schuster, 1991.

Hochberg, Julian. *Perception*. Englewood Cliffs, N.J.: Prentice-Hall, 1978.

Hornung, Clarence P. *Handbook of Designs and Devices: 1,836 Basic Designs and Their Variations*. New York: Dover Publications, 1959.

Hothersall, David. *History of Psychology*. New York: McGraw-Hill, 1990.

Jones, Owen. *The Grammar of Ornament*. New York: Portland House, 1986.

Joyce, Carol. *Textile Design*. New York: Watson-Guptill Publications, 1993.

Kaplan, Peter, S. Hilliard, L. Jenkins, and D. Scheuneman. "Sensitization of Infant Visual Attention: Role of Pattern Contrast." *Infant Behavior & Development* 11 (1988): 265–276.

Kaplan, Rachel, and S. Kaplan. "Environmental Preference: A Comparison of Four Domains of Predictors." *Environment and Behavior* 21 (1989): 509–530.

———. "Aesthetics, Affect, and Cognition: Environmental Preference from an Evolutionary Perspective." *Environment and Behavior* 8 (1987): 3–32.

———. *Cognition and Environment: Functioning in an Uncertain World*. New York: Praeger, 1982.

Kasmar, Joyce. "The Development of a Usable Lexicon of Environmental Description." In *Environmental Aesthetics: Theory, Research, and Applications*, edited by Jack L. Nasar, 144–155. New York: Cambridge University Press.

Kaufman, Lloyd. *Sight and Mind*. New York: Oxford University Press, 1974.

Kondo, Michiaki, and Nakamizo Achio. "Dynamic Wallpaper Phenomenon and Fusional Hysterisis. *Japanese Journal of Psychology* 53, no. 5 (December 1982): 288–295.

Kort, Marie, and M. Teittinen. *Wallcoverings over the Years*. Kyroskoski, Finland: Oy Kyro Ab Publisher, 1989.

Leuwenberg, E. L., and Buffart. *Formal Theories of Visual Perception*. Chichester, England: John Wiley & Sons, 1978.

Lloyd, Christopher. *1,773 Milestones of Art*. New York: Crown Publishers, 1985.

Luscher, Max, and Ian Scott. *The Luscher Color Test*. New York: Washington Square Press, 1969.

Mahnke, Frank, and Rudolf Mahnke. *Color and Light in Man-Made Environments*. New York: Van Nostrand Reinhold, 1987.

Marberry, Sara, and Laurie Zagon. *The Power of Color: Creating Healthy Interior Spaces*. New York: John Wiley & Sons, 1990.

Matlin, Margaret. *Perception*. Boston: Allyn & Bacon, 1983.

McNall Burns, Edward. *Western Civilizations: Their History and Their Culture*, 8th ed., vols. 1 and 2. New York: W. W. Norton & Co., 1973.

Miller, Mary C. *Color for Interior Architecture*. New York: John Wiley & Sons, 1997.

Moller, Clifford. *Architectural Environment and Our Mental Health*. New York: Horizon Press, 1968.

Oman, Charles, and Jean Hamilton. *Wallpapers: An International History*. New York: Harry N. Abrams, 1982.

Nasar, J. L. *Design by Competition: With an Analysis of Eisenman's Wexner Center*. New York: Cambridge University Press, 1998.

Nasar, J. L. *The Evaluative Image of the City*. Thousand Oaks, Calif.: Sage, 1997.

Neutra, Richard. *Survival Through Design*. New York: Oxford University Press, 1969.

Niesewant, Nonie. *Tricia Guild's Country Color*. New York: Rizzoli International Publications, 1994.

Paint and Decorating Retail Association. 1050 North Lindbergh Boulevard, St. Louis, Mo. 63132-2994.

Paolicchi, Juliann. "Children Thrive When Challenged Early." *The Columbus Dispatch,* 11 May 1997, sec. C.

Pennartz, Paul, and M. Elsinga. "Adults, Adolescents, and Architects: Differences in Perception of the Urban Environment," *Environment and Behavior* 22, no. 5 (1990).

Piirto, Rebecca. *Beyond Mind Games: The Marketing Power of Psychographics.* Ithaca, N.Y.: American Demographic Books, 1991.

Posner, M. I. "Abstraction and the Process of Recognition." In *Psychology of Learning,* vol. 3, edited by G. H. Bower and J. T. Spence. New York: Academic Press, 1969.

Proctor, Richard M., and Jennifer F. Lew. *Surface Design for Fabric.* Seattle: University of Washington Press, 1995.

Proshansky, H. M., W. H. Ittelson, and L. G. Rivlin. "The Influence of the Physical Environment on Behavior: Some Basic Assumptions." In *Behavioral Research Methods in Environmental Design,* edited by W. Michelson, 180–234. Stroudsburg, Pa.: Dowden, Hutchinson, and Ross, 1975; distributed by Halsted Press.

Rappoport, Amos. "Identity and the Environment: A Cross-Cultural Perspective." In *Housing and Identity,* edited by James Duncan. London: Croom Helm, 1981.

Restak, Richard M. *The Brain: The Last Frontier.* New York: Warner Books, 1979.

Rochberg-Halton, Eugene. "Object Relations, Role Models, and Cultivation of the Self," *Environment and Behavior* 16, no. 3 (May 1984): 335–368.

Rodemann, Patricia. Thesis follow-up research, study ten. ©1998, 1999. New Movers.

———. Study nine. ©1998, 1999. Selected information derived from National Consumer Design Study.

———. Study eight. ©1997. Selected information derived from National Consumer Design Study.

———. Study seven. ©1997. Selected information derived from National Consumer Design Study.

———. Study six. ©1996. Selected information derived from National Consumer Design Study: The Rooms of America I.

———. Master's thesis, Studies one through five. The Ohio State University, Columbus, Ohio. ©1991.

Rossbach, Sarah, and Lin Yun. *Living Color: Master Lin Yun's Guide to Feng Shui and the Art of Color.* New York: Kodansha America, 1994.

Sadalla, Edward, Vershure, and Burroughs. "Identity Symbolism in Housing." *Environment and Behavior* 19, no. 5 (1987).

Sanoff, Henry. *Visual Research Methods in Design.* New York: Van Nostrand Reinhold, 1991.

Schroeder, Herbert W. "Environmental Perception Rating Scales: A Case Method for Simple Methods of Analysis." *Environment and Behavior* 16 (1984): 573–597.

Segall, Marshall, D. T. Campbell, and M. J. Herskovits. *The Influence of Culture on Visual Perception.* New York: Bobbs-Merrill Co., 1966.

Shibukawa, Ikuyoshi, and Yumi Takahashi. *Designer's Guide to Color 2–5.* San Francisco: Chronicle Books, 1984.

Smith, Lauren, and Rose Gilbert. *Your Colors at Home.* Washington, D.C.: Acropolis Books, 1985.

Somerson, Mark. "Children Thrive When Challenged Early." *The Columbus Dispatch,* 11 May 1997.

Sommer, Robert, and Barbara B. Sommer. *A Practical Guide to Behavioral Research.* New York: Oxford University Press, 1986.

Soso, M. J., and Dawn A. Marcus. "Migraine and Stripe-Induced Visual Discomfort." *Archives of Neurology* 46 (1989): 1129–1132.

Soso, M. J., E. Lettich, and J. H. Belgum. "Pattern-Sensitive Epilepsy I: A Demonstration of a Spatial Frequency Selective Epileptic Response to Gratings." *Epilepsia* 21 (1980): 301–312.

Strohm, Bob, ed. *Patterns in the Wild.* Washington, D.C.: National Wildlife Federation, 1992.

U.S. Bureau of the Census. "Average Annual Expenditures of All Consumer Units." In *Statistical Abstract of the United States,* 117th ed., no. 715. Prepared by the Economics and Statistics Administration of the Bureau of the Census. Washington, D.C.: Government Printing Office, 1997. 464.

———. "Expenditures by Residential Property Owners for Improvements, Maintenance and Repairs, 1980, by Type of Property and Activity," Current Construction Reports Series C50. In *Statistical Abstract of the United States,* 117th ed., no. 1208: 729.

———. "Money Income of Households Percent Distribution, by Income Level, Race, and Hispanic Origin in Constant (1995) Dollars: 1970 to 1995." In *Statistical Abstract of the United States,* 117th ed., no. 717: 465.

———. "1992 Census of Manufactures and Annual Survey of Manufactures Manufactures Summary, by Industry: 1992 and 1995." In *Statistical Abstract of the United States,* 117th ed., no. 1219: 739–740.

U.S. Bureau of Labor Statistics. "Employment Status of the Civilian Population 1950 to 1996," Bulletin 2307. In *Statistical Abstract of the United States,* 117th ed., no. 619. Prepared by the Economics and Statistics Administration of the Bureau of the Census in cooperation with the Bureau of Labor Statistics. Washington, D.C.: Government Printing Office, 1997. 397.

Wagner, Carleton. Color Communications Incorporated (formerly Color Research Institute), 4000 West Filmore Street, Chicago, Ill., 60624.

Walch, Margaret, and Augustine Hope. *Living Colors: The Definitive Guide to Color Palettes Through the Ages.* San Francisco: Chronicle Books, 1995.

The Wallcovering Pattern Guide and Source Directory, P.O. Box 5107, Clearwater, Fla. 33756.

Walsh, David. "Aging and Visual Information Processing: Potential Implications for Everyday Seeing." *Journal of the American Optometric Association* 59, no. 4 (April 1988): 301–306.

Ward, Lawrence M., and J. A. Russell. "Cognitive Set and The Perception of Place." *Environment and Behavior* 13, no. 3 (1981).

Weinstein, Art. *Market Segmentation: Using Demographics, Psychographics, and Other Niche Marketing Techniques to Predict Customer Behavior.* Chicago: Probus Publishing, 1994.

Weiss, Michael. *The Clustering of America.* New York: Harper & Row, Perennial Library, 1988.

What Today's Home Buyers Want. Washington, D.C.: National Association of Home Builders and Fulton Research, Inc., 1996.

Whiton, Sherrill. *Interior Design and Decoration.* J. B. Lippincott Co., 1974.

Wilkins, A., I. Nimmo-Smith, A. Tait, et al. "Neurological Basis for Visual Discomfort." *Brain* 107 (1984): 989–1017.

Wohlwill, J. "The Environment is Not in the Head." In *Environmental Design Research,* edited by W. Preiser. Stroudsburg, Pa.: Dowden, Hutchinson & Ross, 1974.

Yoshimoto, Kamon. *Textile Design in Japan.* 4 vols. Singapore: Page One Publishing Pte., 1994.

Zeki, Semir. "The Visual Image in Mind and Brain." *Scientific American* (September 1992): 69–76.

Special References for Visual Images

Archives of Columbus Coated Fabrics, Div. Borden, Inc.

Cooper Hewitt Museum of Decorative Arts, Smithsonian Institution, New York

Eisenhart Wallcoverings

Formica Corporation

FSC Wallcoverings: Village, Greef, Gramercy, Waverly, Raymond Waites

Gencorp: Essex, Chapters, Genon, Sanitas

Albert Haynosch, designer

IHDG Imperial Home Decor Group: Imperial, Carefree, Sunworthy

Mannington Commercial

Pantone, Inc., 590 Commerce Boulevard, Carlstadt, N.J. 07072-3098.

Patricia Rodemann, Designed for Success

Jared Schneidman, designer

York Wallcoverings: Carey Lind, Three Sisters, Ronald Redding, Antonina Vella, J. Chesterfield Studios

To contact the author for more information, clarification, or to inquire about the annual Rooms of America® survey and ongoing research: parodemann@aol.com or Designed for Success, P.O. Box 108, Lewis Center, OH 43035-0108. Specific statistical references and percentages for studies six through nine are considered proprietary and are not available beyond the Designed For Success client base.

INDEX